Luminos is the Open Access monograph publishing program from UC Press. Luminos provides a framework for preserving and reinvigorating monograph publishing for the future and increases the reach and visibility of important scholarly work. Titles published in the UC Press Luminos model are published with the same high standards for selection, peer review, production, and marketing as those in our traditional program. www.luminosoa.org

Knowing about Genocide

Knowing about Genocide

Armenian Suffering and Epistemic Struggles

———

Joachim J. Savelsberg

UNIVERSITY OF CALIFORNIA PRESS

University of California Press
Oakland, California

© 2021 by Joachim J. Savelsberg

Suggested citation: Savelsberg, J. J. *Knowing About Genocide: Armenian Suffering and Epistemic Struggles*. Oakland: University of California Press, 2021. DOI: https://doi.org/10.1525/luminos.99

Library of Congress Cataloging-in-Publication Data

Names: Savelsberg, Joachim J., 1951– author.
Title: Knowing about genocide : Armenian suffering and
    epistemic struggles / Joachim J. Savelsberg.
Description: Oakland, California : University of California Press, [2021] |
    Includes bibliographical references and index.
Identifiers: LCCN 2020039753 (print) | LCCN 2020039754 (ebook) |
    ISBN 9780520380189 (paperback) | ISBN 9780520380196 (epub)
Subjects: LCSH: Genocide—Sociological aspects. |
    Armenian massacres, 1915–1923.
Classification: LCC HV6322.7 .S385 2021 (print) | LCC HV6322.7 (ebook) |
    DDC 956.6/20154—dc23
LC record available at https://lccn.loc.gov/2020039753
LC ebook record available at https://lccn.loc.gov/2020039754

30   29   28   27   26   25   24   23   22   21
10   9   8   7   6   5   4   3   2   1

For Pamela

CONTENTS

ILLUSTRATIONS AND TABLES

FIGURES

MAP

TABLES

PREFACE

Purpose, Author, and Acknowledgments

This book brings together the topic of genocide and a comprehensive sociology of knowledge (360 degrees, as one reader suggested). The empirical focus is on the Armenian genocide.

I ask how repertoires of knowledge emerge, among Armenians and Turks and in world society, and what dynamics they unfold. Importantly, by *knowledge*, I do not mean certified knowledge but simply humans' taken-for-granted assumptions about the world.

Everyday exchanges, or micropolitics, lay the foundation. They involve conflicting pressures to silence, deny, or acknowledge. Knowledge entrepreneurs, actors with privileged access to channels of communication, often set the parameters for such exchanges, exercising epistemic power. Some practice radical denial, even against overwhelming evidence—a pattern that reaches beyond the issue of genocide, especially in the current era of authoritarian populism (denial of global warming is but one example).

Knowledge entrepreneurs also initiate large collective rituals to confirm a sense of community among their followers and to solidify knowledge.

Finally, when radically distinct repertoires of knowledge face one another, conflicts and struggles erupt. They unfold in distinct social fields such as politics and law, embedded in national contexts *and* in world society with its pronounced human rights scripts since the end of World War II.

Each of these points is the subject of one or more chapters of this book. The final chapter argues that denialism in the context of (partial) human rights hegemony likely produces effects that are counterproductive in the eyes of those who deny mass atrocities.

Now a few words about me, the author, and about institutions and individuals who contributed, speaking to the context and conditions of this book's production of knowledge about genocide knowledge.

THE AUTHOR

I was born in 1951, six years after the end of the Shoah, in a small conservative town in Germany, the country of the perpetrators. I grew up in a world in which World War II was an ever-present, albeit somber, theme, unavoidably in light of the physical traces it had left and the missing family members. It was also a world in which our elders, at home, in school, and in much of the public sphere, thoroughly silenced the Holocaust. Only in the late 1960s did my generation begin to learn, in piecemeal fashion, the horrifying facts of the Shoah. As children of the perpetrator generation, we acquired cultural trauma; we were horrified, shaken in our basic assumptions about the world we lived in and about our elders.

This exposure preceded, by a few years, my entry into the study of sociology, economics, and public policy at the University of Cologne (Köln), continued in the doctoral program of the University of Trier. A series of positions, including postdoctoral fellowships at Johns Hopkins and Harvard universities and employment at the University of Bremen and at the Criminological Research Institute of Lower Saxony (KFN) in Hanover, led to my appointment as a professor at the University of Minnesota. Along the way, I specialized in the sociology of law and criminology and worked on various issues, such as white-collar crime legislation, sentencing guidelines, comparative punishment rates, and the sociology of criminology. Only the events of the 1990s, with their genocides and international criminal tribunals, enabled by the end of the Cold War, encouraged me to apply my professional expertise to issues that had preoccupied me for decades, as a private person and as a citizen. Biography met history, and a new line of work resulted.

I began to examine how legal proceedings color collective representations and memories of mass violence. That work is reflected in my books *American Memories: Atrocities and the Law* (with Ryan D. King, Russell Sage Foundation, 2011) and *Representing Mass Violence: Conflicting Responses to Human Rights Violations in Darfur* (University of California Press, 2015). I developed an undergraduate course on violations of human rights norms and wrote a small accompanying volume (*Crime and Human Rights: Criminology of Genocide and Atrocities*, Sage, 2010), supplemented by a graduate seminar in the sociology of knowledge and collective memory. I organized the latter along a line of theoretical approaches that provide the structure of this book. The seminar inspired several dissertation projects and motivated the writing of this sociology of genocide knowledge.

ACKNOWLEDGMENTS

The present book was made possible by particular opportunities, including residences at two institutes for advanced study, funding and other support, critiques and inspiration by colleagues, and collaboration with research assistants.

The Arsham and Charlotte Ohanessian Chair at the University of Minnesota provided me with resources to advance a research agenda through several interlinked projects that helped me to examine many of my expectations in light of empirical evidence. Outside of Minnesota, I benefited from 2018–19 fellowships at the Stellenbosch Institute for Advanced Study (STIAS) in South Africa and at the Institut d'Études Avancées de Paris (IEA) in France, the latter with the financial support of the French State, programme "Investissements d'avenir," managed by the Agence Nationale de la Recherche (ANR-11-LABX-0027–01 Labex RFIEA+).

The institutes, with their facilities and staff, provided ideal environments for writing and for exchanges with colleagues from many countries and disciplines, guarding against parochialism. STIAS enhanced my understanding of other societies' engagement with dark pasts. Many fellows, especially from diverse parts of the African continent, enriched my experience. The IEA served as a basis from which to engage with the rich intellectual life of Paris and to reach out to civil society and political actors. I built on benefits received during the summer of 2016 as a guest of the Fondation de la Maison des Sciences de l'Homme.

More individuals than I can mention merit special mention. I ask those left out for forgiveness. The names of numerous interviewees in Paris, Massachusetts, and Minnesota have to remain anonymous. To them I am especially grateful.

In Paris, Liora Israël and Jacques Commaille laid the foundation for a series of successful research visits, and John Hagan and Philip Smith helped pave the way to the French capital. Boris Adjemian, Olivier Baruch, Johann Michel, Claire Mouradian, Jacques Semelin, Michel Wieviorka, and Julien Zarifian enriched my understanding of French-Armenian history, genocide knowledge, and memory legislation.

At the IEA, Saadi Lahlou, as director, created an intellectually engaged atmosphere. Gretty Mirdal, previous director and guarantor of continuity, enriched the experience with her intellect and personal warmth. Simon Luck's advice was decisive in guiding us through (what may appear to outsiders as the jungle of) Parisian academic life. Many fellows, especially those concerned with issues of violence, enriched my thought. Hakan Seckinelgin merits special mention. We worked on related fronts, co-organized events, and co-adventured into Parisian intellectual life. Kei Hiruta, Michael Jonik, Andrew Kahn, Adam Mestyan, and Penny Roberts explored painful histories of violence, and I appreciated their solidarity. Many conversations with Gregory Bochner (on realism), Denis Walsh (on agency), Marylène Lieber (on gender), and Adam Frank (on intersections of art and intellectual life) provided further inspiration.

At STIAS, the former and incoming directors, Hendrik Geyer and Edward Kirumira, stimulated intellectual and social life. Christoff Pouw provided us with access to sectors of South African society that would have been difficult to gain without his help. Fellow Fellows Duncan Brown, Kelvin Campbell, Manuel Castells, Abdallah Daar, Charles Fombad, Peter Gärdenfors, Nkatha Kabira,

Marlize Lombard, Susanne Lundin, Henrietta Mondry, and Izuchukwu Ernest Nwankwo are among those who provided inspiration and community. Chielozona Eze, philosopher, literary scholar, survivor of the Biafra War, and author of *Survival Kit*, became a special companion.

At the University of Minnesota, Ohanessian Chair funds allowed me to bring to campus, as Annual Ohanessian lecturers, Bedross Der Matossian, Timothy Snyder, and Fatma Müge Göçek. Each enriched me far beyond the moment of their visit. I am grateful to Dean Jim Parente, who awarded me the Chair, and Dean John Coleman for twice extending the term.

The Ohanessian Chair, supplemented by a series of grants, including a Human Rights Initiative grant, Graduate Student-Faculty Collaborative grants, Undergraduate Research Opportunity grants, and first-year student opportunity grants, allowed me to work with several gifted undergraduate and graduate students as research assistants. They are impressive young people and their contributions to this project are essential. I am most grateful for their engaged work.

Graduate student Brooke Chambers was a crucial collaborator, especially on the *Griswold v. Driscoll* court case. She collected the data and contributed to the writing up of results. Accordingly, Brooke became coauthor of chapter 8. Caitlin Barden, then an undergraduate student at Minnesota, now a successful lawyer, had collected basic information, on which Brooke and I were able to build. Jacqulyn Kantack (then Meyer), as an undergraduate research assistant, did impressive work analyzing French legislative records. Jackie has since earned her Master of Human Rights degree and works with Human Rights Watch.

Prashasti Bhatnagar, now a graduate student in a joint program at Georgetown and Johns Hopkins universities, worked in the Minnesota History Archives, tirelessly and reliably. Dr. Lou Ann Matossian, eminent Minnesota historian with an unparalleled knowledge of the history of Armenians in her state, provided the lead to the Thomas and Carmelite Christie files in the Minnesota History Archives.

Several undergraduate and graduate research assistants contributed admirably to the coding of media reports and VAN (Vigilance Arménienne contre le Négationnisme) data and to the analysis of resulting data sets. They include, again, Brooke Chambers, Jessica Faulkner, Erez Garnai, Miray Phillips, Renée Rippberger, and Ellie Stencel. Abby Vogel and Kate Dwyer did outstanding work analyzing a set of documentary films on the Armenian genocide and Armenian survivor interviews from the Shoah Visual Archives, respectively.

Erez Garnai accompanied this project with his organizational abilities, his artistic skill in the preparation of graphs and tables, and his editorial care for detail. His outstanding work on my book *Representing Mass Violence*, early in his graduate studies, suggested that I employ him again for this book (now, as he gets ready to defend his dissertation).

Intellectual inspiration is hard to trace. I do know that John Hagan motivated me to work on issues of mass violence a good dozen years ago. He must have done a convincing job, as this is the fourth book I have since written on related themes. David Garland's insights into the interaction between elite actors and conditions of people on the ground, articulated for the realm of criminal punishment, inspired my thoughts on similar interactions in the formation of genocide knowledge. Jeffrey Olick and Daniel Levy invited me into the world of memory studies. At Minnesota, Alejandro Baer, director of our Center for Holocaust and Genocide Studies (CHGS) and descendant of refugees from Nazi Germany, is my companion in the intellectual journey through this challenging and painful terrain. I also benefited from advice by Artyom Tonoyan, CHGS research fellow, who combines sociological insight with profound knowledge of Armenian affairs. Past coauthorships on related issues with former advisees Ryan King and Hollie Nyseth Brehm (both now on the faculty of The Ohio State University), Wenjie Liao (Rochester Institute of Technology), James Nicholas Wahutu (New York University), and Susan McElrath (Montana State University) have undoubtedly affected this work as well, as did collaboration with current advisees Jillian LaBranche, Brooke Chambers, Nir Rotem, Michael Soto, and Nikoleta Sremac.

I am especially grateful to Alejandro Baer and Philip Smith, who read parts of an earlier draft of the manuscript, and to Pamela Feldman-Savelsberg, who closely read the final version, all providing most helpful feedback. Fatma Müge Göçek and Lois Presser reviewed the initial submission to UC Press. They waived their anonymity, enabling communication where I had questions. They went far beyond the call of duty. I thank them for their detailed and profound criticism and suggestions. I, of course, am solely responsible for any remaining imperfections or mistakes.

Maura Roessner, my editor at UC Press, combines professionalism and enthusiasm in ways that instill confidence in authors who have the good fortune of working with her and her colleagues, especially Jessica Moll and Madison Wetzell, reliable communicators. I am most grateful to Richard Earles for his thorough and masterful work as copy editor.

Finally, Pamela Feldman-Savelsberg accompanied me every step along the way, at home, sometimes in the office (at times hard to keep apart), in Minneapolis/ Saint Paul, Stellenbosch, Paris, and Berlin, through smooth and difficult stretches, always between cultures. I am more grateful than I can ever say. To her, I dedicate this book.

Joachim J. Savelsberg
Stellenbosch, South Africa / Paris, France /
Twin Cities of Minnesota, 2018–20

Introduction

Epistemic Circle and History of the Armenian Genocide

This book sheds light on seemingly paradoxical times. Heads of state increasingly apologize for atrocities committed by their countries, and humankind builds institutions to prevent, or to respond to, mass violence. Some even speak of a justice cascade. Yet mass violence, silencing, and the denial of genocides continue. We also live in an era in which populist leaders deny what overwhelming evidence documents. They tell their followers, for example, that "global warming" is a hoax, even a Chinese conspiracy, advanced to damage the American economy. In countries as diverse as the United States, the Philippines, Brazil, China, and Russia, they present themselves as saviors and spew falsehoods, "alternative facts," that fly in the face of solid scholarly evidence.

Closer to the theme of this book is denial of repression, mass atrocity, and genocide. We encounter this denial, against overwhelming evidence, in places such as Burma (Myanmar) with regard to the Rohingya; in Sudan with regard to the Fur, the Masalit, and the Zaghawa; in China with regard to the Uighurs; and in Turkey, where, despite great historical distance, political leaders continue to deny the genocide against the Ottoman Armenians committed during World War I. Populist political leaders are not alone in their denial. The populace often follows suit and at times encourages politicians' denialist practices. At times, silencing takes the place of denial. The long American history of silencing the near extinction of the American Indian population is but one example. The silencing of the Holocaust in this author's native Germany during the 1950s and 1960s is another. Even victim groups often silence the violence they experienced, albeit for different reasons, and this book speaks to that too.

In this contradictory and puzzling context, I ask how we know about genocide. Why do various collectivities and their leaders deny, silence, or recognize the same event of mass violence differently? Why do some insist on defining events as genocide, while others forcefully reject the label? This book is specifically about the emergence of radically distinct repertoires of knowledge about the Armenian genocide, which moved from broad acknowledgment to denial among Turks and from silencing to determined recognition among Armenians. The time span of more than a century during which this drama played out allows for insights into historical shifts and their drivers that the study of a more recent event would not grant.

This introduction summarizes themes, central theoretical ideas, and the chapters organized along those ideas. It speaks to empirical evidence, the data I use to illustrate and examine the validity of theoretical ideas. It specifies for whom I wrote this book, and it finally offers a brief historical overview of the Armenian genocide.

KNOWLEDGE ABOUT GENOCIDE—THE SUBJECT OF THIS BOOK

As I engage with the sociology of knowledge, I draw on and contribute to classical and contemporary strands of this sociological perspective. I show that each of them also applies to knowledge about genocide. Throughout this book, *knowledge* does not mean certified knowledge. Instead, as noted in the preface, the term simply refers to that which humans take for granted, to the perceived "certainty that phenomena are real and that they possess specific characteristics" (Berger and Luckmann 1966: 1). Repertoires of knowledge are clusters of such certainties that pertain to a particular set of phenomena, for example historical events.

Interactionist traditions in sociology show how humans produce an understanding of social reality (knowledge) in their daily interactions, communications, and thought processes. The literature, biographies, diaries, interviews, and observations of those who were touched by mass violence—as victims, as perpetrators, or as their descendants—serve as data. They document the unfolding of silencing, denying, or acknowledging when members of families, neighbors, friends, or humanitarians address (or avoid) the topic of genocide, as chapter 1 shows. Inner conversations supplement social interactions. They unfold, in George Herbert Mead's terms, between the I and the Me, the part of the self that assumes patterns of attitudes among others. Going beyond Mead, I see these patterns as embedded in social fields.[1] Such inner conversations become visible in correspondence and diaries kept by humanitarians and other observers, which I examine in chapter 2.

Peter Berger and Thomas Luckmann, in *The Social Construction of Reality*, show how knowledge constructed through self-reflection and millions of interactive situations becomes sedimented. It solidifies into knowledge repertoires of collectivities, "carrier groups" in the words of Max Weber and Karl Mannheim. Yet, where Berger and Luckmann suggest harmony, we may in fact find disagreement and—importantly—diametrically opposed sets of knowledge across social groups.

Such an outcome becomes visible in debates about mass atrocities, including—with particular intensity—the Armenian genocide.

We also see that not all actors have equal chances to contribute to the construction of knowledge, a point overlooked by Berger and Luckmann. Asymmetries in power and communicative capacities affect outcomes. Knowledge entrepreneurs, acting from privileged institutional positions, shape and spread their group's definition of social reality to wider audiences. They also seek to manipulate, intensify, mobilize, or alter knowledge repertoires of carrier groups with which they are associated. Constructionist social problems theory, and scholars of reputations such as Barry Schwartz and Gary Fine, highlight the role of entrepreneurs in the construction of knowledge, in instilling in larger publics a specific definition of reality. These insights also apply, as Jeffrey Alexander has shown, to the role of entrepreneurs in the processing of horrendous experiences that threaten the existence or self-understanding of a collectivity, in the generation of cultural trauma after genocide. Finally, knowledge is not as stable as Berger and Luckmann suggest. It is at times dormant. Entrepreneurs may mobilize and alter it. In chapter 3, I deposit these theoretical concepts and ideas in a toolbox from which I draw in subsequent chapters.

The process of sedimentation of knowledge about the Armenian genocide among Armenians, in their own country and in the diaspora, is the subject of chapter 4. Chapter 5 examines the evolution and sedimentation of Turkish knowledge. Throughout these chapters, I draw from literature that provides analyses of memoirs, banners displayed at demonstrations, memorial sites, news media, and textbooks.

Where different collectivities generate radically distinct repertoires of knowledge, their encounter with "the other" becomes a challenge they need to address. One option is the enactment of public rituals through which each group seeks to protect and reinforce its identity and knowledge. Armenian genocide commemorations, across the diaspora and centrally in Yerevan, Armenia's capital city, held on each April 24, provide an excellent example. The Turkish state instead has developed rituals to cleanse the memory of the Ottoman Empire and to celebrate unambiguously its history, disregarding its dark sides. Émile Durkheim and a new school of neo-Durkheimian thought explores the role of rituals in public life: their capacity to evoke a sense of group integration and collective effervescence and to solidify shared beliefs. This literature provides us with valuable tools for the analysis of Armenian and Turkish rituals, the focus of chapter 6. Ethnographic observation is the key method here.

Yet collectivities and their leaders do not just seek to solidify knowledge repertoires within their own groups. They also openly attack those of "the other" in conflictual processes. The Turkish state has attempted, with growing intensity, to challenge knowledge about the Armenian genocide. Armenians have fought, in return, for the recognition of their history. The form such conflicts take, and their outcomes, vary by social fields in which actors carry them out (politics and law, for example). Each field follows, in the terms of Pierre Bourdieu, its own rules of the game. Yet players in these fields also enjoy discretion. They improvise, with at times unpredictable outcomes. They finally act within institutions that differ across countries, while also being connected to world society.

Politics is a central social field in which conflicts over knowledge unfold. In chapter 7, I explore political struggles over knowledge pertaining to the Armenian genocide in France, using interviews and document analysis as key methods. The French case is most relevant, because the country is home to the largest Armenian diaspora per capita and because conflicts over historical knowledge feature prominently in French politics. At stake are "memory laws" promulgated by legislative bodies. They reach from simple statements of acknowledgment to laws that criminalize denialist utterances. Many countries have recognized the Armenian genocide over the past two decades, often through legislative votes. Examining the French case under a microscope sheds light on the specific struggles and mechanisms of power at work.

The legal field is another battleground. Past research has focused on the contributions to knowledge and memory of trials against perpetrators of mass violence. Chapter 8, cowritten with Brooke B. Chambers, deals with a different type of legal engagement, formally a fight over free speech rights. We examine an American court case, *Griswold v. Driscoll*, in which Turkish interest groups mobilized young civil liberties enthusiasts toward such ends, using a free speech lawyer as a go-between. The plaintiffs insisted that each repertoire of knowledge has to be represented evenly—for example, in curricula or textbooks—for freedom of speech to be secured. We detail the unfolding of this exemplary case in the federal courts of Boston, Massachusetts, and its consequences for knowledge about the Armenian genocide. The United States is a most appropriate setting in which to examine such a conflict in the realm of law, because it is home to one of the largest Armenian diasporas, second only to Russia, and because in the United States, compared to other Western democracies, the legal arena is most prominent in the settling of conflicts. Again, interviews and the analysis of documents provide core evidence.

Finally, chapter 9 examines the counterproductive outcome of denialism in the context of a (partial) human rights hegemony. Here I return to the American and French cases to show the blowback that denial caused those who engaged in it. Their attempts resulted in substantial ethnic mobilization and support by human rights organizations and state actors, who used various means at their disposal toward a solidification of genocide knowledge among the victim group. I supplement these case studies by an analysis of the public sphere, specifically news media and documentary films.

The overall model sketched here is depicted in figure 1. It leads from social interaction and interventions by knowledge entrepreneurs to a group-specific sedimentation of knowledge, attempts to solidify such knowledge against

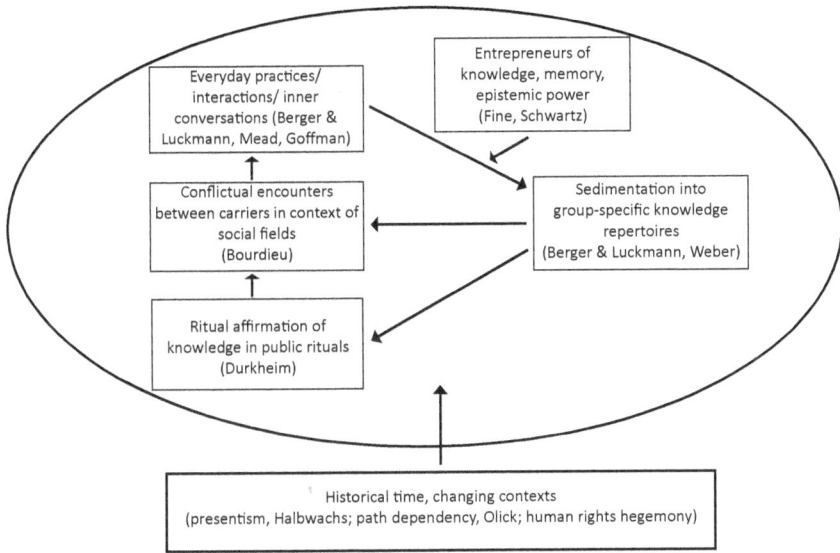

FIGURE 1. Epistemic circle: Formation of genocide knowledge in a multicausal process.

competing views through rituals, and conflictual engagement with challengers in the fields of law and politics. All of this unfolds in specific nation-states with their particular institutions, as well as in a global realm in which human rights principles have gained a hegemonic status. Once sedimented and secured, knowledge repertoires then feed back to the micro-level through socialization processes. The epistemic circle, or circle of knowledge, closes.

In line with a broad constructionist approach, I am not concerned with knowledge produced by specialists, but with knowledge generated in the context of practical action, in everyday life and in fields of law and politics (in line with Swidler and Arditi 1994). The study of knowledge about the past, in the form of collective memory (Olick 1999; Schwartz and Schuman 2005) or cultural trauma (Alexander et al. 2004), aligns well with such constructionism. Note, however, that knowledge produced by specialists (Camic and Gross 2001; Collins 2000) may, at times, and possibly with substantial lags, feed into an understanding of reality in everyday life. The common view of our world as a globe circling around the sun is one example from the natural sciences.

To avoid any misunderstandings, I must state that this book is *not* an attempt to answer the question of truth—even though I have my own understanding of the history of mass violence against the Ottoman Armenians. My understanding is consistent with overwhelming historical scholarship and expressed in the language I use. Throughout, I refer to this catastrophic chapter of mass violence as the Armenian genocide. Yet, working in a sociology of knowledge frame, I take

seriously the knowledge repertoires on all sides. Those who endure denialist prov-
ocations, especially, should have an interest in understanding the knowledge that
so radically clashes with their own and the conditions that generate, solidify, and
diffuse that knowledge.

This book is also *not* a sociology of genocide; I do not seek to explain causes
of genocide. Yet I *am* interested in the contending parties' knowledge about the
conditions of genocide, because they are part of genocide knowledge. Importantly,
the outcome of struggles over genocide knowledge may affect the likelihood of
future genocides.

Finally, this book is *not* an exhaustive evaluation of literature, neither in the
sociology of knowledge nor on the history or sociology of (the Armenian) genocide. It is instead an effort at bringing core elements of these two distinct bodies of
literature into a conversation.

FOR WHOM I WROTE THIS BOOK—CHANCES AND RISKS

I wrote this book simultaneously for those interested in the sociology of
knowledge and collective memory; for those concerned with the denial
and recognition of genocide and other forms of mass violence, specifically of
the Armenian genocide; and finally for those interested broadly in the buildup
of contradictory repertoires of knowledge and the dynamics that unfold
between them.

For readers with an interest in the sociology of knowledge, my project confirms
the applicability of this sociological specialty to the social and cultural processing
of mass violence. By drawing on a wealth of classical and contemporary traditions,
I simultaneously show the value added by each approach and potential gains from
its application to the difficult theme of genocide. For those concerned with collective memory, I suggest that opening up the broader toolbox of the sociology of
knowledge provides new perspectives.

While the promises are substantial, by addressing genocide through a sociology of knowledge perspective, I also enter into dangerous terrain. Seeking to avoid
misinterpretations, I did not adapt Berger and Luckmann's famous title, *The Social
Construction of Reality*, into *The Social Construction of Genocidal Reality*. As a
sociological constructionist, I recognize that our understanding of social reality
and history is always culturally processed. Yet, as a philosophical realist (Ferraris
2014), I know that the pain, suffering, humiliation, and death of those who fell
victim to genocides and other forms of mass violence are all too real. While the
term *genocide* is a judicial construction, and while our knowledge about genocides
is the result of cultural processing, there is most certainly a real referent to the
phenomena the term *genocide* covers.

I am simultaneously writing for readers who are concerned with recognition and denial of genocides and other forms of mass violence generally, and of the Armenian genocide in particular. I hope that helping these readers look at familiar themes through a sociology of knowledge lens will supply them with fresh, and maybe surprising, insights. I also hope to answer some questions that almost certainly plague these readers: How can "the other side" insist on denial even in the face of massive evidence? What kinds of strategies do its protagonists use to spread denial? What are their chances at succeeding? How do members of victim groups respond? Which of their responses are helpful in enhancing recognition, and which are counterproductive?

Finally, and more broadly, I wrote this book for those who are desperate to understand the coexistence of, and interaction between, radically opposed repertoires of knowledge; their emergence, their solidification, and their confrontations; and, closely related, the denial of well-established facts, especially by populist leaders and their followers. Such confrontation is increasingly common, and it is destabilizing. This book thus speaks to all concerned with the dynamics that today contribute to a destabilization of our social and political world.

GENOCIDE AGAINST THE OTTOMAN ARMENIANS IN CONTEXT

Again, this book is *not* about the history of the Armenian genocide. It is instead a sociology of genocide knowledge, examining how different collectivities know and tell this history. Yet some basic historical information is in order. I thus conclude this introduction with a nutshell summary of the prehistory, history, and post-history of the violence, to which subsequent chapters add detail. I here focus on basic information on which historians have reached an overwhelming consensus, even if disagreements on details and specific aspects remain. These historians, supplemented by historical-comparative sociologists, include Fikret Adanir, Boris Adjemian, Taner Akçam, Donald Bloxham, Hamit Borzaslan, Bedross Der Matossian, Vincent Duclert, Fatma Müge Göçek, Richard Hovannisian, Raymond Kévorkian, Hans-Lukas Kieser, Bernard Lewis (despite his rejection of the genocide label), Claire Mouradian, Ronald Grigor Suny, Yves Ternon, and Uğur Ümit Üngör.[2]

This is not the place, of course, to tell the more than three-thousand-year history of the Armenian people. Historians trace this people's migration from the Caucasus region into Asia Minor, its early Christianization in the first century CE, its establishment of a territorial state with shifting boundaries, most expansive in the first century, and the invention of its own alphabet in the fifth century. Nor is this the place to tell the history of the Ottoman Empire, which arose in the fourteenth century. At the time of its greatest expansion, from the sixteenth through the nineteenth centuries, the empire controlled much of the Middle East and the Arab world, the North African coastal regions, and Southeastern Europe. By the sixteenth century, the empire had also incorporated the Armenian people.

The decline of the Ottoman Empire, conflicts among its neighbors, and the rise of ethno-nationalism became crucial preconditions for the Armenian genocide. In 1804–13 and 1826–28, two Russo-Persian wars resulted in the incorporation of Eastern Armenia (Yerevan and Karabakh) into the Russian Empire. Most territories with predominantly Armenian populations, however, remained under Ottoman rule. Armenians, and other minorities, now enjoyed limited equality within the millet system of relatively autonomous self-administration. Yet they suffered substantially higher tax burdens and were prohibited from bearing arms. In addition, military defeats suffered by the Ottoman Empire resulted in the scapegoating of minorities and increasing repression, culminating in the mass killings of more than two hundred thousand Armenians in 1894–96 under Sultan Abdülhamid II (the Hamidian massacres). Simultaneously, Armenian movements formed and radicalized, including the Dashnaks, a nationalist and socialist political party founded in 1890 in Tiflis (Georgia).

The Young Turk revolution of 1908 and the overthrow of the sultan brought hope to the country's minorities, but that hope was short lived. For Armenians it ended in 1909 with a massacre of thousands in the city of Adana. For the postrevolutionary Ottoman Empire, hope was crushed by military defeats during the Balkan Wars of 1912 and 1913. These wars resulted in the loss of the most economically developed parts of the empire, the forced resettlement of hundreds of thousands of ethnic Turks from the Balkans into Anatolia, and—in reaction—a massive campaign of Turkification of space, people, and the economy.

The catastrophe suffered by the Ottoman Armenians unfolded soon thereafter in the context of World War I (1914–18), during which the Ottoman Empire was allied with Austria-Hungary and the German Empire. The Young Turk government now defined the Armenian minority, small and radicalized segments of which had risen up in opposition, as an internal tumor. It set up the Special Organization, a militia force dedicated to the repression of internal opposition and minority groups. The first deportations of Armenians began in March 1915. On April 24, 1915, the regime rounded up, deported, and killed hundreds of Armenian intellectuals, silencing their voices in anticipation of an outcry that would have accompanied the following events. These events included the killing of tens of thousands of Armenian men and the deportation, by train and by foot, of hundreds of thousands, mostly women and children, to concentration camps in the deserts of Syria and Mesopotamia. Thousands perished from exhaustion and starvation along the way. By March 1916, half a million subsisted in camps, where many died from starvation. Most fell victim to mass liquidations. Map 1 represents crucial elements of this process.

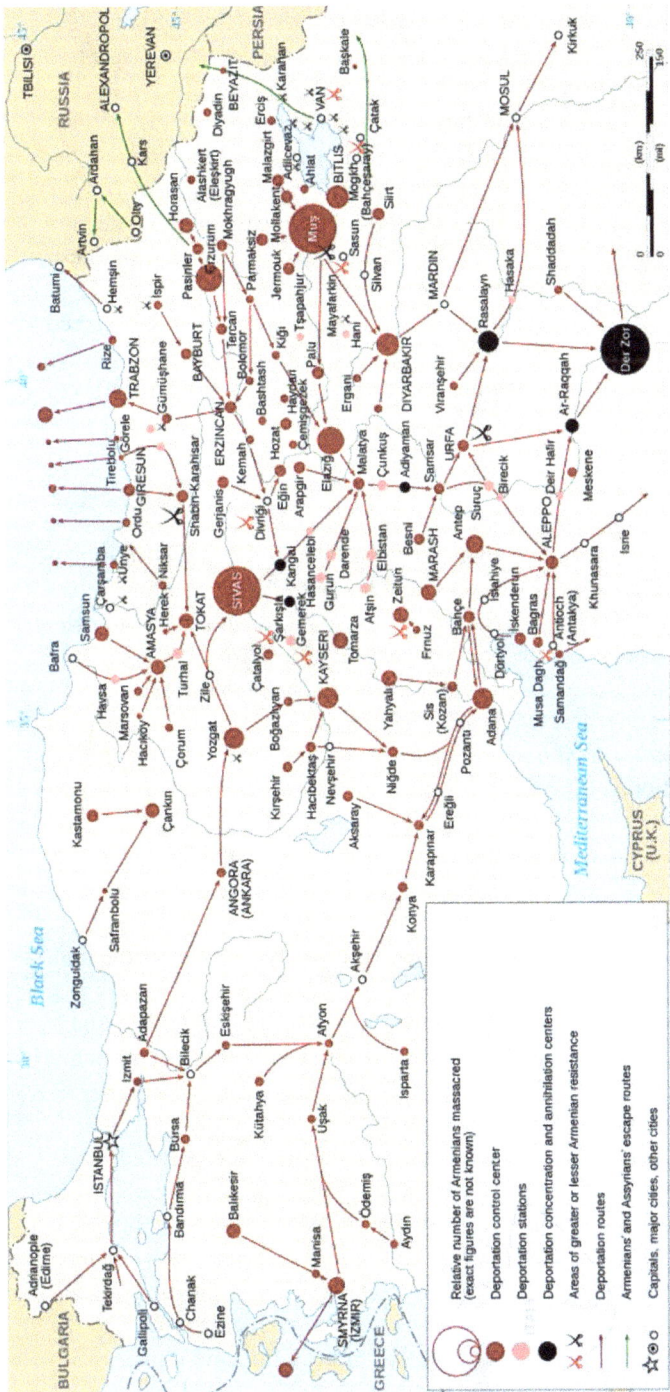

MAP 1. Map of the genocide against the Ottoman Armenians, 1915. This is a replica of map 224 in Robert H. Hewsen, *Armenia: A Historical Atlas* (University of Chicago Press, 2001), p. 232.

Source: Wikipedia (https://en.wikipedia.org/wiki/File:Armenian_Genocide_Map-en.svg).

- Each dot denotes a massacre. There are three types of massacres: in a control center (red dot), in a station (pink dot), in a concentration and annihilation center (black dot). Size of dot indicates relative number of Armenians killed.
- Each pair of swords denotes an area of Armenian resistance: greater resistance (red swords) or lesser resistance (black swords). Different sizes of swords mean nothing; some are smaller to better fit on the map.
- Dots in Black Sea represent Armenians (mainly women and children) drowned in the sea.

While historiography largely agrees on the basic facts, differences pertain to the specific conditions and the pattern of the unfolding genocide. Some scholars place greater emphasis on religion and continuity of violence or nationalism, while others highlight demographic engineering; further, while some focus on one moment of decision making, others see a cumulative policy radicalization, stressing the contingency of the unfolding events (see overview by Der Matossian 2015).

Events shortly before and after the end of World War I further determined the fate of the Armenians in the postwar order. Initially, the Russian Revolution of 1917 provided opportunities for nationalist Armenians to create an independent Armenia (May 1918). Hopes were further elevated by the Treaty of Sèvres, signed on August 10, 1920, the outcome of negotiations between the victorious powers of World War I and the Ottoman Empire. This treaty promised vast territories to the new Armenian state, reaching far into today's Turkey.

Almost simultaneously, however, the Turkish National Movement under the leadership of Mustafa Kemal (Atatürk) established the Turkish Republic, overthrew the sultan, moved the capital from Constantinople to Ankara, and engaged in a war of independence against the occupying powers. The new Turkish government did not recognize the Treaty of Sèvres. Working to neutralize some of the losses resulting from defeat in World War I, its leaders coordinated with the new Soviet Union an attack on Armenia, with Soviet troops invading from the north and Turkish troops from the south. The northern part of Armenia was incorporated into the Soviet Union, and major territories of the short-lived Armenian state were returned to Turkey, including those eastern sections where Armenians had been the dominant population group before 1915. The year 1920 thus marked the end of the short-lived first Armenian republic. The Soviet authorities eventually merged what remained of Armenia with Georgia and Azerbaijan into the Transcaucasian Socialist Republic (1922–36), until they eventually allowed for the establishment of a separate Armenian Soviet Republic (1936). These moves contributed to a replacement of the Treaty of Sèvres by the Treaty of Lausanne (1923), which, for the time being, ended all Armenian hopes for an independent country.

Meanwhile, the new Turkish Republic, under the leadership of Atatürk, stabilized during the 1920s and 1930s. It remained neutral during World War II, and in the war's aftermath joined the United Nations (1945) and the North Atlantic Treaty Organization (1952). Civilian governments took turns with military rule after several successful coups. In the 1990s and early 2000s, Turkey negotiated, albeit unsuccessfully, for membership in the European Union. Secular since Atatürk, the republic displayed a more religious orientation beginning in the early 2000s, under the populist and increasingly authoritarian rule of prime minister, and then president, Recep Tayyip Erdoğan and his Justice and Development Party (AKP). Throughout, Turkey sought to eradicate remnants of Armenian culture and the memory of Armenian contributions to the history of the Ottoman Empire.

The former Soviet Republic of Armenia, for its part, declared independence from the Russian Federation in 1994. The relatively poor country, with a population of some three million people and its capital city of Yerevan, is in close exchange with a much larger diaspora of an estimated eight million ethnic Armenians, mostly in France, the United States, and Russia.

What, then, do Armenians, Turks, and world society know about the mass violence against the Armenians during World War I? How did their knowledge change over time and under what conditions? These questions are the subject of the following sociology of knowledge explorations.

PART I

Interaction and Micropolitics
of Genocide Knowledge

1

———

Social Interaction, Self-Reflection, and Struggles over Genocide Knowledge

Carmelite Christie—missionary, school administrator, and educator in the town of Tarsus in Turkey—writes observations about the Armenian genocide, which unfolded around her and throughout the Ottoman Empire, in her diary entries of 1915–19 (Minnesota Historical Society [MHS], n.d.). Christie's first preserved entry confirms scholarship according to which killings and deportations were in full force by the fall of 1915. On October 1, 1915, she notes that

> Prof. Zenop Bezjian spent one night in Tarsus en route for Constantinople, whither he goes as the ecclesiastical representative for the Protestants of all Turkey. He told us of 60,000 exiles encamped between the end of the RR [railroad] journey, Osmania and Aleppo,—sent from home and business all the way along the line from Constantinople,—and not wanted in the regions to which they go. Multitudes are starving. They are without money, no work to be had, food scarce, even for those able to pay, sickness of all kinds prevalent, numbers dying every day. (MHS Box 28:2–3)

Christie writes about massacres in villages near Yozgat, the dead left unburied:

> They told of a village of 300 where 200 had been butchered. There were many murders on the road, and women outraged in the usual manner, and young women stolen and taken away. Robbery was a daily occurrence. . . . I heard today of a poor woman at Gulek [Gülek] Station, who was without any money or food. . . . [The woman] threww [sic] her two little ones into the shallow stream . . . the inhumanity of man to man, of which we take daily knowledge is almost past belief. (MHS Box 28:2–3)[1]

This testimony, together with that of hundreds of other observers and the experiences of thousands of survivors, accumulated, over the past century, to form a body of knowledge about the Armenian genocide. Testifying is often challenging. Even for a worker in the field of humanitarian aid like Christie, it takes courage to note the cruelties. After all, she has to operate under the regime that is responsible for the suffering she seeks to alleviate. While entrusting a private diary with testimony for posterity is less risky than testifying publicly at the time of the atrocities, a diary writer still has to overcome a sense of caution and accommodation to the surrounding powers. The temptation to hold back information is encouraged by prevailing silences on the part of victims and perpetrators, and by denial, especially by the perpetrators.

Unlike Christie, most do not document their observations in writing. Yet they communicate, or seek to avoid communication, in millions of day-to-day interactions in which they silence, deny, or acknowledge. Through these exchanges they generate knowledge, an understanding of present and historical reality. Which aspect of reality prevails depends on which of these strategies dominates in a given collectivity. Most who grew up in post-atrocity eras know the mechanisms well. Born in 1951 in Germany and growing up in the decades following the Holocaust, this author's knowledge about the world missed essential aspects of the immediate past. Parents, teachers, clerics, neighbors—all to whom children and adolescents look up and from whom they seek to learn—silenced the Shoah. Only in the mid- to late 1960s was this silence broken. Acknowledgment set in, slow initially and then accelerating. When silencing was no longer an option, many responded with various forms of denial.

This generational experience motivates and informs this first chapter. Here I address patterns of communication in personal interaction and written texts as the first stage in the buildup of repertoires of knowledge about genocide. Eventually, millions of micro-level communicative exchanges aggregate into macrosociological outcomes. They become part of group-specific knowledge repertoires in a process of sedimentation that is the subject of subsequent chapters.

KNOWLEDGE: WHAT WE TAKE FOR GRANTED

We all have answers to questions about the world. They reach from the banal—say, what the safest place is to cross the street—to more challenging matters such as what type of education leads to occupational opportunities, or what family arrangements provide a healthy upbringing for children. They include difficult issues, for example questions about the origins of human life, human contributions to global warming, or the safety of nuclear energy or genetically engineered food. Closer to the subject of this book, many of our contemporaries have answers when asked about the Armenian genocide that began in 1915 or about the number of Jewish lives extinguished during the Holocaust. We consider our answers to these questions part of what we know about the world. Yet almost none of that knowledge results from our own scholarly or otherwise systematic exploration. Again, *knowledge*—in the sociology of knowledge tradition—is not certified knowledge, but simply the perceived "certainty that phenomena are real and that they possess specific characteristics" (Berger and Luckmann 1966:1). Knowledge consists of "matter of course assumptions" (Schütz [1932] 1967), which, in aggregate, constitute a "relative-natural world view" (Scheler 1992)—relative, in that it is specific to a collectivity's place in the world.[2]

Some of our knowledge concerns the here and now—phenomena that surround us at the current time and in the places in which we live, work, play, or endure. Yet the meaning of the here and now is not always clear to us. We encounter new situations that appear to be chaotic and confusing. Consider exposure to mass violence and the disorientation it evokes. Noted Armenians such as Aurora (Arshaluys) Mardiganian, Kaspar Hovannisian, and the parents of Arsham and Sita Ohanessian, and hundreds of thousands of others less well known suffered the cruelty of eviction from their homes in the Ottoman Empire and the exhaustion of death marches from their villages and towns into the Syrian Desert. They saw their brothers killed and their mothers raped. Just a quarter of a century later, Jean Améry, Paul Neurath, Primo Levi, Maurice Halbwachs, and Jorge Semprún lived through pain and humiliation in Nazi Germany's torture chambers and concentration camps. Deprived even of basic markers of their identity, they nevertheless communicated with others, even at the time of suffering, and through such exchanges, some made sense of their experience (e.g., Semprún 1981; Neurath [1943] 2005).

Most of our knowledge, however, concerns events and phenomena far removed from our own experience. We learn about them through mediators: some close, such as grandparents or parents who experienced the past directly, or friends who have traveled to distant places; others more removed and formal, such as history books, the internet, or news media. When knowledge about the past is shared, acknowledged, and reaffirmed by members of a collectivity, we refer to it as *collective memory* (Coser 1992). Unlike the firsthand knowledge of Aurora Mardiganian or Jorge Semprún, the collective memory of mass atrocities is, for most of us, part of the body of mediated knowledge. We did not gain it through personal experience.

Addressing communication that supplies us with knowledge about genocide, I build on a branch of sociology that was inspired by pragmatist philosophy and phenomenology. It includes lines of work that purists separate strictly, but that have basic features in common. Its contributors share the notion that knowledge about the world is constructed through social interaction. Charles Cooley (1926), Alfred Schütz ([1932] 1967), Herbert Blumer (1969), Erving Goffman (1967), and Peter Berger and Thomas Luckmann (1966) are among the prominent representatives of this approach to the understanding of society. Closely related is the notion that knowledge is constructed through thought processes, inner conversations between the I and the Me (Mead 1934). When documented through writing, thought processes become externalized and objectified, subject to transmission to others, including new generations. Throughout chapters 1 and 2, we encounter such knowledge construction in the form of letters, diaries, and memoirs.

While scholars in the interactionist tradition thus focus on the micro-level of social life, they know that social interactions in the here and now do not occur in empty social space. Instead, they unfold in a world of social facts of which actors have to be mindful. They also know that social interaction has consequences. It leaves traces, solidifying and altering, albeit in microscopic steps, the social reality in which it takes place.

The history of the term *genocide* offers an example. At the beginning stood a dispute over the notion of state sovereignty, carried out between Raphael Lemkin, then a law student, and one of his professors at the University of Lviv. Lemkin, well informed about the mass violence against the Armenian people, was disturbed by the trial conducted in Berlin against Soghomon Tehlirian, the young Armenian assassin of Talaat Pasha, one of the main responsible actors in the genocide. In debating his professor, Lemkin came to challenge the notion of state sovereignty, ingrained in international law since the end of the Thirty Years' War and the West-phalian Peace Treaty of 1648, a principle that allows a government to act toward its subjects as it sees fit, with no legal recourse or threat of outside intervention. Lem-kin developed the concept of genocide over subsequent decades, in publications, conference contributions, and manifold discussions with legal scholars, activists, and politicians. He fought desperately and succeeded in convincing the newly founded United Nations to draft and vote on the Genocide Convention—formally, the Convention on the Prevention and Punishment of the Crime of Genocide—adopted unanimously by the UN General Assembly in 1948. *Genocide*, according to the Genocide Convention, "means any of the following acts committed with intent to destroy, in whole or in part, a national, ethnical, racial or religious group, as such: (a) Killing members of the group; (b) Causing serious bodily or mental harm to members of the group; (c) Deliberately inflicting on the group condi-tions of life calculated to bring about its physical destruction in whole or in part; (d) Imposing measures intended to prevent births within the group; (e) Forcibly transferring children of the group to another group."[3] What began with communi-cative interaction, a dispute between student and professor, solidified and became a central concept in modern international human rights law.

A MICROSOCIOLOGICAL PERSPECTIVE
ON SILENCING, DENYING,
AND ACKNOWLEDGING GENOCIDE

Victims and perpetrators of genocide, and their descendants, face special chal-lenges when they communicate about the history of genocide. They need to repair their spoiled identities and to manage stigma (Goffman [1963] 1986; Giesen 2004a; Savelsberg 2021). In interactions, they often silence the past, or they deny, challeng-ing truth claims of the "other." In the alternative, they recognize and acknowledge the deadly past. Acknowledgment among perpetrators, or those to whom perpe-trators have passed on the stigma of perpetration, may take the form of confession.

Silencing is a common strategy in the immediate aftermath of genocide. So is denial, especially among perpetrator peoples once silence is broken and information about the genocide begins to seep to the surface of social life. Today, in fact, many have listened to testimonies that survivors of the Holocaust gave to school classes or have watched archived video recordings of survivor interviews.[4] They may have viewed documentary films such as Claude Lanzmann's *Shoah*, with its ten hours of interviews with surviving victims and perpetrators, or one of the many documentaries on the Armenian genocide. Many today have read biographical texts, memoirs, or diaries, or have spoken with survivors and their descendants.

In the following, I draw on such sources in examining how various actors engage in silencing or denying the Armenian genocide, or in acknowledgment and recognition. I make use of autobiographical accounts, family histories, and memoirs as quarries from which pieces of information about interactive situations can be broken off and analyzed. Secondly, at a different level of analysis, I use autobiographical accounts, memoirs, and diaries themselves as data, as examples of inner conversations by the authors, or their conversations with imagined audiences. While elsewhere I examine strategies used by authors and in everyday interaction as forms of stigma management for post-Holocaust Germany (Savelsberg, 2020b), here I am primarily interested in the contribution of these strategies to repertoires of knowledge among Armenians and Turks.

Silence and Silencing

Silence is a state, silencing an activity. In social interactions, we may silence ourselves. "Biting one's tongue" is a familiar expression, and we can all think of times when we were about to utter a statement but stopped ourselves at the last second (or did not, but should have). We may instead silence others, by imposing rules of speech, cutting others off, or interrupting their utterances with discouraging comments or gestures (Smith-Lovin and Brody 1989). Silencing a dark past is common practice among victim as well as perpetrator groups.

Consider Peter Balakian, who grew up in an Armenian American family and became a writer, a Pulitzer Prize recipient, and a scholar. He wrote prominently about the Armenian genocide in *The Burning Tigris: The Armenian Genocide and America's Response* (Balakian 2003). In an autobiography written a few years earlier—*Black Dog of Fate: An American Son Uncovers His Armenian Past* (Balakian 1997)—he tells his readers about family interactions that involved the fate of his ancestors, including stories about silencing. Consider young Peter secretly observing his grandmother, a survivor of the genocide, as she took a long ivory pipe out of her purse, prepared it, and smoked "in long puffs." Occasionally, she made the sign of the cross and repeatedly uttered "Der Voghormya" (Lord have mercy) and "Sourp Asdvadz" (Holy God)—while watching television news about the Cuban Missile Crisis in 1962. Daring to ask his mother, albeit after some delay, about his grandmother's strange rituals, Peter was told: "Oh, in the old country, at a certain age, women smoke pipes once in a while. It's a sign of wisdom" (Balakian 1997:16).

Not surprisingly, his mother's answer, by silencing much, raised new and more urgent questions in the boy's mind. He knew that "the old country" meant Armenia, but his notion of Armenia was a blurry one, and he did not know why its mention made him feel uneasy. When he sought to inquire, adults would change the subject. If it is not "really around anymore," as his mother told him on another occasion, where had it gone? An absence of physical markers accompanied the silence. Where others to whom a place is dear might display a map or a photo, there was emptiness in the Balakian home, adding to young Peter's unease.

Peter Balakian's story is neither universal nor unique. It is one of millions of moments of silencing among survivors and their descendants, inhibiting the transmission of knowledge across generations. Simultaneously, Balakian's story shows that silence is rarely *total* silence. While his mother avoided the difficult topic of genocide, she did refer to "the old country." Silences, especially partial silences, may speak. Balakian's mother thus communicated not just a void to her son, but unease. This transmission of unease may not be generalizable, but the way silence speaks is again not unique to the Balakian family.

Recent interviews with French citizens of Armenian descent reveal similar stories about silencing.[5] For example, a prominent Armenian-French man— editor-in-chief of a renowned ethnic magazine and a leader in organized French Armenian life—tells me about his grandparents, who had survived the genocide and migrated to France from Greece in 1920: "They did not speak to their grandchildren about the genocide, to protect them; but they talked among each other and expressed their hatred of Turks" (paraphrased). His parents, however, did speak to their son about the Armenian experience during World War I. Another prominent French person of Armenian descent, editor-in-chief of a prestigious academic journal dedicated to Armenian issues, similarly reports that he talked with his parents, but not with his grandparents, about Armenian issues. And a young Armenian-French scholar shared the experience of learning little from his grandfather, who had escaped the genocide, about his suffering.

Across the Atlantic Ocean, in the thin Armenian diaspora of Minnesota, an Armenian American revealed his experiences at an event entitled "How it was to grow up Armenian in...," organized by the Armenian Cultural Organization of Minnesota. He spoke to his audience about the absence of April 24 commemorations in his childhood, and recalled that his parents did not talk much about the Armenian past. He attributes their silence to their fight against outsider status in their new country, to which their own parents had migrated from the Ottoman Empire, but in which they were born.

Silencing comes in different shapes. A leading activist for the cultural association Vigilance Arménienne contre le Négationnisme, for example, grew up in a dense Armenian-French community, and she remembers attending somber annual ceremonies on April 24, the Armenian day of genocide commemoration. Yet elders did not explain the meaning of those ceremonies, leaving her with a diffuse awareness of something dark. The shock came—and the silence was broken—at age eight, when she discovered a book with images of the genocide.

Again, silencing histories of mass atrocity is not universal, and below we will encounter different stories, ones of active denying and of acknowledging. Yet silencing is widespread, and Armenians share it with other groups whose history involved genocidal victimization. Vered Vinitzky-Seroussi and Chana Teeger write about "social silences," with a focus on the Jewish experience. They distinguish between overt silence, a literal absence of speech, and covert silence, "covered and veiled by much mnemonic talk and representation" (2010:1104). Both types may serve the aim of either memorializing or forgetting. A "moment of silence," for example during Israel's Memorial Day for the Holocaust, serves the preservation of memory. It contrasts with overt silence practiced by groups that "actively do not wish to remember" (2010:1110). On the side of covert silence, Vinitzky-Seroussi and Teeger identify "bland commemoration," a selective way of memorializing, in which some aspects of history are silenced (e.g., the genocide) while others are cultivated (e.g., music and culinary traditions). From this, they distinguish "cacophonous commemoration," exemplified by days of commemoration of troubling events that are coupled with the commemoration of one or several other occurrences. Consequently, the undesirable event is crowded out.

In the interactive situations reported above for Armenians, social actors typically engage in two of these four types of silence: overt silence with the goal of forgetting and covert silence by way of "bland commemoration." Yet their stories show that even overt silence with the goal of forgetting is never complete silence. Occasional referents to the repressed past tell recipients that something unpleasant is being avoided, that there is a proverbial elephant in the room (Zerubavel 2006).

At times, silence is only verbal silence. Cultural anthropologist Carol Kidron (2009) interviewed fifty-five descendants of Holocaust survivors in her native Israel. While her respondents confirm the preponderance of verbal silence, they simultaneously report nonverbal forms of communication. Examples include embodied practices such as the habit of keeping one's shoes close to the bed, passed on to children and grandchildren. Getting into shoes quickly might confer enhanced chances of survival in the camps. Respondents also report about person-object interactions, such as the spoon a respondent's mother used in the Auschwitz camp to eat her soup. The spoon had become a matter-of-course object in the household with which she fed the interviewee as a little child. The daughter adds: "Look, she won, she survived with that spoon" (Kidron 2009:11). While such statements reveal triumph rather than trauma, other quotations appear to reflect at least ambivalence. Kidron quotes one of her interviewees who reports how her mother's nightly screams woke her frequently when she was a child: "I didn't know why she was crying, I knew she was having a bad dream, that it must have been something very frightening or painful and that it was about the Holocaust. I think my father may have told me it was because of the Holocaust. I didn't know what she was dreaming about the Holocaust or really what the Holocaust was, but . . . *I knew it was about what I didn't know*" (Kidron 2009:5–6). Obviously, the cries of this respondent's mother provided some knowledge, further advanced by her father's words (Holocaust as a "painful" experience that, decades later, causes nightmares—"bad dreams"); but other knowledge was missing ("what the Holocaust was"). The situation Kidron's respondent reports thus reveals awareness (knowledge) of ignorance (not knowing), resulting from a mix of verbal and non-verbal communication. I heard similar accounts from non-Jewish Polish friends whose parents had survived the camps.

Kidron's second major point challenges much of the literature on silence. She argues that the effect of verbal silence is not necessarily disturbing or traumatic. Instead, silent traces transmit tacit knowledge of the past within everyday family life. These arguments pertain to the quality of knowledge, in that it matters if knowledge is verbally articulated or embodied. They speak secondly to the affective consequences of verbal silence in combination with nonverbal communication. Kidron's conclusion certainly contrasts with the unease that quotations from the interviews and biographies above overwhelmingly reflect. Might it be that Kidron's findings and conclusions are reflective of the specific Israeli context, characterized by a sense of relative cultural safety in a new, post-genocide state (as opposed to diaspora) and surrounded by a world in which many share in the respondents' experiences? Contrast this with stories about Jewish life in the diaspora.

Philippe Sands, an international lawyer and professor of law at University College London, conveys such stories in *East-West Street* (Sands 2016). The author tells us that he learned little about his grandfather Leon's life before 1945, in Lemberg (today, Lviv) and Vienna. "The past hung about Leon and Rita [his wife], a time before Paris, not to be talked about in my presence or not in a language I understood" (16). He remembers his grandfather's words "C'est compliqué, c'est le passé, pas important" (17) (It's complicated, it's the past, not important). He also remembers—similar to Peter Balakian—the "absence of photographs" (15), and he quotes psychoanalyst Nikolas Abraham: "What haunts us are not the dead, but the gaps left within us by the secrets of others" (7). If Kidron is right that the silenced past of her respondents is not necessarily haunting, then Philippe Sands's experience might have been different had he grown up with his grandfather in Israel.

In short, the experience of silence is crucial in social interactions between survivors of genocide and their descendants, be they survivors of the Shoah or of the Armenian genocide. Silence may take different forms, but it is never total silence. At times, it is but verbal silence, paired with nonverbal forms of communication. At other times, it is partial silence, whereby participants in interactive situations communicate something verbally, but in a way that leaves obvious gaps. On yet other occasions, silencing consists of aborted or disrupted utterances. No matter the form of silencing, silence may or may not be traumatizing, depending on context. Most importantly here, social silence is one form of social interaction and communication that contributes to the generation of knowledge—often ambiguous, at times troubling—about a horrific past.

Silence is an experience shared by descendants of the victim group and of the perpetrator group, but the motivations and consequences differ. We find similarities to this author's memories of silence in post–World War II Germany in many biographical accounts of the children and grandchildren of (at times just suspected) German perpetrators (e.g., Leo 2014; Schenck 2016; Mitgutsch 2016). Such literature shows how silence among the perpetrator people is profoundly disturbing to at least some, especially when paired with information from other sources. Different from what Kidron observed, social silences do not easily enter into the calm flow of everyday life where the silence of perpetrators is concerned. Silence instead interweaves with a sense of secondary guilt—guilt for loving (or having loved) those who perpetrated (or possibly perpetrated), and guilt for not inquiring decisively about their past. The inheritance is associated with stigma. It is dyed into the fabric of those who succeed their elders. Those who are born into the collectivity out of which evil had grown inherit shame and stigma, be they Germans or Turks.

If some survivors of the Armenian genocide and of the Shoah practiced silence, and if silencing the history of the Holocaust was common in Germany, then we may assume that silencing was also a common practice in the perpetrator people of the genocide against the Armenians. Yet perpetrators and their descendants may also be tempted to engage in another strategy of managing stigma or a spoiled identity. They may deny, and that denial mixes with silencing to produce particular repertoires of knowledge.

Denial and Denying

Among the three concepts at the center of this chapter—silence, acknowledgment, and denial—the latter is the dominant subject of scholarship, and probably of everyday talk. A Google book search shows at least a hundred titles that include the word *denial*. A well-known example is historian Deborah Lipstadt's (1993) *Denying the Holocaust: The Growing Assault on Truth and Memory*. In 1999, historian Richard Hovannisian edited *Remembrance and Denial: The Case of the Armenian Genocide*. Two years later, Stanley Cohen (2001) published *States of Denial: Knowing about Atrocities and Suffering*, a criminologist's take on denial of government repression and mass violence. Finally, 2015 saw the appearance of historical sociologist Fatma Müge Göçek's magnum opus, entitled *Denial of Violence: Ottoman Past, Turkish Present, and Collective Violence against the Armenians, 1789–2009* (2015). The latter book is the most impressive effort thus far to document and explain denial of the Armenian genocide. Göçek's volume, based on a detailed analysis of more than three hundred memoirs of prominent Turks, addresses denial in four stages of Turkish history.

All these books treat denial as something morally abominable. Given that *denial* can also refer to a rejection of falsehoods and outrageous claims, the authors cited above obviously mean something more specific. They generally refer to the denial of historic events documented by overwhelming evidence, including scholarship.[6]

Types of denial.   Denial is a difficult and even confounding concept, in that it embraces distinct phenomena. Thankfully, Stanley Cohen helps by distinguishing between three forms of denial. The first is *literal denial*, "the assertion that something did not happen" (2001:7). This can also be called *factual denial*, and cognition is at stake. The second type, *interpretive denial*, poses greater challenges. Here "the raw facts (something happened) are not being denied [but instead] . . . given a different meaning from what seems apparent to others" (2001:7). This type of denial concerns *morality*. Yes, someone argues, many human lives were lost, but those losses were not the result of murderous violence but rather the unavoidable side effect of war. A more specific instance of interpretive denial can occur when meaning is captured in legal terms. When social actors categorize mass killings as genocide, for example, this form of denial challenges their attempt to subsume evidence under the legal category; most prominent in this regard are challenges to the subsumption of intent.

Criminologists know interpretive denial well, recognizing such strategies of neutralization as enablers of deviance (Sykes and Matza 1957). Deviant actors neutralize by denying responsibility, victimization, or injury; by condemning their condemners (e.g., accusing them of having provoked the violence or having engaged in even worse atrocities); or by appealing to higher loyalties (e.g., the nation's honor over norms of international law). In all these cases, they do not deny that others have been harmed, but they seek to defend their identity as moral actors and upright citizens, shielding it from potential moral and legal damage.

Factual and interpretive denial often overlap, and their deployment begins *during* genocidal regimes. Raul Hilberg ([1961] 2003) reveals such strategies in the first major historical study of the Holocaust. He shows how the regime built an arsenal of defenses, including social mechanisms of repression, to help its murderous agents overcome moral scruples that result from a long civilizing process (Elias [1939] 2000). Such mechanisms include hiding the ultimate aim of the actions (controlling information); forcing those who know what is occurring to participate, in order to secure their silence and denial ("blood kit"); prohibiting criticism; eliminating destruction as a subject of conversation; and cultivating camouflaged vocabulary (e.g., avoiding the term *killing*). Once introduced, these strategies likely spill over into the post-genocidal era, no longer motivated by the desire to enable mass killings, but by the need to face a new world that abhors the evils of the immediate past.

Cohen distinguishes a third type of denial: *implicatory denial*. Such denial accepts the facts and their conventional interpretation, but "what are denied or

STRUGGLES OVER GENOCIDE KNOWLEDGE   25

minimized are the psychological, political or moral implications that convention-ally follow" (Cohen 2001:8). This type of denial again concerns *morality*, in terms of not accepting responsibility.[7] Historians of genocide also engage with impli-catory denial. Again, Hilberg ([1961] 2003) provides an example, writing about mechanisms of collective and individual rationalization. The former may include justification of the destruction process as a whole, for example by defining the target as evil. While such collective rationalization still falls under the category of interpretive denial, individual rationalization involves methods through which actors seek to claim helplessness in the face of larger forces, even if they were directly involved in the killings. They include reference to the doctrine of supe-rior orders, also found in the famous Milgram experiment (Milgram 1963) and in Arendt's (1963) notion of the banality of evil; insistence that no personal vin-dictiveness was involved, for example by telling stories about one's "good deeds" toward Jewish neighbors; blaming others; or diminishing one's own importance ("I was just one among many"). In other words, those engaging in implicatory denial accept that terrible deeds were committed, and also accept their definition as genocide, but they insist that they could not really do anything about them; they were tools in the hands of others, deprived of agency. Implicatory denial comes even more easily to bystanders than to perpetrators.

Like the practice of silencing, denial occurs at different levels of social life. We find it in official pronouncements, where it is easily institutionalized (a subject of subsequent chapters). Yet it is also common at the micro-level. There it leaves its traces in social interactions and inner conversations reflected in diaries, memoirs, or other autobiographical texts.

Denial by Turkish memoir writers.   Perpetrators most commonly practice denial. Accordingly, Göçek's analysis of more than three hundred memoirs of promi-nent Turks focuses on related strategies. Let us consider two of her examples. The first is Dr. Mehmet Şahingiray, a member of the Committee of Union and Progress (CUP; the Young Turk party) and of the Special Organization, the chief executor of the mass killings. Şahingiray, reflecting on the mass violence against Armenians in 1915, claims there was intense hostility and armament among the Armenian population in the Ottoman Empire, aiming to "drive the Turks from [the latter's] beloved ancestral homeland of eight or ten centuries" (quoted in Göçek 2015:249–250). He continues by asking his imagined audience: "[Why should] the Armenians not be punished? Which 'civilized government' would have remained just an onlooker? Which government would expose its political survival to such danger? Just as the government is obliged to undertake precautionary measures, it is also natural for there to be a danger for the Muslim populace to get carried away by their emotions, reacting in kind to the rapacious and terrible murders of the [Armenian] element with which they had lived for so many centu-ries, considering them [fellow] citizens and brethren" (quoted in Göçek 2015:250).

Göçek challenges Şahingiray's arguments by reminding the reader of crucial distinctions in the size and nature of suffering between Turks and Armenians: yes, two million Turks lost their lives in the violence of World War I, but those deaths occurred mostly on the battlefield, in the fight against Allied soldiers, absent any contacts with Armenians. "Armenian suffering [instead] was empire-wide, with the Ottoman state, government and military forcibly and systematically removing and subsequently destroying civilian Armenian communities of mostly women, children and the elderly" (Göçek 2015:250). In Cohen's terms, Göçek considers Şahingiray's reflections a form of interpretive denial. Her second refutation concerns (at least partial) literal denial: the equation of the scale of Armenian militancy, which destroyed an estimated sixty thousand Muslim lives, and the death toll of at least eight hundred thousand among the Armenians.

Göçek provides another example that links factual and interpretive denial. She quotes from the memoir of an Ottoman officer who writes of how he encountered "on the two sides of the road [between Meskene and Deyr Zor] unburied corpses of those among the [Armenian] refugee convoys who had fallen sick and died" (Göçek 2015:205). While expressing sorrow, he continues thus: "The CUP government was forced to remove these Armenians from the regions near military conflict due to the inevitability of [the conditions] of war. But during this migration executed without any organization or transportation, some among the Armenian refugees died due to exhaustion and disease. Yet, according to our calculation at the time, THE LOSS OF THE TURKISH POPULACE WAS MUCH MORE THAN THAT OF THE ARMENIANS" (caps in original; quoted in Göçek 2015:251). Again, equalizing the numbers of deaths constitutes at least partial literal denial, while attributing the deaths to unavoidable exhaustion is an example of interpretive denial.

Denial is not limited to the perpetrators themselves. It extends, in many cases, to their children (e.g., Sands 2016:240) and even to their children's children, who grew up with the love grandchildren develop for their grandparents, though they may learn later about the dark chapter in their grandfathers' past (Welzer et al. 2002). Welzer and his collaborators have found, in the case of Germany, that grandchildren tend to redefine, minimalize, and rationalize their grandfathers' involvement in Nazism. They also find that this tendency intensifies in the context of growing public recognition of the horrors of the Holocaust. In other words, acceptance in public life motivates implicatory denial at the family level. Denial and acknowledgment at the macro- and micro-levels of society move in opposite directions.

Importantly, in all cases of implicatory denial, by the perpetrator generation or its descendants, literal and often interpretive acknowledgment are implied. At times, implicatory denial is a reaction to acknowledgment of fact. Boundaries between acknowledgment and denial are thus blurry.

In short, when a collectivity acknowledges involvement in mass atrocity, implicatory denial is a common practice in everyday communication and individual reflection. Alternatively, by practicing factual or interpretive denial, collectivities offer individuals an escape from challenging situations. Many former Young Turk politicians and military laid the ground for such denial, as Göçek convincingly shows in her study of memoirs. The new Turkish Republic, eager to engage them in its service after its foundation in 1922, embraced their interpretation. Later chapters show how their seed bore rich fruit within Turkey—how denial in individual reflections, in memoirs and in everyday communication, became sedimented. Yet today's broad public recognition of the Armenian genocide in the contemporary West suggests that, despite denial and silencing, acknowledgment was at work as well.

Acknowledging and Bearing Witness

Traces of acknowledgment of the Armenian genocide occasionally appear in writings by agents of the perpetrator state, even those written while the atrocities were still unfolding. In addition, and following a long period of silencing and denial, acknowledgment today advances cautiously among some courageous Turkish intellectuals. Within the victim group, pulled for many decades between silencing and acknowledgment, recent decades have witnessed organized efforts to document survivor testimonies, archive them, and make them available in places such as the Visual History Archive of the USC Shoah Foundation. Such testimonies merge personal and collective knowledge that has accumulated over decades, and they reinforce collective memory.

Perpetrator people: Turkish acknowledgments.   One of the Turkish memoirs analyzed by Fatma Müge Göçek was penned by Ahmed Refik, director of dispatches of the Ottoman government in the early phase of World War I. With the imperial capital under threat of occupation during the 1915 battle of the Dardanelles, Ahmed Refik was sent to the town of Eskişehir to coordinate the possible relocation of the seat of the Ottoman government. Having arrived in Eskişehir, Ahmed Refik witnessed the violence committed against the Armenian population. He was horrified by his observations, and his memoir provides one of the strongest examples of acknowledgment, embedded in the sea of denialist statements by his compatriots that Göçek collected in her volume. Refik writes:

> [When gathered at the train station for deportation,] no one wanted to move for all [the Armenians] believed that a fearsome force awaited them there [death]. Forests around the mountains were filled with the armed bands the CUP government had sent from İstanbul. In order to stay alive, the people were willing to stay in Eskişehir. . . . [Additional observations justified such fear:] Rivers are filled with human torsos and heads of children. This view tears one's heart to pieces. But won't people be one day called to account for this? . . . No government at any historical period has committed murders with such cruelty. (quoted in Göçek 2015:153)

Göçek, a Turk of the grandchildren's generation, writing a century after Refik, herself engages in acknowledgment. She does so through scholarship that lays open what Turkish witnesses of the Armenian genocide observed, and how they simultaneously engaged in denial. In the autobiographical preface to *Denial of Violence*, Göçek introduces the book as "the end result of a long journey, one that was not only scholarly but also intensely personal" (Göçek 2015:vii).

Having grown up as the daughter of an upper-class family in cosmopolitan İstanbul, availed of the best educational opportunities her country had to offer, she also became aware of "prejudicial and discriminatory behavior" (Göçek 2015:viii) against non-Turkish and non-Muslim groups. Yet only as a graduate student at Princeton University did she learn from one of her mentors, the renowned Middle East historian Bernard Lewis, "the role non-Muslim minorities had played in the empire. . . . [N]ot only was the role of non-Muslim minorities unrecognized, but their presence and participation had gradually dissipated during the ensuing republican years" (Göçek 2015:ix). Göçek writes about the silencing of various other episodes of violence and repression in Turkey's past. She summarizes her previous scholarship and her efforts to bring violent occurrences into some temporal ordering. Her account culminates in an epiphany, a recognition of how this intellectual journey led her "to arrive at the foundational violence that had not only triggered but also normalized the subsequent practices: it was through this line of inductive reasoning that I arrived at what had happened to the Armenians in the past, in 1915 to be exact, because it was the earliest instance of collective violence that had still not been accounted for by the Turkish state and society" (Göçek 2015:ix).

Göçek's work thus challenges silence and denial of the foundational violence of the Turkish Republic. She seeks to help break Turkey's path-dependent history of violence and to advance its democratic potential. Importantly, she is not the only Turkish scholar to work toward acknowledgment. Other examples include Taner Akçam (2006), Seyhan Bayraktar (2010), Hamit Bozarslan (2013), Hakan Seckinelgin (2019), Buket Türkmen (2019), and Uğur Ümit Üngör (2015).

In addition to these scholars' public and political mission, a confessional function may be a motivating force for perpetrators or their descendants who acknowledge. German sociologist Alois Hahn (1982) traces historically how new methods, including the writing of diaries and biographies as well as testimonials in psychotherapeutic settings, supplement traditional, religious forms of confessions (see also Berger and Luckmann 1966). Engagement in scholarship about the dark past of one's own nation and of one's forebears may be but one mode of responding to (collective) responsibility (or even to a sense of guilt). The goal today is the overcoming of traumata, and, possibly—in line with David Riesman's notion of the "other-directed self"—a new form of adaptation to externally generated pressures or expectations (Riesman et al. [1950] 2001).[8]

Scholarship is only part of this new engagement with the past. Göçek, in the final substantive section of her book, elaborates on "three spheres of knowledge production and reproduction where the Turkish official narrative has begun to be contested and countered . . . : newly transliterated and penned texts [as the 1928 script reform had made many documents inaccessible to young Turks], activities at newly established private universities, and public interpretations of a new generation of Turkish journalists and intellectuals" (Göçek 2015:466). Her expression of hope preceded the new authoritarianism during the late reign of Recep Tayyip Erdoğan, a brutal rigidity especially evident after the failed coup attempt of July 15, 2016.

The victim people: Armenian voices in the visual history archives.   Acknowledgment plays a more prominent role among the victim people, despite early temptations to silence the painful past.[9] In some cases, the transmission of knowledge sets in early, in historical eyewitness accounts and lines of communication from survivors to their children and grandchildren. Claire Mouradian, one of my interviewees, was raised by her grandmother, who had endured terrifying experiences and survived a massacre under a pile of corpses. She told her granddaughter about the great catastrophe of the Armenian people, including her personal experience, inspiring Mouradian to enter a life of scholarship dedicated to the fate of her ethnic group, a case to which I return in detail below.

We find similar intergenerational transmission of knowledge among Armenians in the United States. Kaspar Hovannisian, having escaped from the Ottoman Empire, arrived in the United States on August 30, 1920. His son Richard Hovannisian (1971) wrote the first history of the Republic of Armenia, and Richard's son Raffi Hovannisian became foreign minister of the newly independent country after the breakup of the Soviet Union. In *Family of Shadows: A Century of Murder, Memory, and the American Dream* (2010), Garin Hovannisian, Raffi's son, writes about the fate of his family, and the cultivation and transmission of knowledge about the Armenian genocide. The process began in the first generation, with his great-grandfather Kaspar in Tulare, California, where he had settled after immigrating. Kaspar was intensely involved in Armenian life and immersed in the Armenian newspaper *Hairenik*, delivered daily from Boston. Yet the transmission of knowledge was gender-specific, excluding his newlywed wife, Siroon. In Garin's words, Siroon "did not know the man she served. She did not understand . . ." (Hovannisian 2010:44).

Growing temporal distance allows for new forms of acknowledgment. Consider testimony by Armenian genocide survivors and witnesses, made available by the Visual History Archive of the USC Shoah Foundation, in the form of interviews conducted between the 1970s and the early 2000s by J. Michael Hagopian, himself a survivor of the genocide and creator of the Armenian Film Foundation, producer of the recordings. Encounters between Hagopian and other survivors are interactive situations, but they differ from those examined above. They do not unfold in everyday life. Instead, their very purpose is the establishment of a record of testimony about the genocide.

In analyzing a random sample of sixty videotaped interviews among those conducted in English, we coded statements about forms of victimization, references to perpetrators, public responses to atrocities, attitudes toward Turkey and Turkish people, and explanations of the genocide. Merging accumulated knowledge absorbed by respondents during their lifetime with personal memories, these statements reinforce sedimented genocide knowledge. Many themes well known from the historiographic literature appear in these sixty depictions: deportations (thirty-nine); forced marches (twenty-nine); starvation and dehydration (fifteen); robberies (twenty-five); and massacres and killings (forty-three), specifically shootings (twelve), mutilation by stabbing or cutting (ten), decapitations (seven), beatings (eight), and rapes (seven). Perpetrators are most often referred to neutrally as "they" (forty-two), frequently also as "Turks" (thirty-four), with some specifications such as "Turkish soldiers" (twelve), "gendarmes" (twenty), "police(men)" (twelve), "Turkish government" (twelve), and references to members of the Young Turk ruling triumvirate generally or by specific names (eleven). We find only one reference to "Muslims." In the following paragraphs, I focus on accounts of victimization.

Interviewees report generally known facts, probably not based on their personal observations—for example, that the first victims of the genocide were male intellectuals, and that other men and boys between the ages of fourteen and sixty-five were targeted next. Some refer to personal observations, though, when they report how perpetrators used guns, bayonets, and daggers to massacre people. Women, too, experienced violence, often in a gendered form. Emma Modrisoff recalls Turkish civilians and soldiers invading Armenian homes, butchering their inhabitants, raping young girls, and mutilating pregnant women. She reports how bodies were thrown out of windows and piled several feet high in streets and alleyways. One survivor, Haroutune Aivazian, describes soldiers forcing women, with children in their arms, from their homes and whipping them through the street.

Other survivors report that the genocide began with deportation notices. They recount that sometimes lists of three hundred to five hundred families were posted on churches; other times, notices were hung directly on homes; and occasionally, town criers announced upcoming deportations. Some victim-witnesses tell how families were given days' or weeks' notice, while others were taken the same day. Only few families were fortunate enough, they report, to prepare food and purchase caravans and donkeys to carry some of their possessions, which they typically lost during the marches. Once evicted from their homes, victim-witnesses observed Turkish civilians and soldiers plundering them, setting looted homes aflame, burning churches and destroying religious texts and artifacts.

Many testimonies speak to the fate of children. Survivors of forced marches regularly describe their mothers carrying their infant siblings in their arms, many of whom died from starvation. Some women decided to end their young children's lives instead of letting them endlessly suffer; others abandoned their children on the sides of streets, hoping that someone with more resources would take care of them.

Some victim-witnesses report decapitations before and during the marches. Agnes Dombalian, a child at the time of the genocide, recalls Turkish soldiers separating men and women and forcing women to identify their husband or father. Soldiers then forced the man's head on a log and cut it off with an axe. Dombalian was among the children who lost their fathers that day. Often, mutilated bodies were thrown into rivers. Two survivors report that decapitations and stabbings were so common that the Euphrates River ran red. Abductions and rapes by civilians and soldiers were also routine, according to the surviving witnesses.

Interviewees further report that soldiers and civilians stole from dying or dead victims, including clothes and shoes. Occasionally, people suspected of swallowing pieces of gold were cut open. Krikor Baldikian recalls a Turkish man nearly cutting off his finger for a ring before his mother freed him from the man's grasp.

On the deportation marches, deprived of food and water, victims were forced to walk for hours until their feet were too swollen to continue. One survivor, Sarah Koltookian, describes soldiers forcing her and others to climb repeatedly up and down a mountain, beating to death with clubs and rocks anyone who stopped. Survivors recall drinking from mud piles created by animal footprints and from rivers in which corpses floated. They ate any plants they could find on the ground and cooked the stems with contaminated water. The desperation of victims was so extreme that they began feeding on the flesh of corpses. George Messerlian remembers a young boy in the Syrian Desert telling his mother, "Mother don't cry. When I die, don't give my meat to nobody. You eat [it] yourself." Gendarmes shot and killed those dragging behind. Corpses surrounded the deported on all sides, in rivers, on the sides of streets, under bridges, and next to campsites. Once arrived at their desert destinations, many victims were abandoned and left to starvation. Survivors returning to these sites found piles of bones, many belonging to young children.

These victim-witnesses were mostly young children during the genocide. They survived, but most lost family and home, and some lost their identity. Paranzan Narcisian, orphaned, is among the typical cases; she bemoans the loss of her family. Only a few survived with their parents or as a complete family. J. Michael Hagopian, in his interview, explains the pain of losing one's home: "I've come to realize that leaving your native land is probably the worst punishment you can get; to be exiled, that you can never go back to your home is a horrible thing." Finally, some survivor-witnesses report assuming Turkish identities under pressure. Harry Kurkjian, for example, describes his forced conversion to Islam and denigration of his heritage when he was coerced to urinate on Armenian graves. While many survivors regained their Armenian identity, some, like Jirair

Suchiasian, report that the violence left them with no knowledge of who their parents were or where and when they were born. Suchiasian says, "I am somebody, but I am nobody"—spoiled identity indeed. The interview does not reveal how long it took this survivor to break the silence.

CONCLUSIONS: INTERACTIVE STRUGGLES OVER GENOCIDE KNOWLEDGE

Silencing, denying, and acknowledging in the aftermath of genocide and mass atrocity unfold at different levels of social life. This chapter has focused on the micro-level—on communication and thought processes, and their externalizations in written texts or video recordings—during times of violence and in later periods. When a troubling past has left actors with the spoiled identity of victims or perpetrators, silencing and denial are tempting responses (Goffman [1963] 1986). Yet confessing, providing eyewitness testimony, and acknowledging are realistic alternatives, and their chances increase over time. They became a rich source of knowledge on many episodes of mass atrocity, including the Shoah and the Armenian genocide.

Importantly, social interaction, communication, and negotiation over an appropriate understanding of troubling experiences are rarely harmonious. Often, survivors and their descendants confront members of the perpetrator group. Within the perpetrator group, intergenerational conflict intensifies when children of the perpetrator generation challenge their elders. They may condemn their parent generation's involvement in or toleration of past atrocities and demand acknowledgment. Alternatively, descendants of perpetrators may hope to free family members (or their group or nation) from stigma through continued silencing and denial. Even on the side of victim groups, silencing is common, despite substantial variation across contexts and time.

Finally, and again, this exploration of silencing, denial, and acknowledgment is part of a sociology of knowledge project. It addresses the social construction of reality. It does not challenge the notion of reality: the history of violence is very real. Millions were killed; were starved; lost their limbs, health, and dignity; were raped and driven from their homes and ancestral lands. Yet we know about such atrocities only through cultural processing. As this chapter has shown, social interaction and reflection play a crucial part in the generation of this type of knowledge. Another form is the systematic documentation by eyewitnesses—for example, in the form of diaries that humanitarians on the ground in Turkey wrote during the genocide. These diaries are the subject of the next chapter.

2

Diaries and Bearing Witness in the Humanitarian Field

Structural contexts, including the nature of social fields, affect whether and how actors engage in acknowledgment, silencing, or denying.[1] In the case of the Armenian genocide, embeddedness in fields that transcend the boundaries of the Ottoman state encouraged acknowledgment. A dense trail of testimony left behind by international eyewitnesses has fed into today's body of knowledge about the Armenian genocide. Reports by consuls and ambassadors, and especially diaries by missionaries involved in humanitarian aid work in Turkey during World War I, feature prominently. In this chapter, I focus on one example from the field of humanitarianism from which I quoted at the outset of the preceding chapter: a diary written between 1915 and 1919 by Carmelite Christie, an American school administrator and humanitarian in the Turkish town of Tarsus.

In the symbolic interactionist tradition, I think of diaries as objectivations—thoughts written down and reflecting, in the words of George Herbert Mead (1934), inner conversations between the "I," that responds to a social situation, and the "Me," that part of our minds that anticipates and takes into account patterned reactions of others to our utterances. Importantly, those others are not free floating, but are themselves embedded in social fields in which they act and form a habitus (Bourdieu 1984). Introducing the terms *field* and *habitus*, I take the unusual step of linking George Herbert Mead's theory of thought with Pierre Bourdieu's field theory. *Field*, for Bourdieu, refers to a set of actors who pursue specific goals such as accumulating power (political field), finding truth (field of scholarship), practicing justice (judicial field), or providing aid (humanitarian field). Fields also impose particular rules of the game on participants, and they form the participants' habitus, or relatively stable dispositions (Bourdieu 1984). The stress is on "relative": habitus leaves room for improvisation, and this is where symbolic interactionism (with its focus on fluidity) and field theory (with its stress on structure) converge.

Workers in the humanitarian aid field are oriented toward alleviating suffering and saving lives. This mission may motivate them to depict the suffering and plead to the outside world for help. Their writings should thus constitute one of the clearest examples of acknowledgment. Yet humanitarians also act in the context of states and their enforcement apparatus, and those states may well be—as in the Ottoman context—perpetrators themselves. Such context likely inserts caution into the testimony of humanitarians, possibly as accommodation to state authorities. The history of humanitarianism is rich with examples of this tension. The failure of the International Committee of the Red Cross to ring the alarm bells after inspecting the Nazis' Terezin Concentration Camp, all for the sake of neutrality, is one of the low points of humanitarianism. Organizations such as Médecins Sans Frontières (Doctors Without Borders), formed in reaction to such constraints during the Biafran War in Nigeria, are determined to bear witness. Yet, in concrete situations, they too have to accommodate repressive political regimes, unless they are ready to pay the price of expulsion from the field (Weissman 2011). The work of Médecins Sans Frontières in—and its eviction from—the Darfur region of Sudan is but one recent example (Savelsberg 2015). In short, humanitarians desire to bear witness, but they are constrained by the perpetrating state on whose collaboration, or at least toleration, they often depend.

Diaries are a partial way out of this dilemma. Their authors write in private, not for (immediate) publication. In addition to the desire to bear witness, the writing of diaries also serves as a tool toward surviving challenging contexts. It helps their authors manage difficult, at times seemingly unbearable, situations. Anne Frank's diaries, written in her hiding place in Amsterdam, are but one famous example. A more recent case in point is Antjie Krog, who reported for the South African Broadcasting Corporation about the excruciating testimony of suffering and perpetration before the South African Truth and Reconciliation Commission. Experiencing each session and interviewing many victims and perpetrators, Krog was able to continue her work only by writing down what she heard. Her reflections resulted in a disturbing text, later published under the title *Country of My Skull* (Krog 1998).

The fact that authors of diaries preserve their writings—even if they do not (at least initially) seek publication—indicates that their purpose is not just therapeutic. Might some want their writings preserved as a record of the world in which they lived and suffered, as testimony of their experiences? In fact, some authors, such as Krog, or their surviving relatives, such as Anne Frank's father, do eventually publish diaries written privately under trying circumstances. While neither Carmelite Christie nor her descendants published her writings, the texts did survive and later generations decided to make them accessible as archival documents.

CARMELITE CHRISTIE AND HER DIARIES: TARSUS, TURKEY, 1915–1919

Sarah Carmelite Christie, née Brewer, was born in 1852 in small-town Illinois as the daughter of a minister and farmer and his housekeeper wife. She attended Rockford Seminary, from which she graduated in 1871. She briefly worked as a schoolteacher until she married Thomas D. Christie, a Civil War veteran and Congregational missionary, in 1872. As a child, Thomas had emigrated with his parents from Ireland to settle in Wisconsin.

In 1877, the couple, with their first living child, moved to Turkey, where, for sixteen years, they were engaged in missionary work in the mountainous town of Marash (Maraş), about a hundred miles north of Aleppo. In 1893, two years before the Hamidian massacres of hundreds of thousands of Ottoman Armenians under Sultan Abdülhamid II, the family, now with five living children, moved to Tarsus, a town west of Adana, close to the Mediterranean coast. There, Thomas Christie assumed the presidency of the Saint Paul Institute, a privately funded college. He traveled much, to missionary outposts and to raise funds, the college's benefactor having died shortly after he took over the presidency, leaving the institution without adequate funding. Consequently, Carmelite was often alone in Tarsus, raising the children and working on behalf of the college, especially toward the education of women. In 1915, shortly after the beginning of the mass violence against the Armenians, Thomas traveled to Constantinople, seeking to intervene with the government on behalf of several teachers whom the authorities threatened with deportation. Not only did the government not grant his request, it did not allow him to return to Tarsus. Carmelite now had to fend for herself and for the Saint Paul Institute throughout the remainder of World War I and beyond, from 1915 until 1919. She managed to keep the institute open initially, and she worked to provide humanitarian aid to the displaced and to victims of war after its closure on November 26, 1915. In 1920, more than a year after the war ended, the couple, now reunited, returned to the United States.

Data: Archives and Selection

The following pages are based on the Thomas and Carmelite Christie and Family Papers, archived by the Minnesota Historical Society (MHS, n.d.), which contain "Correspondence, diaries, and other papers documenting the lives of a family of Protestant missionaries from Minnesota serving in the Turkish cities of Marash and Tarsus."[2] According to the file description, "Family letters, essays, and diaries by Carmelite and Mary [a daughter] detail the sufferings of the Armenian people during the 1895, 1909, and 1915 massacres, and the missionaries' efforts to give them refuge and relief" (see note 2). Given my interest in knowledge about the genocide, I selected, from this wealth of materials, the diaries Carmelite Christie wrote between 1915 and 1919.[3] In addition, I analyzed *The Treatment of*

Armenians in the Ottoman Empire 1915–16, a compilation of consular and mission-ary reports published in a British government series.

Reading all her diaries of this five-year period, my research assistants and I documented all instances in which Carmelite Christie describes the suffering of Armenians and others affected by violence and disease, the constraints imposed by the Turkish government against intervention, and finally the compromises Christie accepted so that she would be able to continue her humanitarian work while simultaneously bearing witness to suffering and persecution. Her testimony is acknowledgment, but a conservative one in light of the threatening context in which she operated.

In Her Own Words: Torn between Desire to Bear Witness and Constraint

Carmelite Christie intensely experienced the conflict between her desire to bear witness, to document, and to acknowledge, on the one hand, and the necessity to navigate threats and demands by the Turkish state while seeking to provide aid to the suffering population on the other. Impediments in communicating to the outside world, due to censorship and control by the Turkish government, are among the constraints about which Christie reports repeatedly. For example, on October 18, 1915, she writes about a ship heading to America and her attempt to send even modest communication to the outside world: "A little gift of mine in an envelope to Agnes [a daughter] for Christmas was kept because I had written a few words on a slip of paper about it, and enclosed. Four 'officers of the Law' were present at the examination" (MHS Box 28:15). Again, on December 7, 1915, Christie mentions difficulties in communication to and from America. She describes an exceptional opportunity to do so, but expresses her general resignation: "Under ordinary circumstances it is impossible to get messages from America by cable or wireless" (MHS Box 28:37). Given such impediments against communication with the outside world, the writing of diaries was not just a therapeutic exercise for Carmelite Christie. It was also the only way to document her observations, possibly in the hope that they might one day reach the public.

The Turkish government did not merely restrict communication to the outside world. It also imposed constraints on delivery of aid to refugees from persecution and severely punished those who did not obey. On April 29, 1916, Christie writes in her diary,

> We hear that the Priest is in Adana to be tried for the crime (!) of trying to hide exiles. He had none in his house: but probably knew where certain others were, and helped them. Awful threats are made against those who do anything for exiles, and the feel-ing against all Christians is increasing. . . . It seems best to *lie a little low* [underlined in original] just at present. . . . It would be disastrous for us to try to shelter fugitives. With so many soldiers on the premises and all about us, we could not hope to escape

detection. . . . We are practically *buying* [underlined in original] the goodwill of those [who] might make life uncomfortable for us. (MHS Box 28:66, 67)

Carmelite Christie must have been a woman of extraordinary determination and courage. While she is reluctant to shelter refugees, her efforts to engage in relief work continue unabated, albeit with a cautious eye toward the authorities. An entry of April 9, 1917, states: "It would be hard on the poor should my hands be tied so that I could not continue relief work. I have an idea that if worse came to worst, that I might offer to superintend a Red Crescent Hospital on our premises on condition of retaining our present servants, cooks, table-boys, etc. I know nothing of such work, but might piece out guess work by self assurance and sympathy and smiles! These are times when one must use her wits for all they are worth,—and a little more" (MHS Box 28:117).

Another strategy that allows Christie to continue her humanitarian work is going under the radar of the authorities. In the same context, she thus writes in April 1917: "The govt is not in sympathy with relief work, so I do nearly everything so quietly that very few have any idea of how much I am doing. I am supposed to be simply a kind neighbor, by the Turks" (MHS Box 28:145).

Government intervention not only makes the hiding of refugees dangerous and aid provision difficult; it also infringes on the regular functions of the institute for which Christie is now responsible. On October 4, 1915, she describes the possession of school buildings by the government: "From Adana comes word that the Govt want the premises and buildings of the Girls' School (American) for a hospital. Already they have all their own school buildings, the Protestant school and church (from which they have moved the bell), the Gregorian schools and churches, and all the fine large buildings used for boarding schools by the Catholics" (MHS Box 28:7). A few weeks later, on October 25, 1915, she reports: "We . . . also lose [*sic*] our gymnasium, eight furnished recitation rooms, and a lot of dormitory space" (MHS Box 28:19).

The decisive moment for Christie's own institution comes on November 26, 1915, when her school closes and police take over. "He [government agent] told us briefly that within 2 hours he was to have a full list of our students, place of residence, parents' names etc, and that day pupils should be separated and dealt with by themselves. Mr. Nute [Carmelite's son-in-law] asked for his authorization papers. He said they were not necessary. . . . Our good Kaimakam [Provincial Administrator] has been sent elsewhere, and his 'Vekil' [representative] is the judge who is the arch enemy of foreign institutions. It seems the order is direct from the Vali [Provincial Governor]" (MHS Box 28:30–31). Much remains in the dark in this diary entry. Why would the police want all the student information? Clearly, the intent was not friendly.

The pressure to accommodate the Turkish authorities continues throughout the following years. For example, on August 28, 1917, Christie writes about needing to prioritize favors to the Turks to live safely and for the sake of "the distribution on the sly of relief funds, fearing each day that you will be called to account for it. . . . In my place they would understand that to some extent, to keep the peace one must in Turkey 'do as the Turks do'" (MHS Box 28:158). A few months later, on November 4, 1917, she reports that their yard is still full of Mersin prisoners—Syrian Arabs, mostly—and troops coming and going, and sick soldiers brought here for convalescence. "We couldn't refuse without losing the goodwill of one whose favor may be useful to us. I have to think of the Armenians in our service" (MHS Box 28:192). Even at this late stage, it seems as though Armenians in the service of international institutions could still survive. Christie's sense of responsibility for these survivors simultaneously intensified the pressure she felt to accommodate the authorities.

In sum, Carmelite Christie, missionary and school administrator in Tarsus, Turkey, describes in her diaries of 1915 to 1919 how she initially sought to continue the functioning of her college and worked throughout to help refugees and others who sought aid. She experienced dilemmas faced generally in the field of humanitarian aid. To provide aid, humanitarians need to accommodate the authorities in order to retain access to those in need, even if the same authorities are responsible for much of the suffering the aid worker seeks to alleviate. It is under such conditions that Christie, during times of violence, observed and sought to find a balance between aid delivery and bearing witness in the form of diaries. The quotations above show that constraints posed by the Turkish state entered into Christie's "Me" (in the sense discussed above). What, then, does Christie tell us in her diaries about the violence and the suffering of the population? How does she bear witness and acknowledge these, in line with her position in the humanitarian field, but cautioned by the powerful role of state actors whose goodwill she had to secure? The following section provides exemplary observations.

A Humanitarian's Local Knowledge: "We Hear of Terrible Things, and of Massacres"

While Carmelite Christie's writings are constrained by the context in which she operates, they nevertheless provide rich testimony regarding the mass violence against the Ottoman Armenians. Christie writes about those who suffer, but also about those who perpetrate. Her pages make clear that she is not driven by resentment against Turks. In fact, she extends help to Turks, at times under pressure, to keep the authorities on her side, at other times voluntarily, especially toward the end of the war and in face of the suffering of the local Turkish population. Throughout, some themes repeat: massacres, deportations, authorizations of violence, misery of the evicted on their trek toward the deserts in the Southeast, forced conversions and the abuse of girls and young women. To convey the unfolding of events over time, I present a selection of Christie's diary entries about victimization and atrocities in chronological order.

Available diary entries begin on October 1, 1915, five months and one week after the deportation and killing of hundreds of Armenian dignitaries and intellectuals on April 24, and continue in the following weeks of the same year.[4] Christie's first entry confirms scholarship according to which killings and deportations were in full force by the fall of 1915. I quoted earlier from her entry of October 1, 1915, in which she writes about massive displacements, misery, and deaths of the suffering as well as massacres (MHS Box 28:2–3). Four Red Cross nurses ("Catholics from Germany") confirm the conditions of refugees described there: "[On their way from Constantinople to Beirut] they told of the suffering multitudes that filled the way all along the route. There were oh so many old people, lame and bent, and so many little children and so many who were ill, and they saw people dying by the roadside. The majority were on foot" (MHS Box 28:8). On November 2, 1915, Christie mentions theft of property, exiling, and massacres: "Many who worked near Tarsus during the summer, now have no homes. Their families have been exiled. Nearly all Armenians have at least lost their property. In some cases parents have been massacred" (MHS Box 28:21). Six days later, on November 8, Christie says more about massacres: "Our streets still swarm with soldiers. . . . We understand that the Arab soldiers now here came via Oorfa [Urfa]; and are the ones who massacred there. I fear there was an attempt at self defense which made matters much worse, the Armenians being always the weaker in means and numbers. It is only occasionally one hears of their giving trouble to their persecutors" (MHS Box 28:22).

At times, visitors come through Tarsus and describe what they observed on their travels. For example, on November 13, 1915, Christie writes: "Miss Ditson of Hadjin came yesterday and went on today. She told us of the burning of Hadjin, that of about 3000 houses, only 300 remained, and those are the very poorest, and a few Moslem houses. . . . It is an open secret that the city was destroyed by an order of the Govt. under special superintendance" (MHS Box 28:23).

Christie's observation regarding the "open secret" is significant. What the sultan did publicly, the Young Turks executed primarily through their Special Organization, with an attempt to leave no traces, no proof, as little documentation as possible. Yet officials were told of these actions informally, and people knew because they witnessed the violence.

Displacement accompanied the destruction of Armenian settlements, and so the observations on the following page are not surprising: "Awful accounts come to us from those in camp at Külek [Gülek] Station[5]. . . . One of our church men assists in the soldiers' hospital at Külek Station, and so sees the people camping about. He tells of a family of 12 who were gathering grass and roots and boiling them for food. . . . We hear of terrible things, and of massacres" (MHS Box 28:24).

Book 2 of the diaries starts the way Book 1 ended. On November 17, 1915, Christie reports: "People are not allowed to remain long at Külek Station where they are actually dying from hunger. Our agents are giving secretly food and money to as many as possible, since money has come by telegram 'on John's account.' I keep women at work making coarse underclothes and warm petticoats for some of the poorest who were robbed en route, and are penniless and without change og [sic] garments" (MHS Box 28:25).

The remaining diary entries of 1915 similarly report mass violence. On December 18, an acquaintance "tells of auful [sic] conditions in Osmania, and says the treatment given Armenian children can't be told, and that numbers of such children were carried off by the Turks to be made Moslems" (MHS Box 28:41). Later: "Several old and feeble—near dead people, were buried with five corpses in a common pit! One woman, still alive, pushed her hand through the earth and waved it to call attention. Later the dogs came and ate the hand! This horrible incident called forth a remonstrance even from the cowed Armenians, and the Pasha receiving it, forbade a repetition of this inhuman treatment of human beings" (MHS Box 28:41–42). A subsequent entry includes reports of massacres in Urfa, Armenian attempts at resistance that were crushed, "and then followed a most horrible butchery with knives and bayonets and guns etc., the Moslem women following and sometimes smashing in skulls with stones!" (MHS Box 28:45). Again, massacres are accompanied by the taking of property. On December 20, 1915, Christie writes about the government's "open robbery in seizing Armenians' property—houses and lands and even the bales of rugs and bedding and bureaus etc." (MHS Box 28:42).

In short, Christie's diary entries of late 1915 speak to atrocities committed by the Turkish military, the Special Organization, and at times civilians against the Armenian population. Mass killings, arson, deportation, and robbery are part of the unfolding events.

Descriptions of victimization and suffering are less frequent in the diary entries of 1916. Yet what we read speaks to the continuation of mass evictions and killings begun in the preceding year. For example, on April 6, travelers report of recent massacres: "They saw awful sights, and tell awful tales" (MHS Box 28:62). On April 17, Christie writes about impediments to aid: "Our sewing has been taken from us. The Govt do [sic] not wish the Armenians to receive favors from foreigners. They promised to give our women work from their depot, and we have sent their names, each carrying our card. Thus far excuses have been made and no work given to those we sent. Others (Turkish and Arab women) got enough" (MHS Box 28:64).

On the evening of the following day, the news is of deaths of those close to Christie: "This time it is one of our old pupils, Gülabi Kouyoumjian, also Eyilmezian and son, and Suren Azirian. Scarcely a day passes in which we do not hear of the death of some Tarsus exile" (MHS Box 28:69).

Entries of 1917 suggest that the government is working to eliminate remnants of Armenian life. On January 30, Christie's bewilderment about massacres of civilians continues, as she writes that "one cannot,—simply *cannot* [underlined in original] understand the cruelty of Turks in treatment of the families of Christians. How can they instigate massacres! Have they no fellow feelings? It's a mystery to me" (MHS Box 28:107).

A March 6, 1917, entry describes again the fate of children:

> Last evening an eye witness who was at the RR [railroad] station when the train came in, saw over two hundred little Armenian orphans taken from five cars and driven by an officer into the garden across the road, and later on up in to the city: They were from four or five years old up to perhaps fourteen, and the majority were boys. . . . They appeared like children who had been under supervision, and were in a uniform dress that suggested the Germans. We have a fear that they may have been taken from the German orphanage in Aleppo which was in charge of Miss Rhoner. We have had vague reports of designs against her work. (MHS Box 28:112)

On August 23, 1917, attention shifts to the Greek population while Armenian survivors are crowded into Aleppo: "The Greek *subjects* [emphasis in original] are doomed to exile, and the Mersine Greeks are now in Tarsus awaiting orders. . . . Aleppo is full to overflowing with Armenian exiles" (MHS Box 28:155). Christie describes local conditions as worsening further.[6]

By early 1918, the defeat of Turkey and the other Axis powers becomes increasingly predictable. The character of Christie's diary entries changes accordingly. Signs of hope and new beginning mix with reports of new atrocities and continuing suffering. On January 19, Christie writes about plans to reopen the school, making it self-supporting. She writes about Muslims asking for such a school. "There will be Greeks and Armenians also—all boys" (MHS Box 28:206).

Some of the exiles manage to return to their places of origin, as an entry of March 27, 1918, indicates: "It's wonderful how people in Exile manage to get back one by one into the region of their former home. Yesterday a Hadjin woman came from Mosul! . . . Her family . . . were massacred some time ago. She was nearly naked and the boy had only a few tatters of one garment clinging about him. They were hungry and penniless. We gave them money and underclothing, and must see about giving them a lodging place" (MHS Box 28:220).

A diary entry of April 10 again reflects hope, but also struggles with the Turkish authorities over the continuation of the extermination campaign:

> People are hearing from Marash, and one person has come from there. There was a time of anxiety and a few were exiled, I believe, *but no massacre* [underlined in original]. The same was true of Adana. Here there was much uneasiness for a few days, as recorded before. It seems that a certain party wanted the Armenians to be sent away, but as no region or city wanted more exiles, there was an intention to dispose of them en route. Orders came, however, from those high in authority in Constantinople that the Armenians were not to be disturbed, save perhaps a few troublers of the peace who were to be exiled. Friday April 5th was the day when something was to have occurred that would have reduced the population, but God turned the hearts of those in influence so that we went to our beds at the close of the day, and slept and

awoke in safety. So it is that God keeps us amidst alarms. Of many dangers we are unconscious. (MHS Box 28:224)

Despite signs of hope, danger and fear continue. On April 4, Christie writes that "still, deportations and massacres come suddenly, so I am not surprised at the frequent apprehensions of the people" (MHS Box 28:223). She sees signs that also the last remnants of minority populations will be destroyed.

On August 12, just three months before the end of the war, notes indicate a mixture of hope and resignation: "There is a report that the new Sultan [Mehmed VI, as of July 4, 1918] has forgiven the exiled Armenians, and that they are free to return to their homes. This is good policy on his part, but what of all the property he confiscated, houses torn down, goods sold, gold appropriated, and all the death and suffering that have come upon a helpless people?" (MHS Box 28:244).[7]

With the end of the war in November 1918, the horrendous state of survivors becomes a central topic of Christie's remaining diary entries. On a trip to Adana, she reports, she

> went over to the American Girls' Seminary where about 900 returned exiles are staying. There are many more in other centers in Adana. Such a crowd! All of them dirty, unkempt and spiritless men and women and children. The men were in minority. There were many young women who had been captives among the Koords [Kurds]. Some had already given birth to children. Others were soon to be confined. The photographer of the expedition took several photos. One was of a group of young women who had hands and faces disfigured. . . . Helpers are to come to us after a while to open orphanages and help in other ways with relief work. (MHS Box 28:289)[8]

Carmelite Christie, a missionary, school administrator, and teacher in Tarsus, writing between 1915 and 1919, thus describes the suffering she observes and about which she learns from travelers and close acquaintances. The expulsions and massacres to which the Armenian population was exposed stand out in her reports.

Several observations are in order from a sociology of knowledge perspective. First, Christie's diary entries are reflections of an inner conversation, including her spontaneous reactions to the violence she observes or about which she learns from eyewitnesses. Second, her "Me"—again, defined as that part of the self that takes into account the imagined other, especially, in her case, the potential reactions of the Turkish state—reflects the habitus of a humanitarian aid worker whose ability to function depends on cooperation by the regime that bears responsibility for the suffering. Because bearing witness under such circumstances is challenging, we have to take Christie's descriptions even more seriously. Third, Christie writes her observations from a local perspective. They are direct, fresh, documented in real time. Yet they only partially reflect the bigger picture. Even information she obtained from others mostly speaks to the part of Turkey in which she resided. Fourth, and finally, Christie's observations became part of the historical record, one puzzle piece among many, contributing to a body of knowledge about mass violence against the Armenians. Her observations alone would certainly not have shaped knowledge in subsequent decades. Yet many other witness testimonies, even if varying by geographic region, overwhelmingly confirm the overall pattern of genocidal violence.

FROM A SINGLE VANTAGE POINT TO A PATTERN OF OBSERVATIONS: THE BRITISH BLUE BOOK

Christie's observations report about a region of the Ottoman Empire where Armenians were relatively wealthy and concentrated in cities. In such places, in conditions that did not apply everywhere, Armenians provided a convenient (and profitable) target. Historical research consequently shows geographic variation in patterns of violence (Kezer 2019), patterns to which the cover picture of this book speaks. French photographer Josephe Marando took that picture in the town of Sölöz, near the city of Bursa, south of Istanbul. The Armenian population was evicted from Sölöz in 1915. Some were saved from deportation into the Syrian Desert by Djelal Bey, governor of Konya, and returned home at the end of the war in 1918.[9] These Armenians were displaced again in 1922, after the War of Independence. Sölöz was taken over by Muslims, originally from Bosnia and Bulgaria, resettled in 1923 to Asia Minor from the region of Thessaloniki and Drama (today Greece). This latter resettlement was part of a massive population exchange approved by the victors of World War I.[10]

Despite such variation, hundreds of pieces of documentation, penned by consuls and other missionaries from all over Turkey during the years of World War I, parallel Carmelite Christie's diary entries. While the intensity of violence varied, the many observations accumulate to a *Gestalt* that reveals the genocidal nature of the aggression committed against the Ottoman Armenians.

Numerous reports are assembled in *The Treatment of Armenians in the Ottoman Empire 1915–16*, a book written by British historian and diplomat James Bryce in collaboration with historian Arnold J. Toynbee (Bryce and Toynbee [1916] 2005). The volume allows us to place the small tile provided by Carmelite Christie into the larger mosaic that emerges from accounts by many observers across the Ottoman Empire. Composed primarily of documentation, supplemented by discussion and analysis, the book appeared in 1916 in the British Parliamentary Blue Book series in the form of a legal report (in the following, I will refer to it simply as the Blue Book). Nearly all of the evidence came from primary sources. Authors of these sources agree that "starting in the spring of 1915, the Ottoman government had embarked on a systematic program to annihilate Armenians in the Ottoman Empire" (Bryce and Toynbee [1916] 2005:vii).

Analyzing the Blue Book, my research assistants and I coded a total of 150 general descriptions or accounts provided by eyewitnesses. Similar to our analysis of the Christie diaries, we focused on reports about bearing witness, providing relief support, conflict between these two goals, and compromises.

Information Constraints and Background of British Information Politics

In a background section included in its "Introduction," the Blue Book speaks to information control practiced by the Ottoman Empire and its German allies. Both "Constantinople and Berlin exercised a strict regime of censorship and misinformation regarding the fate of Armenians" (Bryce and Toynbee [1916] 2005:viii). This depiction is in line with Christie's local observations from Tarsus. The British government initially hesitated to publicize information about the fate of the Armenians. It feared detrimental effects that revelations about the mistreatment of Christians in Turkey could have on its relationship with allied Muslim leaders. Yet "the turning point in the British position came after October 4th 1915, when the United States government began releasing information on the destruction of Ottoman Armenians. This was through a front organisation called the Committee on Armenian Atrocities (CAA), which had direct access to State Department files from Ottoman Turkey" (Bryce and Toynbee [1916] 2005:viii).

Indeed, it appears as though most of the information about the fate of the Armenians was communicated to British authorities from the Ottoman Empire via the United States. A central actor in this transmission was Reverend James Barton, head of the American Board of Commissioners for Foreign Missions, the Committee on Armenian Atrocities, and the American Committee for Armenian and Syrian Relief. Barton, the Blue Book informs us, "was highly respected in President Wilson's administration, [and] had direct access to American consular reports from the interior of the Ottoman Empire" (Bryce and Toynbee [1916] 2005:xiii). Such reporting, collaboration with humanitarian aid organizations, and the channeling of relief funds were possible because the United States was still a neutral power in 1915. In addition, prior to the war, American missionaries had enjoyed excellent relations with the American Department of State (see Sarafian 1994, 2004; Morgenthau 2003).

Yet caution was the order of the day. "In one communication to Bryce, Barton explained, 'Our State Department allows me to make public use of the material if I can conceal the source of information. The Consuls in Turkey have been warned [by the Turkish authorities] against reporting the local conditions. There is a danger that if publicity matter can be traced to the Consuls they may be sent out of the country'" (Bryce and Toynbee [1916] 2005:xiii). Such concerns about disruptions of diplomatic ties have consequences similar to those feared by humanitarian aid workers. Here, as in other cases, they suggest caution in reporting about atrocities (Savelsberg 2015: chapters 6 and 7). Much in line with Christie's specific situation, what aid workers and diplomats report, despite the risks of bearing witness, should be taken all the more seriously. It likely constitutes a conservative assessment of repression and atrocities.

Atrocities Reported in the Blue Book

Segments of the Blue Book speak to the treatment of the Armenian population in the Ottoman Empire in the years 1915 and 1916. The content of these reports from various locales is similar to what we learn from the diaries of Carmelite Christie. While Christie describes massacres, evictions, neglect, and abuse of women primarily from her local perspective, this volume suggests patterns across the empire. A few examples have to suffice in this context.[11] The first is an excerpt from a letter "from an authoritative source," dated August 15, 1915, addressed to an Armenian outside of the empire:

> It is now established that there is not an Armenian left in the provinces of Erzeroum [Erzerum], Trebizond, Sivas, Harpout [Harput], Bitlis and Diyarbekir. About a million of the Armenian inhabitants of these provinces have been deported from their homes and sent southwards into exile. These deportations have been carried out very systematically by the local authorities since the beginning of April last [1915]. First of all, in every village and every town, the population was disarmed by the gendarmerie, and by criminals released for this purpose from prison. On the pretext of disarming the Armenians, these criminals committed assassinations and inflicted hideous tortures. Next, they imprisoned the Armenians *en masse*, on the pretext that they had found in their possession arms, books, a political organisation, and so on—at a pinch, wealth or any kind of social standing was pretext enough. After that, they began the deportation. And first, on the pretext of sending them into exile, they evicted such men as had not been imprisoned, or such as had been set at liberty through lack of any charge against them; then they massacred them—not one of these escaped slaughter. Before they started, they were examined officially by the authorities, and any money or valuables in their possession were confiscated. They were usually shackled—either separately, or in gangs of five to ten. The remainder—old men, women and children—were treated as waifs in the province of Harpout [Harput], and placed at the disposal of the Moslem population. The highest official, as well as the most simple peasant, chose out the woman or girl who caught his fancy, and took her to wife, converting her by force to Islam. As for the children, the Moslems took as many of them as they wanted, and then the remnant of the Armenians were marched away, famished and destitute of provisions, to fall victims to hunger, unless that were anticipated by the savagery of the brigand-bands. In the province of Diyarbekir there was an outright massacre, especially at Mardin, and the population was subjected to all the afore-mentioned atrocities. In the provinces of Erzeroum [Erzerum], Bitlis, Sivas, and Diyarbekir, the local authorities gave certain facilities to the Armenians condemned to deportation: five to ten days' grace, authorisation to effect a partial sale of their goods, and permission to hire a cart, in case of some families. But after the first few days of their journey, the carters abandoned them on the road and returned home. These convoys were waylaid the day after the start or sometimes several days after, by bands of brigands or by Moslem peasants who spoiled them of all they had. The brigands fraternised with the gendarmes and slaughtered the few grown men or youths who were included in the convoys. They carried off the women, girls and children, leaving only the old women, who were driven along by the gendarmes under blows of the lash and died of hunger by the roadside. An eye-witness reports to us that the women deported from the province of Erzeroum [Erzerum] were abandoned, some days ago, on the plain of Harpout [Harput], where they have all died of hunger (50 or 60 a day). (Bryce and Toynbee [1916] 2005:52)

This report indeed is a strong form of acknowledgment. There is no silencing or denial, and the core message resembles that from Carmelite Christie's diaries. The fact that it was written from a distance, in a Christian nation at war with the predominantly Muslim Ottoman Empire and no alien to Orientalism, certainly favored such depiction, but it does not take away from the ontology of the violent excesses. Importantly in our context, it contributes to today's body of knowledge about the Armenian genocide.

Some reports detail conditions in specific places, for example, the following passages we identified in the Blue Book from a *"CABLEGRAM, DATED 4th MAY, 1916, TRANSMITTED THROUGH THE STATE DEPARTMENT AT WASHINGTON TO THE AMERICAN COMMITTEE FOR ARMENIAN AND SYRIAN RELIEF, FROM THE COMMITTEE'S REPRESENTATIVES IN TURKEY"* [caps and italics in original]. This account highlights the need for relief support in different areas based on the conditions and violent acts committed by the Ottoman government.

> *Aleppo.*
> Relief work here supports 1,350 orphans who are only a portion of the destitute children now in the city. It has also furnished food to families in nine destitute centres, including Hama, Rakka, Killis and Damascus. £1,500 (Turkish) monthly are being used at Aleppo for orphans; £600 (Turkish) are being used for the poor of Aleppo; £2,245 (Turkish) are being used in the destitute centres. This is considered to be a minimum allocation, and ten times the amount would not meet the full needs. The work is being overseen by the German and American Consuls. So insufficient are the funds that many exiles in the destitute places have only grass to eat, and they are dying of starvation by hundreds. £1,000 (Turkish) are required each week for the Aleppo centre. [. . .]

> *Aintab.*
> Forty-five hundred Armenians remain here, two thirds of whom are on relief lists. Four hundred refugee women and children in city and neighborhood require £1,000 (Turkish) each month.

> [. . .]

> *Tarsus.*
> This being a station on the route taken by the exiles from the region north of Tarsus, the roads are always full of people in miserable condition. According to Government estimates, 92,000 exiles have passed through Tarsus, while according to other reports, the number is much larger. Typhus is very prevalent. The needs here require £500 (Turkish) a month. (Bryce and Toynbee [1916] 2005:70)

With this last entry, the circle closes. The Blue Book takes us to Tarsus, that town close to the Mediterranean coast, where Christie wrote her diaries. We link back from the big picture to the descriptions of perpetration and human suffering Christie provided from a local perspective, but in great detail and enriched by depictions of the fate of specific individuals. Importantly, the Blue Book was compiled by prominent scholars for publication in a British government series. More than the testimony of a lone humanitarian-missionary such as Christie, it is thus backed by influential knowledge entrepreneurs. It is a powerful contributor to collective memory, backed up by a most influential institution, about the genocide against the Armenians.

Excursus: A Question of Validity

The sociology of knowledge is not concerned with the validity of knowledge, the construction and shape of which it seeks to explore. The reader might nonetheless be interested, and so here I briefly switch gears to summarize debates over the validity of the information provided by the Blue Book. While not an exercise in sociology of knowledge themselves, these debates are part of the massive epistemic struggle with which this book is concerned. They are thus subject to the sociology of knowledge.

Britain was party to the unfolding of World War I, and, generally, caution is advisable when reading war-related information issued by one party against an enemy. Consequently, critiques abound—and, in a newer introduction to the Blue Book, the editors see reason to respond:

> [I]n recent years a number of partisan authors have argued that the Bryce-Toynbee volume was part of a British wartime misinformation campaign against the Ottoman Empire and its allies. Such authors have insisted that the work was based on forged documents with no scholarly merit. Enver Ziya Karal, a former dean of history at Ankara University, dismissed the report as merely "one-sided British propaganda," which was "not worth dwelling upon." Ismet Binark, former general director of the State Archives in Turkey, claimed that "the events described in the reports presented as the records of the so-called Armenian massacre . . . [were] all falsified information taken from the English's files relating to the East." *The Treatment of Armenians in the Ottoman Empire* was "ornamented with massacre stories, unrelated with the truth, biased, written with Armenian fanaticism, and misleading the world's public opinion." (Bryce and Toynbee [1916] 2005:x)

Yet the core messages of the Blue Book are consistent with independent local reports such as those by Carmelite Christie. Many others, like hers, are buried in archives in Armenia, the United States, France, Denmark, Sweden, and Germany's foreign ministry, home of the archives of Imperial Germany. Contained in all of these archives are multiple eyewitness accounts. They include, from the world of American diplomacy, reports by Ambassador Henry Morgenthau, Consul Leslie A. Davis (in Harput), and Consul Oscar Heizer. Note that, when most of these reports were written (1915–16), the United States was not yet involved in the war. Still more significant, in light of Turkish critique of the propagandistic intent of the British Blue Book, is testimony from German sources. They include statements by Paul Graf Wolff Metternich, German ambassador in Constantinople; Walter Rössler, German consul in Aleppo; and Wilhelm Litten, head of the German Consulate in Täbris.

FIGURE 2. Iconic photograph by Armin T. Wegner, a German medic, depicting displaced Armenians on their trek into the Syrian Desert. Image courtesy of the Armenian National Institute, Inc. / Sybil Stevens (daughter of Armin T. Wegner). Wegner Collection, Deutsches Literaturarchiv, Marbach & United States Holocaust Memorial Museum.

Similar reports come from the German allied military. They include testimony by General Friedrich Kress von Kressenstein of the First German-Turkish Expedition Corps; and by Armin T. Wegner, a German medical orderly, to whom we owe much of the iconic photographic evidence of Armenian suffering. Diplomatic and military testimony is supported by journalistic reports, including those by Samuel S. McClure, an American correspondent, and Harry Stürmer, German correspondent for the *Kölnische Zeitung*.

Christie's diary entries about the treatment of the Armenians and the documentation in the Blue Book also find manifold confirmation among humanitarians of the time. Examples are reports by Alma Johannsson and Beatrice Rohner, missionaries from Sweden and Switzerland, respectively; Tacy Atkinson, an American missionary stationed in Harput; Johannes Lepsius, head of the Armenisches Hilfswerk (German Armenian aid organization); Jakob Künzler, a German missionary and physician's aid stationed in Urfa; Martin Niepage, a teacher at a German school; Ernst Christoffel, director of a home for the blind in Sivas; and Karen Jeppe, Danish head of orphanages in Urfa and Aleppo.[12]

Such eyewitness testimonies, supplemented with occasional moments of acknowledgment by Turkish memoir writers (identified by Fatma Müge Göçek; see chapters 1 and 5), with photographic evidence (see figure 2), and with conclusions drawn by an overwhelming number of historians, suggest the validity of information that has today become sedimented in a widely accepted genocide discourse.[13] Such evidence, in combination with the state of scholarship, suggests to me that I should use the term *genocide against the Armenians* throughout this book. Leaving this excursus on the validity of the Blue Book and the Christie diaries behind, I now return to the role of a sociologist of knowledge.

CONCLUSIONS

Social interactions result in knowledge, including knowledge about mass violence. In addition, actors engage in inner conversations and, at times, externalize and objectify such conversations, for example through the writing of reports and diaries. In disorienting contexts, including those of mass violence, they may do so because sense-making becomes a precondition of sanity, the ability to act, and possibly survival. Carmelite Christie's diaries are a powerful example. They provide testimony, even in the context of a humanitarian field, in which Christie has to be mindful of the power of government and military. In the terms we have established, the "I" (spontaneous thoughts and reactions in the face of suffering) is constrained by the "Me" (that part of the self that takes imagined reactions by others into account and that, in the social field of humanitarian aid, codetermines the habitus of the writer). The Blue Book and a multitude of archival sources show that Christie's local observations about the treatment of the Armenians were part of a broad pattern, despite some variation across the Ottoman Empire. The fact that institutions such as the British Parliament backed these observations provides them with particular epistemic power.

Finally, social interactions as well as inner reflections, externalized in the form of diaries, have cultural consequences. Knowledge generated at the microsociological level may become institutionalized, objectified, and sedimented, especially when aggregated by macro-level actors such as the authors of the Blue Book. The outcome of millions of everyday practices, thus supported, is a collective repertoire of knowledge (Berger and Luckmann 1966). It becomes the property of carrier groups (Weber 1978)—that is, collectivities defined by criteria such as religion or nationality that secure the transgenerational transmission of beliefs and worldviews.[14]

Importantly, not all participants in these processes are equal. Powerful entrepreneurs of memory and knowledge, with access to vast resources and channels of communication, have an outsized impact on processes of sedimentation and aggregation. State actors feature prominently among them. The next chapters explore these themes. Chapter 3 provides theoretical and conceptual tools, which help analyze, in chapters 4 and 5, how distinct, in fact radically opposed, knowledge repertoires about the mass violence against the Ottoman Armenians became the property of collectivities, specifically Armenians and Turks.

Sedimentation

Carrier Groups and Knowledge Entrepreneurs

3

Carriers, Entrepreneurs, and Epistemic Power—a Conceptual Toolbox toward an Understanding of Genocide Knowledge

Part I of this book examined how social interactions and inner reflections, some expressed in writing, generate knowledge about ongoing and past mass violence. Silencing, acknowledging, and denying are common strategies, distributed unevenly across groups and over time. Part II explores repertoires of knowledge as properties of social collectivities. Following this theoretical excursus, I specifically seek to display what the Turkish and Armenian peoples know about the events of 1915 and subsequent years. Throughout, I use the word *people* with caution, mindful of variation within each of the two ethno-national groups.

Introducing the term *carrier group*, this chapter recognizes that some knowledge, including knowledge about the past, is the property of groups, transmitted across generations. Different groups may develop, through millions of interactions and reflections, distinct and at times clashing knowledge repertoires—that is, clusters of taken-for-granted notions of specific phenomena (as described in chapters 1 and 2). Knowledge thus negotiated becomes *sedimented* (Berger and Luckmann 1966:67–72) and *relatively* resistant to change. Nonetheless, and in line with Maurice Halbwachs's (1992) thesis on the *presentism* of collective memory, knowledge is subject to later modifications, especially when it is marred by ambiguities, gaps, and contradictions, as knowledge about mass violence typically is. Modifications of established knowledge are also likely when strategic actors in advantaged institutional positions seize opportunities to promote knowledge change. Those actors are *knowledge entrepreneurs* or, where knowledge about the past is at stake, *memory entrepreneurs* (Schwartz 1991, 2003; Fine 2001). These entrepreneurs may hold substantial *epistemic power*. In the following sections, I detail these concepts and arguments. I apply them to the cases of Turkish and Armenian knowledge about the Armenian genocide in chapters 4 and 5.

CARRIER GROUPS AND KNOWLEDGE

Maurice Halbwachs—noted French sociologist, a student of Émile Durkheim, and later a victim of Nazi Germany's concentration camps—examined how knowledge develops in social groups. He famously coined the term *collective memory*, by which he meant knowledge about the past that is shared, mutually acknowledged, and reinforced by a collectivity (Coser 1992). Halbwachs (1992) thereby recognized that memory is the property of social groups. To be sure, individuals remember, but Halbwachs showed how group processes shape what they think about the past.[1] Group boundaries are also boundaries of shared memories.

A different line of sociological thought aligns well with Halbwachs's notion of collective memory, and it provides an additional building block to our understanding of group-specific knowledge, including knowledge about mass violence and genocide. Max Weber (1978) wrote about *carrier groups* to refer to collectivities such as social classes, ethnic groups, and formal organizations that are associated with specific ideas or religious beliefs and carry them across time, even across generations (see Kalberg 1994, 2014; Gorski 2003). Members take these ideas and beliefs for granted, and they reaffirm them. Knowledge and ideas become doxa— that is, taken-for-granted, unquestioned assumptions about the world.

Building on Weber, Karl Mannheim (1986, [1936] 1985) applied the notion of carrier groups to the sociology of knowledge. Like Weber, he highlighted social classes as carriers.[2] He further acknowledged—in fact, he stressed—the overlap of different types of groups or units of social organization. His term *generation units*, for example, refers to groups of persons who are not just part of the same birth cohort, having thus experienced the same historical events in their formative years, but who additionally have been exposed to similar structures of experience (Mannheim 1952).[3] Such structures are likely to vary along lines of social class, religion, ethnic group membership, or skin color. In other words, Mannheim was mindful of the intersectionality of knowledge.

The association between groups and knowledge often results from interest-based affinities. For a prominent historical example, consider bourgeois classes of the eighteenth and nineteenth centuries. Drawing their strength from ownership of capital and their position in expanding markets for goods and services, they experienced the impediment of traditional status-group distinctions embedded in aristocratic society. They were receptive to enlightenment ideas, to principles of formal liberty and the equality of individuals. Intellectuals, philosophers, writers, and poets may have been the producers of these notions. Yet their ideas would have dissipated had they not attached themselves to receptive social classes that provided them with stability and endurance.

As in the case of generations, class membership interacted with other traits, including nationality. In France, for example, enlightenment ideas originated with members of the nobility such as Charles-Louis de Secondat, Baron de La Brède et de Montesquieu. In his 1748 book on *The Spirit of Laws*, Montesquieu had famously proposed the division of government powers, and this notion became one of the foundations of modern democratic constitutions. Class coalitions took different shape in Germany, where Karl Mannheim (1986) closely examined the emergence of a specific type of nineteenth-century conservatism. He identified the royal bureaucracy, nobility, and underdeveloped middle classes as carriers of conservative thought. These groups privileged thinking that was concrete (favoring folk tradition as opposed to abstract ideas of individual rights) and holistic (focusing on the nation as a whole), and they advanced nation-based romanticism (see also Elias [1939] 2000; Kalberg 1987; Gorski 2003). Such a worldview reflected mistrust in the enlightenment, partly in response to the French Revolution with its call for equality, liberty, and solidarity and its abstract notion of rights. Again, the link between group membership and ideological identification may be country specific. It is never straightforward.

Knowledge may also directly grow out of the lived experience of social groups, including the experience of violence. Collectivities exposed to violence are often defined by national, ethnic, or religious characteristics. Their background and experience combine to shape them into carrier groups with distinct memories of atrocity. Knowledge repertoires of perpetrator and victim groups frequently offer the starkest contrast, and they may clash in mnemonic struggles. Chapters 4 and 5 explore Armenians and Turks as carriers of starkly conflicting knowledge repertoires about the Armenian genocide. Chapters 7 and 8 examine struggles.

FLEXIBILITY OR INERTIA OF KNOWLEDGE?

The notion of carrier groups might suggest stability of knowledge over time. Yet the following chapters show flexibility as well. What social forces might then induce shifts in knowledge within carrier groups? What are the limits of such mutability? Thankfully, several lines of sociological scholarship provide us with tools that guide us through the analyses of the following chapters. They inspire a thesis, an antithesis, and a synthesis.

Thesis: Flexibility and Presentism

On one side of the divide, we find Maurice Halbwachs's argument about the presentism of collective memory. By *presentism*, Halbwachs meant that current-day interests and needs of social groups tend to affect their knowledge about the past. Images of historical events, in this line of thought, are always subject to change. Applied to our topic, knowledge about past mass violence likely takes new shape over time and from generation to generation. Halbwachs exemplified his argument by tracing shifting ideas about the topography of the Holy Land over several centuries, as Lewis Coser summarizes in his introduction to Halbwachs's work: "The Jerusalem, say, of the Persians, the Romans, the Jews and the Christian crusaders described a landscape that shifted rapidly in character depending on the various nation-states that dominated the Holy Land over a long span of time" (Coser 1992:28).

More recent empirical evidence supports presentism arguments about the flexibility of knowledge. Weil (1987), for example, shows that an astonishingly high percentage of Germans held on to the notion of Hitler as a great political leader in the immediate years after the end of World War II. Yet these attitudes changed substantially during the 1960s, largely driven by new birth cohorts who were not socialized under the Nazi regime (cohort effect). Older cohorts, indoctrinated under Nazi rule, eventually followed suit (period effect). For the United States, Schwartz and Schuman (2005) identify changes in the popular memory of Abraham Lincoln, especially after the civil rights movement. Of various traditional images of Lincoln, including those of the savior of the Union and the man of the people, the notion of the abolitionist, the great emancipator, eventually prevailed. Even where memories are carved in stone, including memories of violence, later modifications and uses by visitors may change the meaning of the memorial site—for example, from the somber to something patriotic, even heroic. Wagner-Pacifici and Schwartz (1991) offer an impressive example of this in the Vietnam Veterans Memorial.

In short, presentism of memory is a force with which to contend. Knowledge, even if held by carrier groups, is subject to modifications. It is always living knowledge.

Antithesis: Signification, Sedimentation, and Inertia of Knowledge

Despite such support for the notion of flexible knowledge repertoires and the presentism of collective memory, scholarship has also produced arguments that suggest at least relative inertia of knowledge. Peter Berger and Thomas Luckmann (1966), for example, in *The Social Construction of Reality*, write about the objectivation, signification, and sedimentation of knowledge (see also Zerubavel 2016). *Objectivation* is the process through which subjective meanings become part of the intersubjective world, available beyond face-to-face situations. Consider examples surrounding the theme of hate and violence. Hate is a subjective state, often expressed through facial expressions and gestures in the here and now. Once haters throw rocks to smash the window of a church, synagogue, or mosque, the communication of meaning no longer depends on such temporary expressions. The broken window and the rocks represent the meaning that motivated the act.

One important type of objectivation is *signification*, the production of signs that can deliver intended meaning, including hate messages, most powerfully. Instead of breaking a window, anti-Semites may have painted a swastika on the wall of the synagogue. Such signs typically cluster in systems, and language is the most significant sign system in the social world. It is more detachable from face-to-face situations than other sign systems. It transcends the here and now most effectively. Language organizes signs. It builds up classification schemes for things such as gender, zones of intimacy, and types of violence. It allows us, for example, to identify and categorize acts of violence as war, terrorism, self-defense, crimes against humanity, or genocide. Within such semantic fields (fields of signs and meanings), biography and history are (selectively) retained, accumulated, and passed on through time.

Via accumulation, groups build a stock of knowledge and transmit it from generation to generation. In the end, the commonsense world of social collectivities is equipped with specific bodies of *sedimented* knowledge. We know that we share such knowledge with others—and they know that we know. The confidence is mutual, advancing group cohesion and a special sense of trust in other members of our in-groups. Berger and Luckmann also write about language as an aggregate of *sedimentations*, reaffirmed through symbolic objects, actions, and rituals, providing a sense of reality (on sedimentation as a metaphor, see this book's "Conclusions"). Humans communicate such reality to new generations through processes of socialization. Like the work of Mannheim, a revival of Berger and Luckmann's book has great potential for contemporary sociology, including the sociology of knowledge, as several interventions on the occasion of the fiftieth anniversary of *The Social Construction of Reality* show (e.g., a special issue of *Cultural Sociology*, vol. 10, no. 1, 2016; Knoblauch and Wilke 2016; Presser 2018:9).

This, then, is the antithesis: A world (and history) constructed through objectivation, signification, and sedimentation should be solid, not easily manipulated to align with current circumstances—against Halbwachs's notion of presentism. Who is right, then, when we address genocide knowledge?

The Test Case of "Genocide": From Debate to Legal Doxa.   The emergence of legal language about mass violence provides a partial answer to the question just raised. Such language, too, is generated and diffused in personal interaction, and is fluid initially. Eventually, however, legal terms become part of sign systems, doxa, sedimented in the repertoires of law. Remember the conversations in which Lemkin engaged with his professor, and later with international lawyers, conversations that sparked his initial thoughts about the killings of entire social groups (chapter 1). The term *genocide* grew out of those exchanges, and today we take it for granted. It is part of our categorical system when we seek to interpret situations of mass violence. It is codified in the Convention on the Prevention and Punishment of the Crime of Genocide, passed by the United Nations in 1948, and in the Rome Statute of 1998, the foundation on which is built the International Criminal Court, the first permanent international criminal court. We depend on this concept and on related categories such as crimes against humanity (Lauterpacht 1943) or atrocity crimes (Scheffer 2012) when we think and communicate about mass violence. Clearly, international criminal law is an example of a sign system. Symbolic objects, actions, and rituals such as international trials reaffirm the validity of these concepts and the notion that they reflect real phenomena. The category of genocide becomes independent of the interactive contexts from which it emerged.

The Test Case of Genocide: Toward Cultural Trauma.   What applies to the concept of genocide also holds true for knowledge about specific instances of mass killings. Again, social interaction and communication contribute to repertoires of knowledge about events such as the Armenian, Cambodian, or Rwandan genocides or the Holocaust. In communication, these historical events, disturbing and confusing initially, take cultural shape. The process of meaning-making begins in the situation of terror, as we learn from survivor narratives (Neurath [1943] 2005; Levi [1986] 2017; Semprún 1981). Eventually, even those who never experienced violence know what occurred, and they may learn to empathize. The dark past becomes part of their world. They may even experience the cultural trauma of victims or of perpetrators, including their descendants and those who learn to identify with them (Alexander et al. 2004).

The late Berkeley sociologist and psychoanalyst Neil Smelser defined *cultural trauma* as "a memory accepted and publicly given credence by a relevant membership group and evoking an event or situation that is a) laden with negative affect, b) represented as indelible, and c) regarded as threatening a society's existence or violating one or more of its cultural presuppositions" (2004:44). Again, the group is central as a carrier of knowledge, in this case of collective memory or—yet more specifically—cultural trauma. Jeffrey Alexander (2004) adds that cultural trauma is anchored in Émile Durkheim's classical idea of "religious imagination." Such imagination, argues Alexander, forms "inchoate experiences, through association, condensation, and aesthetic creation, into some specific shape" (2004:9). In other words, what once was diffuse and chaotic in the minds of those who experienced horrific events begins to take shape and comes into focus; it becomes organized. Only after such transformation are groups able to communicate effectively about terrifying experiences and potentially share them, as solidified knowledge, with others who were not directly involved.

Like legal concepts, knowledge about specific experiences of mass violence becomes resistant to change, in line with Berger and Luckmann's arguments. This applies to the recognition of genocide, where cultural trauma emerged, for example in the cases of the Shoah or Rwanda. It likewise applies to denial of mass violence, colonialism, and oppression. Consider the memory of Christopher Columbus. Even if today's history textbooks depict Columbus critically, even if social movements portray him as co-responsible for the genocide of indigenous American populations, even if mass media and politicians display sympathy with the victims of the European conquest, the traditional image of Columbus as the "discoverer of America" remains dominant in nationally representative opinion polls (84.7%) (Schuman, Schwartz, and D'Arcy 2005). Few see him as a villain (3.6%). Schuman and coauthors attribute such inertia to the institutionalization of the "traditional Columbus" memory through Columbus Day commemoration in schools, paintings, statues, and literature.

Postcommunist Russia partially, but only partially, confirms the notion of mnemonic inertia. In the late twentieth century, a majority of Russians continued to remember the Stalinist purges of 1936–38, especially those who had lived through the period.[4] They did so despite widespread silencing of this violent chapter of history by the Soviet, and later Russian, state—a case of inertia. Yet the memory dropped off substantially among younger cohorts (Schuman and Corning 2000)—proof of the limits of inertia due to an imperfect intergenerational transmission of knowledge in adverse political contexts.

In short, different strands of scholarship are divided, each supported by empirical evidence. Some suggest flexibility and others inertia of knowledge, including knowledge of past mass violence—thesis and antithesis.

Toward Synthesis: Dialogism and Carrier Group Dynamics

Contemporary scholarship has addressed the tension between inertia and presentism, creatively working toward a synthesis. It holds on to Halbwachs's insights regarding the mutability of knowledge. Yet it simultaneously allows for degrees of inertia, recognizing the weight of sedimentation and endurance of carrier groups. Olick (1999), for example, studied May 8 anniversaries in Germany and asked whether this day in 1945 was commemorated as defeat (of a nation guilty of the crimes of the Nazi regime) or as liberation (of a nation victimized by the Nazi regime). Building on Mikhail Bakhtin's notion of dialogism, in which each utterance is a link in the chain of speech communication, Olick analyzes commemoration of this difficult date for each of the subsequent decades. He finds substantial path dependency, meaning that today's speakers at commemorative events have to take past commemorations (and the reactions they received) into consideration (i.e., inertia). Yet he simultaneously identifies politics of commemoration as speakers take seriously current-day conditions, from the hardship of the immediate postwar era, via exposure to the Frankfurt Auschwitz trial and intergenerational frictions of the 1960s and 1970s, to rightist violence in post-unification Germany of the 1990s (i.e., presentism).[5]

While Olick displays the simultaneity of the past in the present and the present's manipulation of the past, analyses of Armenian versus Turkish knowledge about the Armenian genocide show that specific conditions allow for flexibility, while others promote inertia. The nature of the knowledge at stake matters, as do the different types of actors who seek to change knowledge. Their interests and institutional positions, their narrative facility, and their epistemic power are crucial factors.

AMBIGUOUS KNOWLEDGE, KNOWLEDGE
ENTREPRENEURS, AND EPISTEMIC POWER
IN CONTEXT

Knowledge about difficult experiences is full of ambiguities, as we have seen: perforated by gaps and silences; marred by contradictions; resulting from struggles between recognition, silencing, and denial. Such features of knowledge may create vulnerabilities, opening up opportunities for revision when strategic actors seek to revise images of history. True for participants in everyday interactions, this holds especially for strategic players, often macro-level actors such as representatives of movements or parties, or heads of organizations or governments. Their institutional positions allow them to reach large audiences, and they are chief promotors of presentist adaptations of knowledge to contemporary interests. Scholarship often refers to them as entrepreneurs, including problem entrepreneurs in the tradition of social problems theory (Schneider 1985), reputational entrepreneurs, or mnemonic or knowledge entrepreneurs. Barry Schwartz (1991; 2003) and Gary Fine (2001) have documented, in multiple case studies, how entrepreneurs shape reputations of past presidents or of entire communities. Their success depends on their motivation, driven by material or ideal interests, and on their institutional placements, their ability to reach large audiences. Clearly, what applies to reputations also affects other types of knowledge, including genocide knowledge. Accordingly, the role of knowledge entrepreneurs will show prominently throughout all of the following chapters.

Narrative Facility and Receptive Audiences

Narrative facility advances knowledge entrepreneurship. It manifests itself in the skilled use of analogies and narrativization (Rydgren 2007). Consider analogism, the drawing of conclusions from a partial similarity to a similarity in all other respects. This strategy is attractive because it reduces uncertainty—even if it offends against the rules of logic. During the Yugoslav wars of the 1990s, for example, the president of Serbia, Slobodan Milošević, evoked memories of the 1389 Battle of Kosovo between Serbs and troops of the Ottoman Empire to advance his campaign against Bosnian Muslims. He analogized from the aggressive cruelty of the fourteenth-century Ottoman military to the twentieth-century Muslims of the former Yugoslavia, to whom he falsely attributed aggressive tendencies.

Some literature relatedly uses the term *analogical bridging*—that is, the application of an event that has taken clear cultural shape to a new event that is still confusing. A well-known example is the image of Bosnian Muslims, emaciated, behind the barbed wires of the Omarska concentration camp during the Bosnian civil war. Albeit partially staged, this image, published on title pages of news magazines all over the world, resembled iconic pictures of liberated inmates from Nazi concentration camps and thus evoked memories of the Holocaust. It also contributed to the willingness of Western powers to intervene militarily. Effects of skilled analogical bridging can obviously be substantial.

The second way to display narrative facility is skilled *narrativization*, successful reduction of complexity by bringing events into an order of interconnected sequences. Narrativization often goes along with other forms of simplification, as in Marxist or Christian master narratives that distinguish dichotomously between the righteous and the condemned. Such dichotomization is a common trait of narration in the aftermath of mass violence. Some legal concepts, prominently "genocide," actually require the identification of entire groups as victims—and, by implication, that of other groups as perpetrators. Importantly, narratives about violence not only shape knowledge repertoires, but may also lay the groundwork for future violence or for the slowing of circles of violence, a core theme in narrative criminology (Presser 2018) and in neo-Durkheimian writings about war (Smith 2005). Such narratives may be advanced by rituals, which are the subject of chapter 6.

One additional condition is required to achieve epistemic change: *receptivity of audiences*. Receptivity to simplifying narratives is high in times of uncertainty. In such eras, schematized knowledge is in high demand, and leaders who are trusted on the basis of common ethnicity or positions of authority find the greatest resonance. David Garland (2001), seeking to explain excessively punitive attitudes in late modern societies, cites Anthony Giddens's notion of "ontological uncertainty." He argues that elites would not have succeeded in instilling a culture of control on the populace without a general sense of uncertainty, social isolation, and loss of trust in traditional institutions. Like late modernity, post-genocide periods are rife with ontological uncertainty. Old ties have been torn apart, institutions undermined. Limited contact across groups further enhances receptivity to narratives with clear messages and stark images of the other (Rydgren 2007). Context thus codetermines which narratives reach audiences and "what kind of a hearing particular stories secure" (Polletta 2006:167).

Epistemic Power

Knowledge entrepreneurs succeed best in certifying or modifying knowledge if their narrative facility is supplemented by *epistemic power*. I approach this difficult term by first clarifying what I mean by *power*. For the level of social action, especially suited for concrete decision-making processes, Max Weber provides us with his classical definition. He refers to *power* as "the probability that one actor within a social relationship will be in a position to carry out his will despite resistance, regardless of the basis on which this probability rests" (1978:53). Building on Weber, I have elsewhere coined the term *representational power*. Specifying the notion for the realm of international criminal justice, I referred to representational power as the chance for international criminal justice institutions to affect collective representations and memories, even against resistance, and thereby to impress on a global public an understanding of mass violence as a form of criminal violence (Savelsberg 2020a). More broadly, we may conceive of *epistemic power* as the chance for actors to affect knowledge repertoires, even (but not necessarily) against resistance, in line with their desired understanding of reality, regardless of the basis on which this probability rests.

The means of epistemic power, the basis on which the probability to affect knowledge rests, are diverse. In the context of genocide knowledge, actors may practice power through the initiation and structuration of rituals (a mechanism explored in chapter 6); through the threat of economic or diplomatic sanctions or military force in international relations, or the risk that ethnic blocks will withdraw voter support in electoral politics (mechanisms explored in chapter 7); or by the use of legal resources (as analyzed in chapter 8). All of these strategies may enhance the ability of some actors (and reduce that of others) to certify, diffuse, or regulate knowledge.

In the context of state action, special kinds of power to which social actors attribute legitimacy play an important role. Weber calls them *authority* or *domination*. Submission to the will of others here involves a voluntary element, a belief in the justification of command. Such justification may be based on a "belief in the appropriate enactment of impersonal statutes and regulations" (Kalberg 2005:xxii). A case in point is obedience to legislatively imposed language regulations that criminalize either genocide denial or the articulation of genocide history. Court judgments are another example of legal-rational authority, and struggles over court decisions that pertain to speech rights versus restrictions on hate speech show the importance that current societies attribute to this mechanism (see chapter 8). Perceived justification of authority or domination may rest, alternatively, on charisma, whereby "obedience results from a belief in and devotion to the extraordinary sanctity and heroism of an individual person" (Kalberg 2005:xxii). It may finally be rooted in tradition, when "obedience results from an established belief in the sanctity of immemorial traditions and the legitimacy of those exercising rulership under them (for example, clan patriarchs)" (Kalberg 2005:xxix–xxx). Indeed, obedience based on old age or religion is relevant in our context, because many Armenians and many Turks are closely wedded to religious communities—the Armenian Apostolic Church and the Hanafi school of Sunni Islam, respectively.

The notion of legitimacy also fares prominently in Pierre Bourdieu's concept of *symbolic power*, a tacit mode of cultural domination unfolding within everyday social habits and belief systems (Bourdieu 1984). For Bourdieu, symbolic power is "the form that the various species of capital [economic, social, cultural] assume when they are perceived and recognized as legitimate" (Bourdieu 1989:17). Symbolic capital thus enables its holders to use their economic, social, or cultural capital in order to impose ideas and knowledge on others. They are unlikely to face resistance. The term *hegemony*, to which I return in chapter 9, is closely related.

STRUCTURAL CONTEXTS OF GENOCIDE
KNOWLEDGE: INSTITUTIONS, NATIONS,
AND HISTORICAL TIME

Narrativization and the practice of power happen not in a vacuum, but in the context of social fields—for example, legal and political fields (and the institutions embedded in them). Each social field follows its own rules of the game, and institutions are endowed with specific institutional logics.

Institutions and Their Rules of the Game (Institutional Logics)

Consider criminal trials and the stories, silencing, denial, and acknowledgment they generate. Their narratives tend to focus on individuals, relatively short time frames, and the need to arrive at binary guilty/not guilty decisions. They are also contingent on specific evidentiary criteria that differ from those accepted, for example, in the world of scholarship. Under such conditions, participants act in predictable ways. Defendants, when confronted with overwhelming evidence, tend to respond with implicatory denial. In genocide trials, they tell a story in which they were ignorant of the atrocities, or at least lacked agency, and are thus not guilty. By engaging in implicatory denial, however, they implicitly acknowledge the violence and its interpretation as crime, possibly as genocide.[6] Yet theirs is not the only story told in trials. In the adversarial setting of a criminal court, the other side will challenge the defendant's story and the denial it entails. Victim groups and their representatives contest incomplete confessions.

A series of effective trials advance at least partial acknowledgment. Their force may help explain differences between post–World War II Germany and post–World War I Turkey. International trials in the case of Germany are famous, and domestic trials there extended over decades. In Turkey, by contrast, there were no international trials and the domestic trials took place only in 1919–20. The latter trials reached guilty verdicts against some perpetrators, but opponents successfully challenged the legitimacy of the proceedings (Göçek 2015).

Nation-States as Contexts

In addition to social fields and institutional settings, societal contexts also affect the chances of truth claims to settle in collective knowledge repertoires. Consider country contexts in which institutions and social fields are embedded. Recently, Mark Wolfgram (2019) demonstrated the weight of national contexts on knowledge about the past in his comparative study of legacies of war and genocide in Germany, Japan, Spain, Yugoslavia, and Turkey. His comparison highlights the explanatory weight of generational distance, generated by nation-specific cultural assumptions about strong families, patriarchy, collectivism, and tradition versus individualism. These forces impede critical distance toward the past, including in generations that follow the perpetrators, and Turkey provides a strong illustration (Wolfgram 2019:185ff). In other contexts, where acknowledgment and confessions prevail, they may lead to a contentious coexistence at the societal level that is wholesome for democratic development, as Payne (2008) observes in her study on confessions in transitional justice contexts and as Göçek (2015) hopes for Turkey. Yet at the level of families and communities, a price may have to be paid in the currency of discord and conflict.

Like perpetrator knowledge, knowledge repertoires of victim groups are also contingent on national context, especially a victim group's proportional representation. Wholesome effects of verbal silencing described by Carol Kidron (2009) for the families of Holocaust victims in Israel seem to be weaker or absent in the diaspora, as stories told by Philippe Sands (2016) illustrate (see chapter 1).

Importantly, though, nation-states are embedded in global contexts, in world society. Effects of nation-level action are always contingent on forces emanating from world society (a theme I engage with in chapter 9).

Historical Context and Cohorts

Historical context, especially temporal and generational distance from the genocide, may also affect knowledge repertoires. In Germany in the first decades after the Holocaust, silencing prevailed, as did implicatory denial in specific contexts such as trials. Later, silencing by the perpetrator generation gave way to acknowledgment. At times, members of younger generations struggled for comprehensive, including implicatory, acknowledgment. In other societal contexts, in which silence and denial have been successfully institutionalized, such generational patterns are missing. Turkey is a prime example. Turkish intellectuals such as Fatma Müge Göçek are not alone with their insistence on acknowledgment, but they are exceptions.

Where societies have reached broad consensus about past violence as an instance of mass atrocity and genocide, the pressure on individuals and families to acknowledge those facts intensifies. Yet such acknowledgment sets in motion opposite tendencies at the level of small, intimate groups, especially families, that often seek to redefine actions by elders in ways that exculpate those involved in the history of perpetration (Welzer et al. 2002). Grandchildren who have strong ties with their grandparents experience intense dissonance when affection clashes with information about mass atrocities that is taught in school, described in literature, or uttered in public discourses—atrocities in which their grandparents' generation had been involved. Even if grandpa was a member of the SS in Nazi Germany or of the Special Organization in Turkey, grandchildren will likely find ways to exculpate him. They may reason that he did not join voluntarily, or that he was not in the places where atrocities were committed. Implicatory denial on behalf of a grandparent then becomes a common form of stigma management—but, again, it is associated with factual and interpretive acknowledgment.

CONCLUSIONS: HARVESTING THEORETICAL TOOLS

In sum, repertoires of knowledge, including knowledge about mass violence, past and present, are associated with group membership. Some types of knowledge stick to specific groups with particular ease, especially if they grow out of those groups' experience. We refer to these as *carrier groups*. Knowledge repertoires build up through thousands and millions of day-to-day interactions. They are captured in enduring *signs and symbols*, which are *sediments of social communication*. Consequently, *inertia* is one attribute of such bodies of knowledge.

Yet knowledge is not immutable. Knowledge repertoires, especially those entailing ambiguous knowledge, are receptive to mutations, especially when *knowledge entrepreneurs* are involved. Knowledge entrepreneurs are actors who are motivated to shape knowledge, who occupy privileged institutional positions with access to *channels of communication*, and who master *narrative facility*. An additional condition for their success is *public receptivity*, often the result of uncertainty and social isolation. In such contexts, knowledge entrepreneurs may hold substantial *epistemic power*. Yet they have to contend with *context: social fields, institutions, nation-states, historical time*, and *generational patterns* within which they seek to establish, or revise, repertoires of genocide knowledge.

In short, sociological literature offers us a set of conceptual and theoretical tools with which to trace and possibly explain conflicting knowledge repertoires held by Armenians and Turks about the events of 1915 and subsequent years, their inertia, and their transformations—a task to which I turn next.

Sedimentation and Mutations of Armenian Knowledge about the Genocide

Armenians are, in Max Weber's terms, an ethno-religious carrier group. Many ancestors of today's Armenians are survivors of the mass violence of 1915 and subsequent years. These ancestors suffered through great cruelties and experienced grave losses, and later generations of Armenians are receptive to the accumulated genocide knowledge documented in the first two chapters. While those chapters showed great fluidity of knowledge in its early production and intergenerational transmission, I now focus on Armenian repertoires of genocide knowledge in its sedimented form—relatively stable, but subject to modifications.

Armenians, of course, are not a monolithic group. Some three million live in Armenia, long a Soviet Republic but since 1991 an independent country. Millions of others live in the diaspora, many in France and the United States, where they wage mnemonic struggles against adversaries (see chapters 7 and 8). Armenians are divided further by political convictions, by degrees of involvement in religious life, by levels of participation in Armenian organizations, and by age cohorts and generations. While keeping these distinctions in mind, I first focus on knowledge in Armenia about the mass violence of 1915, and then turn to the diaspora.

GENOCIDE KNOWLEDGE IN ARMENIA

On a hill named Tsitsernakaberd, overlooking the one-million-inhabitant city of Yerevan, capital of the Republic of Armenia, is a memorial complex "dedicated to the memory of 1.5 million Armenians" who perished in the genocide. The complex "consists of three main buildings: the Memorial Wall, the Sanctuary of Eternity (Memorial Hall & Eternal Flame) and the Memorial Column 'The Reborn Armenia.'"

It signifies the memory of the violence the Armenian people endured. The message is explicated on the website of the memorial complex, from which I took the above quotations.[1] It is worth quoting from this text in detail:

> Tsitsernakaberd Memorial Complex in Yerevan is dedicated to the memory of the 1.5 million Armenians who perished in the first genocide of the 20th century, at the hands of the Turkish government. Completed in 1967, the Genocide Monument has since become a pilgrimage site and an integral part of Yerevan's architecture. Set high on a hill, dominating the landscape, it is in perfect harmony with its surroundings. The austere outlines convey the spirit of the nation that survived a ruthless campaign of extermination. . . .
>
> Before reaching the central part of the monument, visitors first observe a 100-meter long basalt Memorial Wall with the names of cities engraved in stone. The names also include the Armenian populations that were massacred by Turks during the Genocide campaign. Since 1996, the last portion of the Memorial Wall houses glass casings that contain soil taken from the tombs of political and intellectual figures who raised their protest against the Genocide committed against the Armenians by the Turks. Among them are Armin Wegner, Hedvig Bull, Henry Morgenthau, Franz Werfel, Yohannes Lepsius, James Bryce, Anatole France, Jakomo Gorini, Benedict XV, Fritioff Nansen, Fayez El Husseyn.
>
> As part of the Monument, an arrow-shaped stele of granite, 44 meters high, reaches to the sky, symbolizing the survival and spiritual rebirth of the Armenian people. Partly split vertically by a deep crevice, this tower symbolizes the tragic and violent dispersion of the Armenian people, and at the same time, expresses the unity of the Armenian people.
>
> At the center of the Monument stands the circular Memorial Sanctuary. Its unroofed walls consist of twelve, tall, inward-leaning basalt slabs forming a circle. The shape of these walls simulates traditional Armenian khatchkars, which are stone slabs with large carved crosses at the center. These slabs also suggest figures in mourning. The level of the floor of the Genocide Monument is set at one and a half meters lower than the walkway. At its center, there is an eternal flame, which memorializes all the victims of the Genocide. The steps leading down to the eternal flame are steep, thus requiring visitors to bow their heads reverently as they descend.

The symbol-rich buildings of the Tsitsernakaberd Memorial Complex represent what collective memory scholars call structural memory, something carved in stone, a monument that endures. Yet the meaning attributed to monuments is subject to variation across social groups and time. The above interpretation is provided by the Armenian Genocide Museum-Institute, part of the National Academy of Sciences of the Republic of Armenia. I conceive of the Museum-Institute as a macro-level actor seeking to offer a binding and universal interpretation of the mass violence committed against the Armenians. In doing so, it does what memory entrepreneurs commonly do: it answers "questions to which a successful process of collective representation must provide compelling answers: A. The nature of the pain . . . B. The nature of the victim . . . C. Relation of the trauma victim to the wider audience . . . [and] D. Attribution of Responsibility" (Alexander 2004:12–14). Below, I address each of these in turn.

The nature of the pain is captured, in the long passage quoted above, in the words *perished, extermination, tragic and violent dispersion,* and the repeated use of the term *genocide,* as in "first genocide of the 20th century," "genocide campaign," and two more times just "genocide." The word *first* gives the events of 1915 historical primacy over the sequence of subsequent genocides, the second of which is the Holocaust. Such primacy must be important to the authors, all the more so as it omits the genocide committed by the German military against the Herero and Namaqua in 1904 to 1908 in Namibia, then German South West Africa. It is unlikely that the authors are not mindful of this event, especially given the historical proximity and the similarity of the main method of extermination: driving the population into the desert so they would painfully perish.

The text also determines the nature of the victims: "1.5 million Armenians," "Armenian populations," and "the Armenian people." The categorization is already implicit in the term *genocide,* defined by the Genocide Convention as acts directed against a "national, ethnical, racial or religious group" with the intent to destroy that group, "in whole or in part." The authors writing for the Museum-Institute also attribute responsibility, defining the perpetrator as "the Turkish government," "Turks," and "the Turks." The text does not speak to its authors' relationship to a wider audience. Yet the annual memorial events of April 24, discussed in detail in chapter 6, do provide an answer. On these occasions, the president of Armenia and the head, or Catholicos, of the Armenian Apostolic Church lead members of the cabinet, a procession of celebrities, diplomats, and scholars from around the globe; and tens of thousands of Armenians into the memorial. Through this representation, and the invitations that precede it, the rituals reach a large international audience.

The text describing the Tsitsernakaberd Memorial Complex provides a distilled narrative of the violence against the Ottoman Armenians during World War I. Mnemonic entrepreneurs—motivated and in a privileged institutional position, suited to reach a wide audience—classify the suffering, the victims, and the perpetrators, and establish a relationship between victims and a world audience. The memorial and rituals provide the tools. Local audiences are likely to subscribe to the narrative, given three conditions the current context fulfills. The first is uncertainty, generated by continuing Turkish challenges to the narrative, an unstable state history, and a neighborhood of potential aggressors. The history of Armenian acts of perpetration—incomparably more limited, to be sure, than those the Armenian people endured—may also play into this uncertainty. The second condition is the sedimentation of knowledge through decades of interpersonal communication. The third is the relative lack of communication between the antagonists.

In short, the memorial site of Tsitsernakaberd hill, supplemented by the text on the website of the Museum-Institute, provides us with a condensed narrative of the Armenian genocide. Shared by Armenian communities around the globe, it is relatively stable, supported by the confluence of knowledge diffused in informal social networks over many decades. Yet this narrative is not the natural outcome of the events unfolding in the Ottoman Empire. Human agency intervened, and knowledge entrepreneurs played a prominent role, leading up to the contemporary understanding.

A series of articles by Armenian scholar Harutyun Marutyan (2007, 2010, 2014a, 2014b) sheds light on the process that cumulatively formed the dominant narrative. Marutyan distinguishes between three major stages: the silence of the 1920s, the definition of victim status resulting in the establishment of the memorial in 1967, and the emergence of a new Armenian identity beginning in 1988. His account provides us with insights into the stability and the flexibility of Armenian genocide knowledge, and into the social forces that contribute to both.

Repression and Quiet Reminders: Postwar Memories

The introduction to this book provides a brief overview of the conquest of the Armenian people by the Ottoman Turks and the 1923 division of the short-lived post–World War I Armenian state between the Soviet Union and Turkey. The Soviet-occupied part was initially incorporated into a Transcaucasian Socialist Republic. Conditions for the cultivation of an Armenian public national memory in the new Soviet Union were poor, and the new multinational country fought, with an iron fist, any nationalist movements. Marutyan (2010) attributes the withering of collective memories of the Armenian genocide in the early years of Soviet domination to this antinational context. Massive displacements of ethnic populations and the internment of Soviet-Armenian intellectuals in the Gulags, especially during Stalin's Great Purge of 1938, further contributed to discontinuities of collective memories (Mouradian 2003; Werth 1998; Polian 2004). Note that this was the second destruction of Armenian intellectuals within less than a quarter century, occurring just twenty-three years after the April 1915 arrests, deportations, and killings of leading Armenians in the Ottoman Empire. The associated memory loss must have been devastating.

At the level of informal social life, Armenian genocide survivors nevertheless cautiously cultivated knowledge about the horrors they and their ancestors had experienced, even if that cultivation was perforated by the kinds of silencing we encountered in chapter 1. Cultivation of knowledge even found written expression: "The national tragedy first appeared in Soviet Armenian literature in the form of literary descriptions of childhood reminiscences. Writers who survived the atrocities of genocide, and lost their motherland, recalled their childhood years and places dear to them, [yet] without actually speaking about the fact of genocide" (Marutyan 2010:24–25). There had thus emerged a knowledge repertoire, a form of cultural capital—tenuous as it may have been—that enabled Armenians to seize the opportunity for public articulation at the moment of de-Stalinization, initiated by the new party secretary, Nikita Khrushchev, and articulated famously in his speech to the Twentieth Congress of the Soviet Communist Party in 1956. Remember also that the international community had established the Genocide Convention eight years earlier. The moment had come to move beyond the vocabulary of "Metz Yeghern" (the Great Crime) that Armenians had used for the mass destruction of their people. The time was right to claim the term *genocide*.

Approaching the Fiftieth Anniversary: Epistemic Shifts of the 1960s

The decade following the thaw of the immediate post-Stalinist moment witnessed a rapid expansion of Soviet-Armenian literature. A series of political events helped as it brought the memory of the genocide into public view, albeit still cautiously. In December 1964, the first secretary of the Central Committee of the Armenian Communist Party, Yakov Zarobyan, wrote to the Central Committee of the Communist Party of the Soviet Union (CPSU) with regard to the memory of the Armenian past (Marutyan 2014b). Zarobyan pointed at the prominent role of nationalist forces in the diaspora for the commemoration of Armenian history and noted that "Soviet Armenia does nothing to commemorate the anniversaries of mass killings of Armenians" (quoted in Marutyan 2014b:65). He depicted this omission as dangerous in light of the fact that "our country neglects the memory of hundreds of thousands of our compatriots, thus actually exonerating the policy of genocide" (2014b:65). He concluded: "We think it appropriate to commemorate the 50th anniversary of the date in the light of the absolute victory of the CPSU Leninist national policy, to signify the great achievements of the reborn Armenian people in the spheres of economy, culture and science" (2014b:65).

The party secretary was mindful of Soviet interests in maintaining constructive relations with Turkey. He stressed that the Armenian tragedy could be commemorated in universalistic terms, without mentioning Turkey's role, in order to move the events from a "level of a solely Armenian tragedy to the level of world history" (Marutyan 2014b:65). The first secretary's letter thus showed great sensitivity to ideological concerns of the Soviet leadership, while simultaneously raising the idea of a memorial. Its author proved himself a skilled and influential knowledge entrepreneur in a sensitive context.

Importantly, mass demonstrations in Yerevan in April 1965, on the fiftieth anniversary of the genocide, followed the initiative by the Armenian communist leadership. Slogans on posters and banners reflected a sense of national renaissance, proclaiming, for example, "Compensate [for] Our Lands" or, with an image of Mount Ararat, Armenia's sacred mountain (on Turkish territory), in the background, "Give a Just Solution to the Armenian Cause" (Marutyan 2010:26).

The skilled moves by the Armenian leadership in combination with these popular demonstrations convinced the government in faraway Moscow that it would be wise to allow for the establishment of a memorial. A competition was held, and construction of the winning design was completed in 1967. It differed substantially from that of monuments in the style of Soviet Socialist Realism, further supporting a sense of Armenian cultural autonomy within the Soviet Union (see figure 3).

FIGURE 3. Tsitsernakaberd Memorial Complex, Yerevan. Photo courtesy of Ministry of Foreign Affairs, Republic of Armenia.

The Armenian public started flocking to the memorial from the beginning, and in 1975, eight years after its construction, the Soviet Armenian leadership began official visits, laying wreaths on April 24, Commemoration Day. The authorities added a Moment of Silence, further sanctifying the memory of those who had fallen victim to the Armenian genocide.

Strategic actors in the Armenian political leadership were initially willing to pay the price of the omission of any attribution of responsibility for the mass atrocities and the celebration of the Soviet Union as a savior of the Armenian people. Further, only pain and victimhood were on display—heroism and nationalist themes were avoided. Yet, while the memory shaped by strategic macro-level actors obviously reflects power asymmetries in Soviet Armenia, the memorial, like all elements of structural memory, is polysemic, open to reinterpretations and modifications that power holders may not be able to control (see Wagner-Pacifici and Schwartz 1991). The continuation of the story is a case in point.

New Opportunities and Analogies: On Polysemy and Reinterpretations of the 1980s

World historical changes, unfolding in the late 1980s, fundamentally affected Armenia and Armenians. They simultaneously left profound traces in Armenian collective identity and affected how Armenians remembered the events of 1915 and subsequent years. The Soviet Union became destabilized. The projects of Glasnost (openness) and Perestroika (restructuring), designed under Mikhail Gorbachev to save the Union, freed up sentiments in peripheral republics that had previously lain dormant. In Armenia, a flurry of interconnected events unfolded between 1988 and 1994:

- In February 1988, in mass demonstrations in the Opera Square of Yerevan, hundreds of thousands of people expressed solidarity with demands by Armenians in the Nagorno-Karabakh region. These Armenians increasingly demanded independence from Azerbaijan, to which a Soviet decision had assigned Karabakh when the Armenian Soviet Socialist Republic (SSR) separated from the Transcaucasian Republic.
- On February 20, 1988, the Soviet of People's Deputies in Nagorno-Karabakh voted to request the transfer of their region from Azerbaijan to Armenia.
- During the last days of the same month (February 27–March 1), anti-Armenian pogroms took twenty-six Armenian lives (and six Azeri lives) in the Azerbaijani city of Sumgait, further fueling nationalist sentiments in Armenia. Conspiracy theories claimed that Armenians had instigated the violence to discredit Azerbaijan. Almost simultaneously, a series of mass demonstrations took place in Armenia, referred to as the Karabakh Movement. Participants in the movement demanded the incorporation of the ethnically predominantly Armenian Nagorno-Karabakh region into Armenia.
- On November 22, 1988, the legislature of the Armenian SSR passed a "Law on the Condemnation of the 1915 Genocide of Armenians in Ottoman Turkey." This law formally designated April 24 as the "Genocide Martyrs' Commemoration Day." The political leadership of the Armenian SSR had abandoned previous caution about naming the responsible country.
- Just two weeks after the passing of the law, on December 7, 1988, a horrific earthquake struck Armenia, taking between twenty-five thousand and fifty thousand lives, injuring many more, and destroying towns and villages. In response, Armenia experienced an outpouring of international aid, especially from the Armenian diaspora.
- In December 1989, the Supreme Soviets of the Armenian SSR and Nagorno-Karabakh passed a resolution on the formal unification of Nagorno-Karabakh with Armenia.
- New violence in Azerbaijan followed. Beginning on January 12, 1990, a seven-day pogrom unfolded against the Armenian civilian population in Baku. Ninety Armenians were killed, hundreds injured, and the majority of Armenians were expelled from the city.
- On August 23, 1990, Armenia declared its sovereignty, and the issue of the genocide was included in the Armenian Declaration of Independence: "The Republic of Armenia stands in support of the task of achieving international recognition of the 1915 Genocide in Ottoman Turkey and Western

Armenia." The new country formally declared independence from the Soviet Union on September 21, 1991. Independence was completed on December 26, 1991.

Many of the above events motivated (or were motivated by) the Nagorno-Karabakh War, an ethnic and territorial conflict that started on a small scale in 1988.[2] It erupted into open warfare in early 1992, unfolding in the enclave of Nagorno-Karabakh in southwestern Azerbaijan, with ethnic Armenians, backed by Armenia, on one side and the Republic of Azerbaijan on the other. By the end of the war, in 1994, Armenians controlled almost the entire enclave and a mountain pass—originally part of Azerbaijan—that connects Armenia with Karabakh. Russia mediated, but a formal peace treaty is missing to this date. The conflict, which displaced 230,000 Armenians from Azerbaijan and 800,000 Azerbaijanis from Armenia and Karabakh, continues to linger, with occasional outbreaks of violence. Violence has again intensified into open warfare in the fall of 2020.

Early Armenian popular mobilization, especially after the pogroms of Sumgait of February 1988, reflect an Armenian understanding of this new conflict in close affinity with the memory of 1915. Analogical bridging was at work—that is, an interpretation of current events in light of memories of the genocide. Marutyan (2007) tells us about these sentiments as he analyzes banners and posters displayed at Armenian demonstrations. He interprets them as "changing icons . . . as an index of the collective understanding of the Movement by its participants . . . [and of the] stages of transformation of ethno-psychological orientations, and the changing identity of the nation as a whole" (Marutyan 2007:85).

What, then, do banners and posters tell us about shifts in collective identity and genocide knowledge at this dramatic historical juncture? Marutyan (2007) identifies several major themes, each expressed by demonstrators and captured best in titles the author chose for section headings. The first set includes "Recognize the Great Genocide of 1915"—presented in the shape of (then familiar) Soviet-style wreaths—and "We Demand of our Soviet Government that the 1915 Genocide Be Officially Recognized." This theme should not be surprising in light of the events of 1965 to 1967, leading up to the establishment of the memorial, and the yearly anniversary commemorations ever since. Yet, at this historic moment, toleration of commemoration no longer sufficed; recognition became the demand of the day. When the government in Moscow did not respond, producers of posters directed their call to global authorities. A banner of April 1989 reads, "We appeal to United Nations to accept the Armenian Genocide."

This first episode in the unfolding drama teaches two lessons. First, the weakening of the Soviet Union provided movement leaders and Armenians generally with opportunities for the expression of nationalist agendas and associated memories, especially memories of the genocide. Second, activists seemingly hoped for a "boomerang effect" (Keck and Sikkink 1998). By appealing to global actors, they bargained that their country's government, not responsive to local voices, would be swayed by changing positions of a world audience.

A second set of posters established a series of causal links and analogies between different events of mass violence: "Sumgait is a sequel to the Genocide" or "Sumgait is a continuation of the Great Genocide." Other banners and posters displayed the dates "1915" (genocide) and "1988" (Sumgait pogroms) against the silhouette of Mount Ararat. They linked the current events in Sumgait, no matter the difference in scale, to the genocide of 1915 and to Armenian identity. Intensifying such analogical bridging, and thereby underlining the message, on the genocide anniversary of April 24, 1988, a khatchkar (traditional Armenian cross-stone) commemorating the victims of Sumgait was erected on the area of the genocide memorial. Other khatchkars followed in later years, commemorating subsequent pogroms.

Another poster of April 24, 1988, engages in further analogism: "Der-Zor, Buchenwald, Sumgait." This message links the Sumgait pogrom to Deir ez-Zor, a city in eastern Syria that had been a core destination of the genocidal deportations during World War I. Tens of thousands of Armenians who had survived the torturous journey perished in nearby concentration camps. Marutyan estimates the number at two hundred thousand. Buchenwald is one of the early concentration camps erected by the Nazi German government. The producers of banners thereby linked both the Armenian genocide and the Sumgait pogroms to Nazi Germany's concentration camps.

Mnemonic entrepreneurs elsewhere in the world drove the analogy between the Nazi crimes and the destruction of the Armenians further. For example, Peter Balakian wrote in *The New York Times* of December 5, 2008: "For Armenians, Der Zor has come to have a meaning approximate to Auschwitz. Each, in different ways, [is] an epicenter of death and a systematic process of mass killing; each a symbolic place, an epigrammatic name on a dark map. *Der Zor* is a term that sticks with you, or sticks on you, like a burr or thorn: 'r' 'z' 'or'—hard, sawing, knifelike." Yet more pronounced is the statement of Armenia's president during a 2010 state visit to Syria, at the Church of Holy Martyrs at Deir ez-Zor: "Quite often historians and journalists soundly compare Deir ez Zor with Auschwitz saying that 'Deir ez Zor is the Auschwitz of the Armenians'. I think that the chronology forces us to formulate the facts in a reverse way: 'Auschwitz is the Deir ez Zor of the Jews'. Only a generation later, the humanity witnessed the Deir ez Zor of the Jews" (quoted in Marutyan 2014b:70–71). The skilled use of analogisms testifies to the narrative facility of mnemonic entrepreneurs. This strategy is especially powerful when analogical bridging links the Armenian genocide with the Shoah.

Other posters at the April 1988 demonstrations in Armenia quoted poetry of mourning from the aftermath of the 1915 genocide. Yet others, with banners reading, for example, "We demand the truth about Sumgait," called for political assessments of the recent pogroms and for the attribution of guilt. Some suggested appropriate answers, proclaiming that the governments of Azerbaijan and the USSR were responsible: "Moscow + Baku = Sumgait."

Increasingly, with the drive for independence intensifying, and the Soviet Union weakening further, opportunity structures became yet more favorable. Demonstrators now identified Moscow as complicit with the perpetrators. Merging the themes of Soviet guilt and Holocaust analogism, and supplementing this thematic pair with a reference to Stalinist crimes, one banner of November 18, 1988, stated: "These are our children. Buchenwald—Oswiecim—Khatin—Experience exchange—Sumgait—Masis—Zvartnots—Shushi—Stepanakert . . ." (Marutyan 2007:100). Depicted on this poster was a soldier of Nazi Germany's Wehrmacht and a Soviet internal forces soldier, shaking hands from which blood drips to the ground. Armenian movement leaders, encouraged by the lack of repressive responses by the reforming and weakening Soviet state, now began to link their memory of the genocide with the history of Soviet repression, including a repression of nationalist sentiments.

A fifth major theme, emerging in this ever-changing field of opportunities, appeared on a poster reading, "We Should Fight, Not Weep . . . ." Here, the narrative moved from one of victimization to one of active, in fact forceful, agitation. Marutyan suggests:

> Perhaps it was due to this, that all of about 60 posters of April 24th, 1990 completely lacked any pleading intonations. Among the posters recorded on that day calling for fight and for getting armed, a text taken from a fedayeen song was depicted in six different posters . . . , 'We should fight, not weep, but fight / to gain back losses of nation by weapons.' The fact that the text of an 80-year-old patriotic song was so often recalled is proof enough of a parallel between the events of the 1900's and the 1980's, as well as of a certain resemblance in the mentality of the Armenian people then and now. (Marutyan 2007:103)

The new Armenian identity as fighters did not replace the memory of victimization; it supplemented it, as many other posters and banners documented on the same occasion.

In short, knowledge about the Armenian genocide in Armenia proper showed both stability, due to the slow accumulation of knowledge through everyday interaction (Berger and Luckman 1966), and change. Mnemonic entrepreneurs made sure that private knowledge became public, but they also drove knowledge change. Their representational power became visible especially in the last phase of Soviet rule, when they incorporated the notion of heroism and nationalism into Armenian collective memory, built analogical bridges between genocide knowledge and repression during the Soviet (and especially the Stalinist) era, and made a further bridge to the Holocaust. Knowledge entrepreneurs initially included leaders of the national branch of the Soviet Communist Party. Later, in the 1980s, social movement leaders and their followers played crucial roles. Today, in independent

Armenia, political leaders are prominent in this regard, in harmony with institutions such as the Museum-Institute of Tsitsernakaberd and the thousands of Armenians who make the annual pilgrimage to the genocide memorial on April 24, the anniversary of the genocide.

In the Armenian drama, as in similar situations elsewhere, some drivers of mnemonic change occupy influential institutional positions. They are highly motivated by ethno-political agendas, and they possess substantial narrative facility, skillfully using narrativization and analogisms (Rydgren 2007). All of the above factors are among the conditions Fine (2001) highlights as preconditions for successful memory entrepreneurship (see chapter 3). Mnemonic entrepreneurs finally recognize and seize opportunities, here the weakening and eventual breakup of the Soviet Union. While this story from Armenia entails central sociological lessons about the generation and mutation of knowledge about genocide, we gain additional analytic leverage when we examine genocide knowledge in the very different context of the Armenian diaspora.

ARMENIAN GENOCIDE KNOWLEDGE
IN THE DIASPORA

Almost a century has passed since survivors of the Armenian genocide, in search of safety and new opportunities, migrated to new countries. The leading recipients were France and the United States. Here, as ethnic minorities, Armenians built up, maintained, reinforced, and defended, in mnemonic struggles, knowledge about the Armenian genocide.

Consider the United States. Today, according to U.S. Census data, 447,580 Americans self-identify as Armenian Americans, about 0.14 percent of the U.S. population. Estimates suggest, however, that the actual ethnic Armenian population is more than twice that size. Some Armenians had already arrived in the United States in the late nineteenth century, but many more followed in the context of World War I and the genocide. These populations are concentrated in California, especially in Fresno and Los Angeles, in New York, and in Massachusetts, particularly in Boston and its suburb of Watertown. Ten percent of Watertown's population are of Armenian descent.

Estimates of the size of ethnic minorities are yet more difficult in France, where the law prohibits census takers from inquiring about origin and ethnic status. Experts on French Armenian issues nevertheless suggest an ethnic Armenian population of about five hundred thousand, approximately one percent of the French people. Most French Armenians are concentrated in the metropolitan areas of Lyon, Marseille, and Paris.

In diasporic communities of both countries, communication about the mass killings was spotty in the decades immediately following the genocide, a pattern similar to that of the former Armenian SSR and its Transcaucasian predecessor. Quotations from autobiographies, interviews, and "How it was to grow up Armenian in…" reports (cited in chapter 1) provide illustrations. In regard to the United States, recall the autobiographical reflections of Peter Balakian, who would later become a Pulitzer Prize–winning writer about the Armenian genocide. Balakian had little knowledge about the genocide far into his adolescence.

In France, Serge Avédikian, a French Armenian actor and a director of powerful films with Armenian themes, and an immigrant from Soviet Armenia, observed that "in the 1970s, the Armenian community of France did not yet have all the structures it has today. One spoke rather little about the Armenians" (Avédikian and Yégavian 2017:37, translated by author). Avédikian continues: "There were not yet those claims of recognition of the genocide as organized, explicated, and written. There were not yet all those associations, and the traditional parties were very closed" (Avédikian and Yégavian 2017:37). Avédikian also writes about Armenian ghettos (*ghettos arméniennes*).

The rather slow development of an ethnic identity and of genocide knowledge in France may be due to several adverse conditions. Early French hostility toward the new immigrants was one factor. In 1923, for example, the mayor of Marseille referred to Armenians as "Cholera and Plague" entering the country (interview with Claire Mouradian). Armenians found themselves lower in the ethnic hierarchies than other "European" immigrant groups (on hierarchy of peoples, see Mauco 1932). Low social status challenged Armenians in everyday life all the more, as their names revealed their ethnic background (on early Armenian immigration to France, see Deschamps 1923; on "hybrid societies" and integration, see Bastide 1948). After all, Armenians had gained citizenship only after World War II. The position of Armenians in France was thus precarious far into the 1960s.

Self-identified as "guests," Armenians in France acted accordingly. They sought to contribute (e.g., serving in the military and the Résistance during World War II). After gaining citizenship, they worked to be exemplary French citizens, not to seek the benefits of the proverbial "squeaky wheel." Additional impediments for the organization of Armenian communities resulted from divisions along political lines, as well as from "snobbism" among those self-identifying as more European than newer immigrants (interview with Claire Mouradian; for details, see Mouradian and Kunth 2010). Yet the 1970s finally brought noticeable change, even against resistance. In 1975, the first major French book on the genocide appeared, and in 1973, the Armenian community of Marseille planned a genocide memorial in one of its churches. The French government, however, intervened and prevented its realization.

Commonalities in the temporal unfolding of Armenian knowledge about the genocide among immigrants to France and the United States and among Armenians in the homeland indicate that the early silence in the Soviet Union was not only a result of Soviet repression. Instead, it reflects a general tendency toward silencing found among many genocide survivors and some descendants.

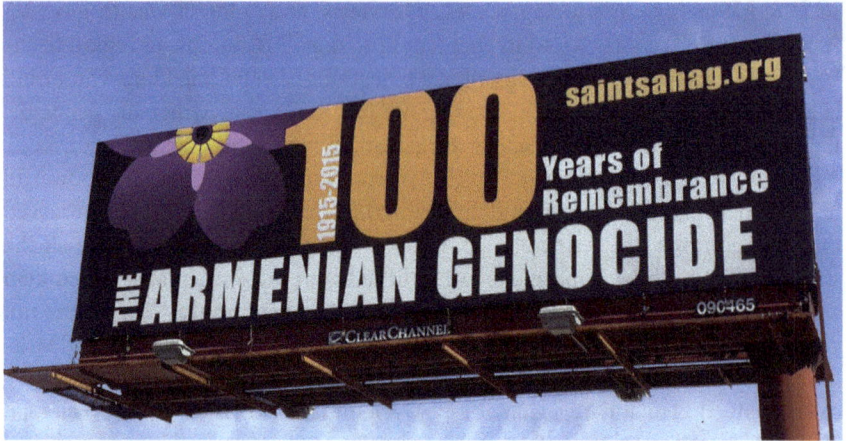

FIGURE 4. Billboard on a highway in the Twin Cities region of Minnesota, March 2015. Photo courtesy of Lou Ann Matossian.

Carol Kidron's work, cited earlier, attests to this pattern in the case of Holocaust survivors. In all of these cases, however, such silence was not to last, and France and the United States are no exceptions.

Indeed, by the end of the twentieth century and certainly by the 2015 centennial of the genocide, knowledge about the Armenian genocide was firmly entrenched in both France and the United States, in Armenian diasporic communities and in parts of the host societies. In today's America, the genocide is a regular subject of public presentations and discussions in Armenian congregations and cultural associations, whose members flock to annual April 24 commemorations. Armenian youth groups travel to the Republic of Armenia, and a visit to the genocide memorial is on their agenda as a matter of course.

On special occasions, such as the one hundredth anniversary of the genocide, Armenian organizations set up billboards along major highway arteries. In Minnesota they displayed the inscription "1915–2015—100 Years of Remembrance—The Armenian Genocide," adding "saintsahag.org," the web address of the Saint Sahag congregation that had initiated this billboard (see figure 4). Also on the one hundredth anniversary, congregations of the Armenian Church held memorial services. In the small diasporic community of Minnesota, for example, U.S. senators, representatives, and state and local officials attended and addressed those assembled in Saint Sahag Church, attesting to the representational power arising from the overlap of ethnic and religious affiliation.[3]

In short, emergence from marginality, strengthening of ethnic self-confidence, opportunities arising as external constraints diminish, and temporal distance from the genocide allowed mnemonic entrepreneurs to articulate forcefully the history of the Armenian genocide, and Armenians to communicate openly. The silence of early decades was broken.

In such situations, chances of finding allies grow, and they materialized in the struggle over recognition of the Armenian genocide as well. For example, university chairs, some endowed by Armenian donors, organize symposia and lectures, as do centers for genocide studies. Academic institutions offer teacher workshops to provide high school teachers and college instructors with materials and strategies designed to evoke their students' interest in the history of Armenians, especially the genocide, a challenge in light of great geographic and historical distance.[4] Initiatives intended to reach broader audiences further include teaching guidelines, issued by state departments of education (the central topic of chapter 8).

Knowledge about the Armenian genocide is as prominent in France today as it is in the United States. Armenian-French communities established a strong sense of identity in the last third of the twentieth century. They began to communicate their memory to the world around them. We will see later (in chapter 7) how these communicative efforts, paired with political strategies, were a precondition for the French legislature to pass a law in 2001 that formally recognized the Armenian genocide and a second law in 2012 that criminalized denial of the genocide—even if the latter was overruled by the Constitutional Council.

What, then, contributed to the transformation of knowledge that had remained hidden in small communities for half a century? How did it accumulate and become a publicly professed memory? Above, we have encountered mechanisms such as status gains of ethnic communities, political opportunities, ethnic and national organization, and the formation of coalitions with fields such as academia and politics. In the following sections, I elaborate on two of these mechanisms in greater depth. The first is an organization effect: the promotion of memory by ethnic organizations and their leadership. The second is a charging effect: the acquisition, by carriers of local knowledge, of universalistic academic capital and, through the latter, the extension of that knowledge into civil society.

Ethnic Organizations as Carriers: An American Illustration

Armenian ethnic organizations are potent contributors to genocide knowledge. Remember that Max Weber identified both ethnic communities and formal organizations as carrier groups. Ethnic organizations thus hold a double promise as carriers of collective memory. It becomes a triple promise, despite impediments resulting from assimilative pressure and internal tensions (Panossian 2006), when ethnicity overlaps with a specific religious identity, as is the case for substantial parts of the Armenian community.[5]

Recent studies by Julien Zarifian (2014) and Ben Alexander (2007) indeed highlight the central role of ethnic organizations for Armenian diasporic life and knowledge held by Armenians in the United States beginning in the early twentieth century. Local party headquarters served as social clubs for members, and each major organization published its own newspaper. Ethnic leaders play a particular role, as Alexander, working in the tradition of John Higham (1979), shows. They strive to build up collective identities and memory among followers, with considerable success.

The division of Armenian American organizations into two adversarial political camps, each with its own organizations, provides a natural experiment in that each set of organizations cultivated a distinct memory of Armenian history, even though both converged on the history of the genocide. On one side is the Armenian National Committee of America, earlier named the American Committee for the Independence of Armenia. Its roots are in the Armenian Revolutionary Federation (or Dashnak [also Tashnak] Party), founded in the early 1890s in Tiblisi, the capital city of Georgia. The Dashnaks pursued a nationalist and socialist agenda. They dominated the first Armenian Republic (May 1918–November 1920) and strongly opposed incorporation into the Soviet Union. Accordingly, they rejected the leader of the Armenian Church in Soviet Armenia, the Catholicos at Echmiadzin, who sought to accommodate the Soviet authorities. Instead, they have recognized, since 1933, the Holy See at Antelas, Lebanon. The Dashnak side of organized Armenian life has published, since 1899 and out of Boston, a weekly newspaper, *Hairenik* (homeland).[6]

On the other side of the divide is the Armenian Assembly of America (AAA), founded in 1972. The AAA grew out of the Armenian Democratic Liberal Party, which dates back to 1921 and is rooted in the Armenakan Party of 1885. Originally embedded in a bourgeois and clerical milieu, this party eventually broadened its base when aligning itself with the Armenian General Benevolent Union and its leader, Boghos Nubar Pasha. Motivated by political pragmatism, this strand of Armenian organizational life favored accommodation with Soviet Armenia and recognized the Catholicos at Echmiadzin. It, too, published a major newspaper to disseminate news and commentary, though the name changed repeatedly, from *Azk* (nation) to *Baikar* (struggle) after 1922, to *Armenian Mirror* after 1933, to *AM-Spectator* after 1939.

Aligned with this division between two major camps within organized Armenian American life, each side cultivated its own version of Armenian history. While the Dashnak side celebrated the 1918–20 era as one of a free and independent Armenia, often using the terms *Armenian people* and *Dashnaks* interchangeably, the AAA side depicted the era of the first Armenian Republic, under Dashnak rule, as antidemocratic, highlighting the preponderance of social problems, economic deprivation, and hunger. The division was so deep that, on December 24, 1933, a group of young Dashnaks assassinated the Armenian Archbishop of New York, Levon Tourian, during a religious service. The bishop had refused, on July 1 of the same year, to be seated under a flag of the Armenian Republic during an ethnic ceremony. Doing so would have demonstrated a rejection of Soviet Armenia and, simultaneously, of the Catholicos at Echmiadzin. The divisions between the two factions of organized Armenian life further deepened after the murder, leading to a formal split of the Armenian Church in America. Not surprisingly, subsequent generations of Armenian Americans would learn different accounts not only of the history of the first Armenian Republic, but also of the assassination of Archbishop Tourian. By 1933, the division and separate sets of knowledge about the first Armenian Republic were institutionalized among followers of both movements (Alexander 2007).

If ethnic leaders, through competing organizations and associated news outlets, succeeded in instilling distinct versions of Armenian state history in their followers, how much more successful must they have been in impressing on them the one issue on which both sides were in full agreement: recognition of the Armenian genocide? They succeeded indeed, and they worked to spread knowledge of the genocide to broader audiences.

The Armenian Museum of America in Watertown, Massachusetts, exemplifies both reaffirmation and outreach. Established in 1985, and affiliated with the Dashnak branch of Armenian American organizations, the museum supplements a display of Armenian material culture with an exhibit on the Armenian genocide. It features artifacts such as the clothing of a boy who was killed, bone fragments, and a Bible that belonged to a victim. Panels tell about the progression of the violence and the American response. The museum's website describes the display as a "stunning visual narrative of the events of the 1915–1923 Genocide, and the continuing aftermath and denial by the Turkish government over generations."

The establishment of the AAA and of the museum coincided, not accidentally, with an era of "ethnic revival" (Glazer and Moynihan 1970). Even if this revival is but an "ethnic myth" (Steinberg 2001), myths contribute to new cohesion among those who believe. In addition, this revival occurred during a time of intensifying Holocaust consciousness (Alexander 2002), when other victim groups were encouraged to articulate their own suffering (Novick 1999; Stein 2014). Armenian group consciousness thus solidified in this era, and Armenian organizations reached out to communicate knowledge about the genocide against their people to a broader public.

Going further, both branches of Armenian life targeted political actors. Despite different histories of political engagement,[7] they have headquarters in Washington, D.C., hold regular meetings with the Armenian embassy, maintain internet sites, and network with members of Congress, especially the eighty-eight-member-strong Armenian Congressional Caucus.[8] In their fight for recognition of the genocide, they have been most successful at the state level. All U.S. states have formally recognized the Armenian genocide. At the federal level, successes include budgetary allocations to Armenia, the blocking of the nomination of a potentially hostile ambassador, and recognition of the genocide by the U.S. Congress in 2020, during a time of heightened tensions between Turkey and the United States. As of this writing, however, no presidential administration has ever recognized the genocide; this is attributable to American political and military ties to Turkey—a

NATO ally in the volatile Middle East—in combination with Turkey's continued staunch denial of the genocide (Zarifian 2018).

This historical account delivers a sociological lesson. Ethnic organizations function as carriers. Their leaders, as knowledge entrepreneurs, are motivated and capable of shaping the identity and consciousness of diasporic communities. Opportunities broaden in times of "ethnic revival," even of "ethnic myth." In the Armenian case, the articulation and diffusion of knowledge about the genocide is a core theme, aided by the simultaneous recognition of the Holocaust. Eventually, leaders and their followers reach beyond the in-group toward broader audiences. Their efforts are likely to succeed in a new era of human rights hegemony, a topic to which I return in chapter 9.

Charging Effect: From Biography via Scholarship to French Genocide Exhibitions

Another path toward objectivation of subjective experiences of genocide leads from biography and exposure to genocide knowledge in family or community interactions, to the world of scholarship, and on to major public statements such as the curation of a national genocide exhibit. Early motivation is charged by new currents from academic life and propelled into public view. The example of Claire Mouradian, a French scholar, illustrates this progression well.[9]

Born in 1951, Mouradian is a French historian, specializing in the history and geopolitics of the Caucasus, specifically Armenia and the Armenian diaspora. She is director of research at the French National Centre for Scientific Research (Centre national de la recherche scientifique, or CNRS), and she teaches at the School for Advanced Studies in the Social Sciences (École des hautes études en sciences sociales, or EHESS) in Paris.

In an interview conducted in her office at the EHESS in the summer of 2016, Mouradian told me about her grandparents, survivors of the Armenian genocide. Her grandfather was a militant (Dashnak), fighting first against the Turks and then against the Soviets. He escaped both struggles with journeys leading from his home in Diyarbekir via Istanbul, Greece, Armenia, Istanbul again, and finally to France. Mouradian also tells about her grandmother Hripsimé, originally from Sasun (Sassoun, Sason), a descendant of a "family of fighters." She reports how her grandmother found herself under a pile of corpses at age fifteen, with massive injuries, how she was taken in (or held captive) by a local Kurdish family, escaped, and eventually arrived in France. Her grandparents raised the young Claire from the age of six, after her mother died in a car accident. They lived in Paris, near Porte Saint-Martin, in the second arrondissement, rue d'Aboukir, at that time a predominantly Jewish and Armenian neighborhood. As mentioned in chapter 1, her grandmother talked with Claire about the genocide, and this transmission of knowledge and the surroundings in which Claire grew up contributed to her decision to become a historian and to specialize in Armenian history.

An impressive career of scholarship and publishing followed. Motivation rooted in biographical experience was charged by intellectual currents, and Mouradian became an ethnic leader and mnemonic entrepreneur. In 1992, she helped reestablish the Société des Études Arméniennes, where she contributed to the publication of the (albeit short-lived, 1994–2001) scholarly journal *Revue du Monde Arménienne Moderne et Contemporaine*. Later she accompanied the French president when he visited Yerevan on the centennial anniversary of the genocide.

In Paris, the path from scholarship to public life is shorter than elsewhere (see chapter 7). Claire Mouradian traveled this path successfully, and in 2015, on the centennial of the genocide, she co-curated, with historians Raymond Kévorkian and Yves Ternon, a major exhibit, hosted by the Shoah Memorial (Mémorial de la Shoah) in Paris. The memorial exhibit was paralleled by a second display in the Hôtel de Ville, the city hall of Paris. Both exhibits reflect and contribute to the objectivation of knowledge about the genocide as it had developed in France by the early twenty-first century. They provide yet another opportunity to lay out the structure of sedimented knowledge of the Armenian genocide.

The full title of the exhibit at the Shoah Memorial was *Le Génocide des Arméniens de l'Empire Ottoman: Stigmatiser, Détruire, Exclure* (Mouradian et al. 2015). As the title suggests, it was organized in three parts. The first part, entitled "Stigmatiser" (stigmatize), provides historical background information, from early Armenian migration into Asia Minor during the times of the Trojan War; to the establishment, the waning and the waxing, and the geographic shifts of Armenia; all the way to its absorption into the Ottoman Empire. Under Ottoman rule, the viewer learns, Armenians and other minorities enjoyed limited equality and self-rule within the millet system, the partial self-administration of ethno-religious communities, but at the price of higher tax burdens and the prohibition of owning arms.

This section of the exhibit also highlights nineteenth-century military defeats of the Ottoman Empire, with substantial territorial losses in the Balkans and Caucasus. It informs the visitor that these defeats initiated a new era of stigmatization of Ottoman Armenians. Increasing repression resulted in the formation and radicalization of Armenian nationalist movements, including that of the Dashnaks. The repression turned into mass killings in 1895–96 under Sultan Abdülhamid II. Under headings such as "The Politics of the Sultan" or "The Times of Massacres," the exhibit informs the visitor that "the outcome is terrible: more than 200,000 dead, tens of thousands of orphans, mass conversions, exile of many survivors to the Russian Caucasus, Persia and the United States" (Mouradian et al. 2015:21, translated). Contemporary posters from France accompany the text tables, showing a blood-stained "Le Grand Saigneur [word play, combining *Seigneur*, or Master, with *sang*, or blood], le Sultan Abdülhamid II" (published in *L'Assiette au Beurre*, a French satirical magazine). Other countries stood by. An American poster, for example, shows John Bull, personification of England, looking at an Ottoman Turk raising his dagger and pistol against a kneeling woman, with the words "C'est difficile de les déranger—C'est un si bon client" (It is difficult to disturb them—it is such a good customer; Mouradian et al. 2015:18). Yet signs of solidarity challenge indifference. At the time of the massacres, France experienced an Armenophile mobilization, overlapping with the movement against the anti-Semitism-inspired trial of Alfred Dreyfus, and including prominent French politicians and writers such as Georges Clémenceau, Jean Jaurès, and Anatole France.

The exhibit next leads the visitor into a brief era of hope following the Young Turk revolution of 1908 (see also Der Matossian 2014). A 1908 poster, with Asia Minor in its center, shows a rainbow reaching from the western shore of the Bosporus to Armenian land in the east, with the word *Constitution* inserted (in the Armenian language). In addition, flags held by representatives of different ethnic groups state, each in their own language, "Autonomy," while the flags held by the Turk sport the words "Union, Equality." Yet hope was short lived. The exhibit leaves unanswered the question of whether the massacres against Armenians in the city of Adana in April 1909 should be attributed to remaining followers of the sultan or to the new Young Turk–led government. It leaves no doubt, however, that the latter responded to new territorial losses during the Balkan wars of 1912 and 1913, and the resulting flow of refugees from the Balkans to Anatolia, with a massive campaign of Turkification of space, people, and the economy.

The second part of the exhibit is entitled "Détruire" (destroy) and subtitled "La mise en oeuvre du génocide" (enacting the genocide). A large photo of the Syrian Desert, the fatal destination of hundreds of thousands of displaced Armenians, accompanies these words. This section introduces the visitor to the events of World War I as a necessary condition for the execution of the genocide. It shows how the war, and its preparation, included the advancement of nation-state ideology, support from Imperial Germany, military mobilization (also of Armenians), and military requisitions, especially directed at Ottoman Greek and Armenian businesses. Most consequential was the formation of the so-called Special Organization, a paramilitary group for combat against *"tumeurs internes"* (internal tumors) under the control of the party. The exhibit also points at responsible actors, detailing names and positions of the Young Turk leadership.

Moving forward in the exhibit, the visitor learns how "The Ottoman offensive on the Caucasian front is accompanied, under the cover of military operations, by localized massacres. . . . Already in late March 1915, the first signs of the genocidal project can be seen: the Armenian populations of Zeytun and Dörtyol are being deported" (Mouradian et al. 2015:35, translated).[10] Fifteen thousand villagers seek refuge in the city of Van from massacres committed by units of the Special Organization: "one counted 58000 victims" (Mouradian et al. 2015:35, translated). Armenian forces, concentrated in two neighborhoods, defend the city against the Turkish military for more than a month until Russian units approach. The exhibit reports how "these events, presented in Istanbul as an Armenian revolt, served to justify the initiation of the plan to exterminate the Armenians" (Mouradian et al. 2015:35, translated). Other elements of the exhibit show the deportation of Armenian intellectuals on April 24, 1915, a mass grave discovered by Russian troops in spring of 1916, and the deportation by train and by foot of mostly Armenian women and children to the "concentration camps" (Mouradian et al. 2015:39, translated) of Syria and Mesopotamia in the following months of 1915:

- April: 8 convoys, 35,500 deportees
- May: 21 convoys, 131,408 deportees
- June: 65 convoys, 225,408 deportees
- July: 96 convoys, 321,150 deportees
- August: 86 convoys, 276,800 deportees
- September: 5 convoys, 10,825 deportees
- October: 11 convoys, 27,500 deportees
- November: 6 convoys, 4,600 deportees
- December: 8 convoys, 7,500 deportees

Part 2 of the exhibit concludes with panels on the "Second Phase of Destruction in the Camps of Syria and Mesopotamia" (Mouradian et al. 2015:40–41). Beginning in October 1915, a department in the Ministry of the Interior set up twenty-five "concentration camps" with a capacity of eight hundred thousand. By March 1916, some "500,000 interned subsist in these camps and some other places of relegation. The Central Committee of the Young Turks now made a final decision, to move ahead with their liquidation. From April to December 1916, two locations . . . were the sites of systematic massacres that caused the deaths of several hundred thousand, primarily women and children" (Mouradian et al. 2015:41, translated; see also map 1 in the introduction of this book).

Part 3 of the exhibit is entitled "Exclure" (exclude). The subtitle specifies: "Exclure du territoire, effacer de l'histoire" (Exclude from territory, erase from history; Mouradian et al. 2015:43). It addresses the small size of the remaining Armenian population in the new Republic of Turkey and the state's efforts to reduce the memory of Armenians to one of "rebels and traitors of the fatherland" (Mouradian et al. 2015:45, translated). It displays images of ruins of formerly Armenian historical sites, especially churches, and, in sharp contrast, a Turkish memorial constructed in 1997 through which Armenians are defined as genocidal killers of Turks (Mouradian et al. 2015:47). The last images of this section show "monuments against forgetting" (Mouradian et al. 2015:48–49), including a 1919 memorial erected in Constantinople (today Istanbul), but destroyed by Kemalist nationalists in 1922; the Tsitsernakaberd memorial discussed above; a memorial church and museum in Deir ez-Zor (destroyed by ISIL in 2014); and monuments in Sydney, Australia, and in Paris. The exhibit depicts these as mere examples of a wave of recognition and commemoration around the globe:

Almost two-thirds of the seven to eight million Armenians live today in the diaspora, far from the Republic of Armenia, spread over all five continents, mostly descendants of those who escaped 1915. The chronology and geography of the memorials they erected . . . allow us to trace the expansion of the diasporic space, the itineraries of exile, the processes of integration, and the status of liberty in the countries after the settlement, in private and public spaces. Virtual exhibitions in cyberspace have recently enlarged the field of expression. Each new monument constitutes simultaneously a place of gathering and a symbol in the battle against the persistent denialism in the Turkish state, which has chosen to celebrate the executioners, set to affirm the "genocide of the Turks by the Armenians." (Mouradian et al. 2015:49, translated)

In short, the exhibit examined here, hosted by the Shoah Memorial in Paris and representing the events of the Armenian genocide, displays several messages. It provides legitimization—and, in fact, celebration—of Armenian life in territories later incorporated into the Ottoman Empire. It represents Armenians as victims of mass violence. The segment on the resistance at Van, displaying Armenians as heroes, is an exception. It specifies the form of victimization (killings, death marches, starvation). It claims applicability of the genocide label, a concept that became part of international law in 1948. It also identifies responsible actors. Different from the Tsitsernakaberd site, it does not refer to "Turks" or the "Turkish State," but instead attributes responsibility more specifically to the "Young Turks," the "Committee of Union and Progress," to specific (named) actors within the government and military, and finally to military units and the Special Organization. The label "Turkish State" appears only late, primarily in the section on denialism. The specification of terms avoids a broad and generalizing attribution of guilt or responsibility. The exhibit finally points to the spread of Armenian genocide knowledge across the globe, as manifested in memorials in many countries. It does not engage in analogism, but it has been relieved of that task by its host, the Shoah Memorial in Paris. Inviting this display at the central site of French Holocaust commemoration in itself establishes a link between the Shoah and the Armenian genocide.

Importantly, the story presented here shows the process of proliferating individual, community-level knowledge. Private memory, communicated in family circles, is charged by currents from scholarship and backed by academic capital. Especially in France, such capital can be converted into political and civil-society capital to reach a broad public. Finally, the outcome of memory formation, crystallized in an exhibition, constitutes a form of structural memory, a reflection of memory in material objects. While different visitors may interpret the displays in various ways, the visual and textual representation of the Armenian genocide reflects the knowledge of Armenians as a carrier group, and it communicates it to a broad public.[11]

CONCLUSIONS

This chapter has examined Armenians, in the homeland and in the diaspora, as an ethno-religious carrier group of genocide knowledge. Such knowledge, however, was not the natural result of the experience of genocide.[12] Over decades, widespread—even if often only partial—silencing turned to acknowledgment. History reveals the externalization and objectivation of thoughts and subjective experiences, their sedimentation as an Armenian knowledge repertoire about perpetrators, victims, and forms of victimization. It further shows both inertia and change of articulated knowledge with shifting historical contexts and ethnic organization, in the diaspora as well as in Armenia. This history finally demonstrates how entrepreneurs are at work to advance genocide knowledge within their ethnic community and to spread it toward a broad audience in their countries and globally. All of these elements, jointly, constitute the ingredients of cultural trauma.

Armenian genocide knowledge includes knowledge about Turkish reactions to and denial of the events of 1915 and subsequent years. The next chapter sets out to explicate Turkish knowledge and to show how it compares and contrasts with Armenian knowledge.

Sedimentation of Turkish Knowledge about the Genocide—and Comparisons

Research on Turkish knowledge about the Armenian genocide identifies deeply ingrained and systematic denial by the Turkish state and most of its citizens. As in the case of Armenians' genocide knowledge, however, scholars find that group-specific memories are not a constant. They solidify over time, as Stanley Cohen observes of the years after World War I: "This is not the usual story of initial unconfirmed rumours giving way to certain truths. . . . Rather, the opposite: truths that were certain at the time and the object of international attention were transformed into speculation, rumours and uncertainties. The initial denials entered collective culture in Turkey and slowly became more prevalent outside: the events did not take place; Turkey bears no responsibility for any loss of life; Armenian deaths were an unintentional by-product of bad conditions; the term 'genocide' is not applicable" (2001:134).

The shift from genocide knowledge as "truth" to its categorization as "uncertainty" and "speculation" poses a challenge to the sociology of knowledge. Who turned "truth" into "uncertainty"? Why and by what means? Was Halbwachs's notion of presentism at work? Who adjusted knowledge to new circumstances, and how? Further, in light of early changes, how can we explain the later solidification of knowledge, the relative inertia of memory?

The explanatory puzzle posed by Cohen is especially pronounced because denial costs Turkey dearly. Bayraktar (2010) rightfully stresses that Turkish denial contrasts with widespread and growing acknowledgment of various historical atrocities around the globe, encouraging official apologies by heads of state for crimes against humanitarian law and human rights norms committed in the name of their countries (see also Bilder 2006). Bayraktar finds Turkish denial of events that unfolded over one hundred years ago even more peculiar in light of modern Turkey's efforts to distance itself from the Ottoman Empire, at least until recently.

Göçek adds to the puzzle, highlighting that, in addition to symbolic costs, Turkey also pays a substantial material and political price: "millions of dollars to prevent other countries from employing the term 'genocide'" (2015:2), a closed border to Armenia with its military risks and barriers to economic development, and the impediment genocide denial poses to membership in the European Union. Why, then, is Turkey willing to pay such a high price in the currency of challenged legitimacy, loss of international prestige, and economic cost?

Thankfully, recent literature provides rich material with which to reconstruct, in condensed form, the evolution and state of Turkish knowledge about the mass violence against the Armenians. It suggests several answers to questions raised above about the conditions of knowledge, its mutations, and later inertia. I seek to show how these answers correspond with, benefit from, and contribute to the sociology of knowledge approaches discussed thus far.

Knowledge entrepreneurs play a central role, for which Fatma Müge Göçek's (2015) book *Denial of Violence: Ottoman Past, Turkish Present, and Collective Violence against the Armenians, 1789–2009* provides crucial evidence. Göçek's analysis of the evolution of Turkish knowledge about the country's violence covers more than a century, divided into four eras. The ensemble of more than three hundred memoirs of prominent Turks she analyzed allows for the construction of a gestalt of collective knowledge as property of those segments of Turkish society that were motivated and able to write such texts. Exceptions notwithstanding, factual denial and, especially, interpretive and implicatory denial were prevalent. They played out especially in the immediate post–World War I era (see also Kaiser 2003).

Further, news media and textbooks diffused knowledge produced by elites to a broad public, and for this, too, recent scholarship provides a wealth of evidence. Seyhan Bayraktar (2010) analyzes Turkish newspapers and their statements pertaining to the Armenian genocide (1973–2009), and several authors examine Turkish textbooks (Adak 2016; Akçam 2014; Wolfgram 2019). Together, memoirs, news media, and textbooks reveal the state of Turkish knowledge about the treatment of Armenians during World War I. Each of the authors cited also provides causal arguments that correspond with and enrich a sociology of knowledge perspective. Consider the sedimentation of knowledge regarding the genocide against the Armenians over four periods Göçek (2015) distinguishes.

THE YOUNG TURK ERA (1908–1918)

Accounts of Turkish knowledge about the Armenian genocide during the Young Turk era, an era that includes the war and the execution of mass violence, are fraught with ambiguities. Recognition is accompanied by denial, repression of information, silencing, media control, and various forms of neutralization, from blaming the victim to attributing responsibility to the Great Powers. Memoir writers, especially Young Turks and members of their administration, are motivated to shape, in an exculpatory manner, public understanding of the events to which they contributed. Like all political leaders, they hope to go down in history as heroes, and they certainly want to dispel any thought of criminal responsibility. They are also in institutional positions to reach a broad audience, and some master substantial narrative facility, capturing ideas in a narrative form that is convincing to many.

Narrating Violence in Memoirs

Early memoirs acknowledge mass violence. I quoted, in chapter 1, from Ahmed Refik's account of the fate of Armenians during the deportations, written shortly after the end of the Young Turk period (1919). Refik described the mournful state of ten thousand to twenty thousand deportees, waiting at the train station of Eskişehir, a "flood of disaster and death" (in Göçek 2015:152), victims of "theft and plunder" whose "houses were burned down to cover their [the perpetrators'] illegal acts" (in Göçek 2015:153). I repeat an earlier quote from this text: "No government at any historical period has committed murders with such cruelty" (in Göçek 2015:153). Yet even Ahmed Refik relativizes by equating violence against the Armenians with violence committed by Armenians against Turks. The title of his book, *Two Committees, Two Massacres*, indicates as much. By "second" committee and massacre he means "the massacres the Armenian revolutionary committee Dashnak committed against the Muslims in 1918 from Erzurum all the way to Trabzon" (in Göçek 2015:154). Refik disregards the massive difference in the scale of violence committed by the two sides, which Göçek depicts as "deaths of up to 60,000 Muslims . . . [versus] at least 800,000 Armenians" (Göçek 2015:250).

Ahmed Refik is not the only Turkish official to have acknowledged the mass violence. A government inspector, also stationed in Eskişehir, writes how houses "had been blockaded, hundreds of Armenian families had been loaded onto carriages, and [many] dumped in streams. Many women witnessing these atrocities had lost their mind" (quoted in Göçek 2015:220). The mayor of Kayseri, a Committee of Union and Progress (CUP) member, describes in detail the organization and staffing of units that were to drive the Armenian population from their villages into collection centers in larger towns (Göçek 2015:221; for a literary account, see Werfel [1936] 1983:152ff). An Ottoman officer describes deportations he observed when traveling to Damascus. He saw "on the two sides of the road unburied corpses of those among the refugee convoys who had fallen sick and died" (in Göçek 2015:223). Four Ottoman Turkish officials describe the Armenian deportations from Diyarbekir (Göçek 2015:224), and ten contemporaneous accounts portray the "deportations and massacres in Aleppo, Damaskus, and Syria . . . in great detail" (Göçek 2015:225). Yet such recognition of mass violence and suffering, and occasional expressions of empathy, pity, and regret, are rare compared to instances of denial with its various strategies.

Denialist strategies are, of course, not unique to perpetrators of the Armenian genocide. I showed (in chapter 1) how Raul Hilberg ([1961] 2003) details, for the Holocaust, ways in which actors at different levels of hierarchy managed to

overcome moral scruples against the execution of atrocity that had been incul-
cated by a long civilizing process. Within an arsenal of defenses, he distinguishes
mechanisms of repression and rationalization. The former include hiding the
ultimate aim by controlling information, prohibition of criticism, elimination of
the destruction as a subject of conversation, and camouflaged vocabulary. Mechanisms of rationalization, comparable to Sykes and Matza's (1957) neutralization
strategies, include a collective form: the justification of the destruction process as
a whole, typically achieved by defining the targets as evil. They further include, at
the individual level, references to the doctrine of superior orders, insistence that
no personal vindictiveness was involved (e.g., the telling of stories about "good
deeds" toward Jewish neighbors), blaming others, and attempts to diminish one's
own importance in the destruction process.

We find many of these strategies in the Young Turk accounts of the years of
mass violence. Consider repression: Göçek reminds us that "the violent and systematic elimination of Ottoman Armenians by the CUP, the government, and
state forces was carried out under the legal cover of 'temporary deportations' [i.e.,
camouflaging vocabulary]" (Göçek 2015:246). Repression by silencing takes two
forms. Memoir writers intentionally silence events that did take place, or they omit
mention of "the actors involved in secret and informal execution of the collective
violence" (Göçek 2015:247). One writer describes the role of Bahaeddin Shakir,
the CUP official who implemented Interior Minister Talat's orders on the ground:
"This issue was not dissected or illuminated even at the most intimate [CUP]
meetings. I do not have a clear, absolute opinion, but from a word used when
other issues were being discussed, a thought that leaked out, jests that could not
be contained, in summary, from all such fine and slight clues . . . he was the greatest motivator and creator of the deportation business" (quoted in Göçek 2015:217).

In addition to repression, neutralization strategies (Sykes and Matza 1957)
come to full display, including collective neutralizations that seek to justify the
destruction process as a whole (Hilberg [1961] 2003). The government inspector from Eskişehir, cited above, reports the words of a CUP official who, in a
speech, compared the Christians in the empire to "snakes and scorpions" (Göçek
2015:220). This language builds on a long tradition in which Ottoman authorities
and intellectuals considered Armenians traitors and internal enemies, especially
after select groups of militant Armenians cooperated with the Russian enemy
during World War I and in previous armed conflicts (Göçek 2015:251). It is also
in line with language used in the buildup and execution of other genocides (e.g.,
Rwanda, Holocaust).

Individual neutralization, partly building on such collective form, appears in
memoirs primarily in the form of "blaming the victim." Remember the words
of Dr. Mehmed Şahingiray, a CUP and Special Organization member, quoted in
chapter 1, who deems it "natural for there to be a danger for the Muslim populace
to be carried away by their emotions, reacting in kind to the rapacious and terrible murders of the [Armenian] element with which they had lived for so many

centuries, considering them [fellow] citizens and brethren" (quoted in Göçek 2015:250).

Göçek observes correctly that the author omits specification of "precautionary measures" (what in fact did the government do?) and that he joins those who falsely equate Turkish and Armenian victimization. In addition, this Young Turk memoir writer blamed the Great Powers (Göçek 2015:246), and he points at a few "black sheep" as responsible for atrocities that even he cannot deny (Göçek 2015:252, 255).

Institutional Position, Motivation, and Popular Receptivity

Importantly, the Young Turk leaders were not only motivated to deny, they also had the means to spread their denialist narrative. They were knowledge entrepreneurs. A paragraph from Göçek's book makes this point quite clear:

> Given the CUP's extensive control of the state, government, and the media, [Interior Minister] Talat had no problem altering the public discourse, claiming that the rumors about the massacres of Armenians in 1915 were "lies and slander the Armenians had started to contrive and fabricate about [some] Turkish and Kurdish massacres." And Talat did so when he had full knowledge that such massacres were occurring, executed mainly by the [Special Organization] armed bands he had personally helped organize and fortify. In 1915 the CUP also published propaganda material to allegedly demonstrate the destructive intent of all Armenians, material originally confiscated by the Ottoman state during the 1893–96 rebellions. (Göçek 2015:248)

The early strategies employed during the peak of the deportations continued as the end of World War I was in sight and CUP leadership had to expect military defeat. Göçek continues thus: "In the aftermath of the Armenian deportations and massacres, the CUP once again published propaganda as early as 1917 and 1918, perhaps due to the limited Armenian massacres of the Turks and Kurds in the east after the withdrawal of the Russian empire from the Great War, leading 'those who had been ashamed by the Armenian deportations to change their views as a consequence of this propaganda, to instead feel animosity toward the Armenians'" (Göçek 2015:248–249).

Göçek also informs her readers about historical conditions that contributed to both the genocide and its denial. She highlights the sultan's modernization efforts, continued by the Young Turks, which lacked a sufficient structural and cultural basis in Ottoman society (Göçek 2015:155–157); the widespread perception of minorities dominating the business world (Göçek 2015:171–172); and the nature of the Young Turks as a movement rather than a formal party. As a movement, they developed a pattern of secrecy, which they imported into government practice after their coup of 1913 under Enver Pasha (Göçek 2015:188). A culture of violence within the CUP supplemented these conditions (Göçek 2015:191, 202), as did the radicalization of the CUP (Bloxham 2005).

One additional factor speaks not just to the motivation of Young Turk leaders but also to the receptivity of the public. Preceding the Armenian genocide, just before the outbreak of World War I, the Ottoman Empire had suffered a devastating defeat in the Balkan War of 1912 to 1913. Göçek writes that "the war was disastrous for the empire; it lost 146,100 square kilometers of land, and approximately a million Balkan Turks were massacred or escaped to the empire with nothing but their clothes on their backs. In the end, the population of the empire decreased by 5 million, corresponding to a loss of about a quarter of all land mass" (Göçek 2015:228). The territorial loss was not just vast; it also included the industrially most developed regions of the empire. The Ottoman leaders believed that the Great Powers had promised a return to the status quo of the prewar era, a promise that was not fulfilled; hence, deprived of land, economic capacity, and population, their sense of betrayal was profound.[1]

The defeat in the Balkan War thus damaged the resource base of the empire, the Ottoman leaders' national pride and political ambitions, and the sensitivities of many leading Young Turks who were native to the lost territories. The wounds also dug deep into the lives of ordinary Turks, as "hundreds of thousands of refugees flooded the empire ahead of the Bulgarian army. . . . The Directorate of Refugees kept sending the refugees 'to Anatolia in droves,' while at least 40,000 to 50,000 ill and neglected ones remained behind in the capital. With this flood, the populace of the imperial capital also witnessed the trauma of the Balkan Wars" (Göçek 2015:235). Meanwhile, the arrival of masses of refugees in Anatolia intensified competition over scarce resources.

We can only imagine the stories about loss and betrayal circulating among the refugees and their struggle to secure an existence in their new settlement areas. Many Turks were pained even more because these displacements followed, by little more than one generation, those resulting from the Ottoman-Russian wars of 1853–56 and 1877–78. The second of these wars especially had already caused substantial loss of territory in the Caucasus and in the Balkans, and it, too, had unleashed a wave of refugees into the empire (Göçek 2015:37). Many Turks' profound suffering and sense of victimhood, we must assume, had lowered their sensitivities toward the victimization and suffering of others, including Armenians during World War I, and increased their receptivity toward denial.

MEMORY FORMATION IN THE EARLY REPUBLICAN ERA (1919–1973)

The Young Turk era ended with the defeat of the Axis Powers at the end of World War I. In Germany, the emperor was forced into emigration, and the foundation for the short-lived Weimar Republic was laid. The formerly mighty Austro-Hungarian Empire split into small nation-states, and the imperial capital of Vienna suddenly seemed out of proportion to the now modest Alpine republic of Austria. Finally, the long history of the Ottoman Empire had reached a shameful and degrading end. Large parts of its territories were occupied by the victorious powers.

What were the conditions for the development of knowledge about the Armenian genocide in this new context, specifically in the early republican era of the new Turkey? Here too, Göçek's analysis of memoirs contributes answers. Marking the beginning of this era with the 1919 onset of the Turkish independence struggle, she considers the war crimes trials of the early postwar era (1919–1922) and the establishment of the Turkish Republic on October 29, 1923, extending this period to include the end of the first half century of the republic's existence. Examining her account through the analytic categories laid out above yields further insights for the sociology of genocide knowledge.

Criminal Trials: Failures of an Otherwise Powerful Cultural Tool

In response to pressure from the victorious Allies, the postwar Turkish authorities initiated and held criminal trials of some actors whom they suspected of having perpetrated violence against the Armenians and of other mass atrocities. Sociolegal theory and empirical evidence from a variety of postwar and post-dictatorship trials suggest that such trials should have generated Turkish recognition of the atrocities. Arguments by Émile Durkheim, further developed in recent sociological literature, consider trials powerful rituals that awaken society's conscience, highlighting and generating a collective understanding and condemnation of evil. This literature interprets criminal punishment as a didactic exercise, a "speech act in which society talks to itself about its moral identity" (Smith 2008:16). The representational power of trials became most visible a quarter century later, through the proceedings of the International Military Tribunal at Nuremberg, which initiated the extension of knowledge of the Holocaust and broad psychological identification with the victims (Alexander 2004). Supplemented by the Eichmann trial in Jerusalem and the Frankfurt Auschwitz trial, these court proceedings produced cultural trauma as members of a world audience developed empathy with suffering they had not experienced themselves.

Not only sociologists, but legal and political practitioners as well have invested much hope in post-violence trials. Prominently, both President Franklin D. Roosevelt and the American chief prosecutor of the Nuremberg trials, Justice Robert Jackson, hoped that the trial—by laying out all the evidence, both written documents and the testimony of witnesses under oath—would certify knowledge, beyond reasonable doubt, of the unbelievable acts Nazi Germany had committed (Douglas 2001).

Trials can indeed serve such a function, even if constrained by a particular institutional logic. Examples abound, as documented in scholarly works on the Frankfurt Auschwitz trial (Pendas 2006), the Nuremberg "Doctors' trial" (Marrus 2008), the My Lai trial (Savelsberg and King 2011), and trials held by the International Criminal Tribunal for the former Yugoslavia (Hagan 2003; Savelsberg and King 2011). A recent example is the impact on Western public opinion generated by criminal charges filed against perpetrators of the Darfur conflict in Sudan, all the way up to the country's (then) president, Omar al-Bashir (Savelsberg 2015; Savelsberg and Nyseth-Brehm 2015).

Yet the trials held in Constantinople between 1919 and 1922 had no such effect. Instead, they stood at the beginning of a period in which denial of the Armenian genocide solidified, and in which former perpetrators were celebrated as heroes of the independence struggle. These trials thus constitute a challenge for the sociology of law and knowledge. What features of the Constantinople trials, and what contextual conditions, contributed to this unexpected outcome?

Some of the context and the constraints under which these trials were conducted become evident through Göçek's description of the judicial proceedings, for which she again provides evidence contained in contemporaneous Turkish memoirs. Challenges associated with setting up the trials included the issue of national sovereignty, which the Allies resolved by allowing the Ottoman authorities to conduct the trials, and legal ambiguities resulting from the informal ties between the Ottoman government and the CUP on the one hand and the illegal, and nonpublic, actions of the Special Organization on the other. These conditions posed substantial impediments in identifying suitable defendants.

Once the court began its work on December 16, 1918, the challenges intensified. First, the court faced fierce resistance. Memoirs document how former CUP members, now in positions of authority, obstructed the trials by warning friends, slowing the flow of correspondence, and destroying documents: "In our sleepless eyes, half drowned by the smoke and dripping with tears, the flames of the things we burned started to take on the color of blood. And we constantly burned the strange thing we call the past" (in Göçek 2015:357). CUP and Special Organization members further sought to obstruct proceedings by infiltrating offices of the Allied forces. They finally sought to delegitimize the courts through media commentaries that linked the trials to the occupation by foreign powers.

Second, politicization of the trials posed a challenge. Unionists, following in the CUP's footsteps and seeking to create an ethnically pure Turkish nation, charged that the Ententists, who pursued the continuation of a multiethnic empire and who constituted the government in the postwar years, cooperated with the occupiers, therefore engaging in a witch hunt against former CUP officials.

Thirdly, and most importantly, multiple efforts to delegitimize the military tribunal and to rehabilitate the perpetrators posed challenges. One memoir writer described the judge as "an enemy of the Turks" (quoted in Göçek 2015:360). Challengers of the court celebrated their greatest successes when the court also sentenced nationalists in absentia.

In the course of the court proceedings, the populace, in its nationalist fervor, and encouraged by Unionist leaders, began to redefine perpetrators as heroes who fought for the country's liberation from the occupying forces. Several memoir writers, in fact, tied the independence struggle to the trials, condemning those who sought to punish the perpetrators of the Armenian genocide. One writer explicitly linked the trials with prominent Armenian actors and their political, and territorial, pursuits: "The one gathering, readying, and transporting the witnesses [to the tribunal] is the (Armenian) Patriarchate. The Armenians are after

Greater Armenia, some . . . after a Kurdistan next to this Armenia, the Greeks after Smyrna, Thrace, and a Pontus Kingdom on the Black Sea shores" (quoted in Göçek 2015:360).

The most convincing evidence of the attempt to cleanse the record of perpetrators results from Göçek's detailed effort to trace the fate of different categories of suspects. Those arrested, charged, and acquitted contributed memoirs that "selectively narrated their past violence, providing irrelevant information while silencing their actual acts of destruction" (Göçek 2015:361). A second category were those the British had exiled to Malta and Egypt, in reaction to mass protests against the first conviction and the hanging of the convicted. Eventually, they were allowed to return to Turkey, in exchange for British citizens who had been sequestered in the empire. Many of these former exiles later became prominent republican politicians. Those among them who wrote memoirs never mentioned the violence against the Armenians or the role they had played in the genocide. Yet another group consisted of those who had escaped arrest, fled to Ankara (outside the reach of the occupying forces), and joined the independence struggle. "They were all very well received in Ankara because the leaders of the independence struggle needed educated CUP officials, officers, and civilians and therefore did not hold the perpetrators' crimes against them" (Göçek 2015:371).

A final category consists of those who were tried and hanged or otherwise killed. Many memoir writers celebrated them as "national martyrs" (Göçek 2015:365). Given the impediments the court faced, their number was quite small (fewer than ten). The redefinition of their reputation began right after the death sentence and execution of Kemal Bey, which shocked those who were imprisoned and awaiting trial but expecting lenient treatment. They and their loyalists' desperate desire to redefine perpetrators as martyrs was helped by the trial against Nusret Bey, in which the court offended against rules of procedure, and—mindful of potential challenges—sped up the convict's execution.

Summarizing this event in the context of judicial (non-)responses, Göçek writes that

> the rationalizing event comprising the few injustices committed at the 1919–22 military tribunals coincided with the independence struggle, enabling the nationalists to gradually transform the former perpetrators into patriots, thereby leaving only a few to be held accountable for the crimes they committed against the Armenians. The majority not only avoided prosecution but escaped to Anatolia to join the independence struggle, and with the victory of the struggle, they reemerged as republican patriots and served the newly established nation-state in high positions. This transformation effectively produced the republican denial of the perpetrators of the collective violence against the Armenians. (Göçek 2015:373)

In short, against Durkheimian expectations and despite positive historical evidence for other post-atrocity trials, the court proceedings in Istanbul did not affirm the history of the Armenian genocide. Instead, the trials strengthened the notion of Armenians as aggressors and the redefinition of former perpetrators as national heroes. Collective amnesia about the victimization and suffering of the Armenians during World War I was the ultimate consequence. The ritual power of trials is contingent, as this experience certifies, on the legitimacy of courts, and circumstances described in this section thoroughly undermined such legitimacy.

Strategies of Denial: Historical and Personnel Decoupling

Following the immediate postwar period and the trials, denial unfolded in two stages. Memoir writers first engaged in what we might call *historical decoupling*. They denied any connection between the independence struggle and the CUP. Nationalist leaders used various strategies. The CUP itself held back the publication of individual memoirs by its leaders in the years immediately following the war (Göçek 2015:375). Leaders blocked the return of CUP top leaders from exile (Göçek 2015:378), and they obscured the continued presence of CUP members—first in the liberation struggle and later in the new republic—and obscured their identities (Göçek 2015:379). A famous 1927 speech by Mustafa Kemal (Atatürk) was crucial. In that speech, he skillfully hid the role of the former CUP in the independence struggle, portraying himself as the undisputed leader of the movement and the new republic (Adak 2003). Many memoirs show that this definition of the new Turkish reality conflicted with the actual historical situation.

A second stage of denial silenced the involvement of perpetrators in the republican cadres, which I refer to as *personnel decoupling*. Nineteen memoirs analyzed by Göçek confirm the continued presence of former CUP members as civil servants in the new republic. Many among them swore an oath not to inform on each other. One memoir writer determines that November 1920 was a turning point. At that time all former perpetrators, CUP and Special Organization members, joined the independence struggle under the condition that they be granted amnesty. "The allied forces and the destroyed non-Muslims had indeed noted and protested the Unionists amid the national forces, but this did not change the future course of events because in the end, they were forced to leave, and the national movement ultimately succeeded. The subsequent national history of Turkey was penned by the winners who whitewashed the past violence against the Armenians as well as the violence they committed in achieving their victory" (Göçek 2015:381).

Additional strategies supplemented and solidified new knowledge repertoires: exclusion of contributions that Armenians and other minorities had made to the Ottoman Empire, and the cleansing from history of the mass violence committed against these populations. Toward that end, state authorities renamed parks and squares and confiscated Armenian property, turning some buildings into schools and theaters.

Perhaps most consequentially, the new republican government introduced changes to the educational system. Republican leaders decided early on to centralize all educational institutions under the Department of Education in Ankara. The department controlled textbook production, teacher training, course content, and examination questions. Textbooks harmonized closely with official nationalist rhetoric. The curriculum highlighted Turkish contributions to the country's development and the righteousness of Muslim Turks, at the expense of other religions and ethnicities. These patterns transcended that era and survived into the late republican period, as an analysis of recent Turkish textbooks shows (Akçam 2014; also Adak 2016; Wolfgram 2019). Political controls reached beyond primary and secondary education to encompass institutions of higher learning. Constraining critical engagement with Turkish history, they tightened in specific moments such as the 1960 military coup. Göçek concludes that "the ensuing system produced public knowledge that instituted, diffused and reproduced Turkish ethnic nationalism, distorting the past and erasing the presence in and contributions of non-Muslims and non-Turks to Turkish history. . . . In summary, early republican modernity, undertaken with the intent to democratize the country and successfully transform former Ottoman subjects into Turkish citizens, instead produced a society hegemonized by the Turkish state and government in particular and the dominant Turkish majority in general" (Göçek 2015:294–295).

Consequently, memoirs written by leading politicians and administrators of the CUP shortly after World War I, but published only decades later, self-celebratory and self-exculpatory, fell on fertile ground. Authors included Talat Bey (Minister of the Interior) and Djemal Bey (Minister of the Navy), both members of the triumvirate of Young Turk rule, and lower-ranked but powerful actors such as Ali Münif, whose career reached from serving as Talat's undersecretary to becoming governor of Lebanon and Beirut (1915, 1916). All were highly motivated to present to their readers a clean and heroic Turkish past, and all mobilized substantial narrative facility to eliminate knowledge of the atrocities they had committed during their reign, or—where elimination was not an option—to justify their actions (Kaiser 2003).

LATE REPUBLICAN KNOWLEDGE
FORMATION (1974–2009)

The year 1974 marked the beginning of a new era of Turkish denial, in response to a global and intensifying Armenian insistence on acknowledgment of the genocide. Destabilizing domestic events sharpened Turkey's reaction. Importantly, in 1973 the conservative wing of the military had intervened in the political process, resulting in a substantial tightening of civil liberties. In the following year, the Turkish military launched an offensive in Cyprus. Turkish troops occupied 40 percent of its landmass, setting off waves of refugees and an exchange of Greek and Turkish populations to split the island into two parts (Bayraktar 2010:99–103).

Simultaneously, a new cultural climate provided fertile ground for the emergence of terrorist organizations across the Western world. In Germany, the Baader-Meinhof group engaged in abductions and killings of prominent politicians and business leaders; in Italy, the Brigadi Rossi pursued similar strategies; and in the United States, groups such as the Symbionese Liberation Army spread terror. In Palestine, Israel, and beyond, the Palestine Liberation Organization (PLO) engaged in terrorism to pursue its goals. It was in this context that members of radicalized Armenian diaspora groups resorted to terrorist strategies. Leading among them was the Armenian Secret Army for the Liberation of Armenia, organized in Beirut and operating in collaboration with the PLO, presumably with support from the Kurdish Workers' Party and the Irish Republican Army (Bayraktar 2010:98). Around the same time, a group named Justice Commandos of the Armenian Genocide, founded in the United States, also took up arms.

Establishment of these organizations resulted in a decade of terrorist violence. The series of murders was initiated, however, by the violent act of an individual. In 1973, Gurgen Yanikian, a seventy-seven-year-old immigrant from Turkey to the United States, who had lost many members of his family during the violence of 1915, assassinated the Turkish consul general to Los Angeles (Mehmed Baydar) and his deputy (Bahadır Demir) (Bayraktar 2010). In a letter to various American newspapers, Yanikian wrote that he wanted to avenge the genocide, and he called on other Armenians to follow his example. Göçek (2015) spells out the deadly harvest: "a total of 110 acts of terror against the Turkish republic in thirty-eight cities of twenty-one countries. Of these, 39 are armed attacks, 70 are bomb attacks, and 1 is an occupation. During these attacks, 42 Turkish diplomats and 4 foreign nationals are murdered, and 15 Turks and 66 foreign nationals are wounded" (Göçek 2015:46–47). This wave of violence against Turkish targets reached its peak in 1979 and finally ebbed in 1986.

Armenian terrorist activities succeeded in breaking Turkish silence about Armenian history (Bayraktar 2010:97). Yet, against the intent and expectation of the terrorists, they did not yield acknowledgment. On the contrary, the violence provided Turkish authorities with new bricks to build their wall of denial and to appeal to the Turkish public at home and the Turkish diaspora abroad. Turkish state actors used Armenian terrorist violence to engage in *reverse analogical bridging*: to color the interpretation of all past violence in Armenian-Turkish relations in light of the present. Current terrorism aided their interpretation of past Armenian violence as aggression and Turkish violence as defense. Göçek concludes:

> In a defensive move that commenced in 1981, Turkish state officials in general and the diplomats in the Foreign Ministry in particular developed an official counternarrative that actually delegitimated and negated the Armenian claims. These officials selectively focused on the past, homing in exclusively on the incidents of Armenian violence to thereby portray the Turks not as perpetrators but as victims. As a consequence, it became easier to argue that what had occurred in the past had been 'mutual massacres.' By doing so, however, the Turkish official stand actualized the last stage of denial, namely, the denial of responsibility for the collective violence committed against the Armenians. (Göçek 2015:456–457)

Narratives of historical processes cannot easily establish causality. Would Turkish denial not have succeeded and further solidified without the wave of Armenian terrorism in the 1970s and 1980s? We do not know. Yet we do know that Turkish discourses on Armenian history were revived at this juncture. They built on past practices of denial and further advanced the sedimentation of Turkish knowledge. Göçek's analysis of memoirs shows that much.

Critical readers may challenge Göçek's account of Turkish denialist representation, noting that it relies primarily on one type of document. They may ask whether memoirs merely reflect knowledge within a small group of actors in positions of authority and in the intelligentsia. Such critics, however, should not overlook analyses, by Göçek herself and other scholars, of news media and textbooks, which are crucial mechanisms through which knowledge entrepreneurs reach a broad audience and pass knowledge on to new generations.

Diffusing Knowledge: News Media

Turkish news media indeed reinforce dominant themes from the memoirs Göçek analyzed, as findings by Seyhan Bayraktar (2010) convincingly demonstrate. Bayraktar analyzed 1,339 Turkish media reports, published between 1973 and 2009, from five distinct newspapers. Included in her sample are the nationalist, populist, and military-friendly *Hürriyet*; the left-leaning, radically secular, and somewhat elitist *Cumhuriyet*; the Islamist-fundamentalist *Milli Gazete*; the liberal *Radical*; and the Islamist-conservative *Zaman*. Bayraktar selects articles specifically addressing "critical discourse moments," historic events that evoke broad public debates about Turkish history.

Working to identify frames through which Turkish media interpret Armenia-related events, Bayraktar first finds a terrorism frame. Reporting on Armenian terrorist activities, media juxtapose "innocent diplomats," good people who dutifully served their nation, to "cold-blooded Armenians" (Bayraktar 2010:106). Yanikian, the initial individual assassin, is portrayed as "vengeful," "uncivilized," and "crazy." Media reports omit, or mention only in passing, his traumatic experiences of 1915. Armenians are "notorious terrorists." One commentary proceeds to link the killing of the Turkish consul-general to the 1921 assassination of Talaat Pasha by a young Armenian, Soghomon Tehlirian, in Berlin (Bayraktar 2010:109). Media also represent Yanikian as a member of the "Huntschak" organization, thereby linking his action to the violent Armenian resistance movement of the 1890s (Bayraktar 2010:111).

Following highly organized terrorist attacks against the Turkish embassies in Vienna and Paris in the fall of 1975, the interpretive frame in Turkish news media shifts from "Armenian" to "international" terrorism. On October 25, 1975, *Cumhuriyet* quotes Prime Minister Süleyman Demirel's words in its headline "Turkish State Target of Murders" (Bayraktar 2010:112). Media reports are careful, however, to interpret the Armenian terrorists as members of the diaspora, contrasting them with "our Armenians" (Bayraktar 2010:115). Such distinction seeks to present domestic Turkish-Armenian relations as harmonious. It also aims to prevent a recurrence of Turkish pogroms akin to those against Greeks in 1955 that had caused major destruction and bloodshed. Yet not all papers apply such caution. *Milli Gazete* more aggressively writes about "minorities in our country that have, throughout our history, pushed the knife into the back of the nation. The minorities include Greeks and Armenians" (Bayraktar 2010:116).[2]

Other media reports reflect more explicitly on Ottoman-Armenian relations throughout history, including the violence of 1915. *Milli Gazete* writes about "The Massacres by Armenians in our History," and a five-part series in *Hürriyet* is entitled "The Truth behind the Armenian Question" (Bayraktar 2010:121). This series reads like a "treatise on Armenian revolts, collaboration and instrumentalization by foreign powers" (Bayraktar 2010:212). Its authors attribute responsibility for violence primarily to "radicalized" Armenian organizations and political parties such as the Huntshaks and Dashnaks. In addition, they seek to identify foreign powers as responsible for the decline in Ottoman-Armenian relations: Armenians "dared to engage in the revolts *only* because they had the back of the European powers" (in Bayraktar 2010:125). Thus, the series concludes, Turks and Muslims are the real victims of history: "Millions of innocent Turks . . . were killed during the Armenian massacres. . . . Yet, Armenians received the appropriate response. . . . They had to receive that response as there are two things Turks cannot tolerate: injustice and cowardly actions" (in Bayraktar 2010:125).

In short, terrorist violence, motivated by rage about Turkish denial of the Armenian genocide, provided the Turkish government and media with ammunition to advance denial further. It helped knowledge entrepreneurs strengthen, at least domestically, Turkish interpretations of the violence of 1915.

A decade and a half later, another historical moment evoked Turkish media engagement with Armenian history. In 1991, Armenia once again became an independent country. After separating from the dissolving Soviet Union, the new republic joined diasporic Armenian communities to push for recognition of the genocide at national and international organizational levels. A new knowledge entrepreneur had thus entered the scene, and a growing number of countries now recognized the Armenian genocide (see chapter 7). Such recognition evoked massive governmental and societal responses in Turkey, where sensitivities were heightened in the context of the country's new status, in 1999, as an official candidate for membership in the European Union.

Challenged and sensitized, Turkey intensified denial. In response to a 2001 French genocide recognition law, *Hürriyet*'s chief editorial writer, Oktay Ekşi, calls for a general boycott of France by Turkish organizations and businesses. Generally, papers express alarm regarding the spread of the "recognition virus" (Bayraktar 2010:202). Using its geostrategic position vis-à-vis the Middle East and Incirlik Air Base (shared with NATO allies) as a bargaining chip, Turkey manages to prevent U.S. recognition of the genocide. Media now open a new line of attack, charging European powers with their own complicity or guilt. *Milli Gazete* reminds its readers that France continues to pay pensions to Armenian veterans (Bayraktar 2010:206), and *Cumhuriyet*, responding to a pending debate of the Armenian genocide in the German legislature (Bundestag), quotes a leading Turkish foreign policy maker who charges Germany with the attempt to relativize the Holocaust.[3]

Eventually, however, Turkey recognized that its version of the events of 1915 was no longer internationally accepted. Armenians had spread, in the words of a commentator in *Milli Gazete*, a "lie for a truth" (Bayraktar 2010:211). Journalists now redirected their writings, as in a commentary in *Cumhuriyet*, against a three-phase plan: recognition, reparation, territorial demands (Bayraktar 2010:212, 216). They also reminded the world of histories of atrocities committed by European powers, including French violence in Algeria, and challenged European "claims of cultural superiority" (Bayraktar 2010:220).

In short, media discourses analyzed by Bayraktar raise similar themes as the memoirs Göçek dissects. Both types of documents generate Turkish knowledge about Armenians and the Armenian genocide. Both involve factual and interpretive denial. Well-known neutralization strategies of blaming the victim and challenging the accuser support such denial (Sykes and Matza 1957). Journalists join government officials and intellectuals in articulating and reinforcing denial of the Armenian genocide.

Intergenerational Transmission of Knowledge: Textbooks

Textbooks do not just reflect knowledge; they communicate it to new generations. The Department of Education in Ankara produces or approves all textbooks, and these textbooks, not surprisingly, reflect official Turkish positions on topics such as the Armenian genocide. Clashing with historical scholarship and radically opposed to Armenian knowledge, they simplify to the extreme. Easily identifiable errors abound (Akçam 2014; Adak 2016; Wolfgram 2019:175–180).

Textbook narratives, like other contributors to cultural trauma, identify the nature of the pain, the nature of the victim, the relation of the trauma victim to the wider audience—and they attribute responsibility. Yet here the account is reversed, advancing cultural trauma about Turkish suffering and victimization. A middle school textbook, approved by the Ministry of National Education's Board of Instruction and Education on December 8, 2011, addresses the "The Armenian Events." It teaches students about Armenian rebellions, initiated by revolutionary organizations. In this narrative, rebels issued instructions to fellow ethnics according to which "if you want to survive you have to kill your neighbor first" (quoted in Akçam 2014).[4] Consequently, "Armenians murdered 'many people living in villages, even children, by attacking Turkish villages, which had become defenseless because all the Turkish men were fighting on the war fronts'. . . . They stabbed the Ottoman forces in the back. They created obstacles for the operation of the Ottoman units by cutting off supply routes and destroying bridges and roads. . . . They spied for Russia and by rebelling in the cities where they were located, they eased the way for the Russian invasion" (in Akçam 2014).

Another textbook, written for the tenth grade and approved on May 4, 2009, addresses the events of 1915 under the heading "The Armenian Problem during the World War I Years." It explains to students that "the entry of the Ottoman state into World War I was viewed as a great opportunity by Armenians. . . . [B]y invading Erzurum, Erzincan, Mus, and Bitlis in Eastern Anatolia, Russia further incited the Armenians in these regions" (in Akçam 2014). This account misses the fact that Russian military invaded the cities listed here only beginning in April 1916, after the deportation of the Armenian population.

Elsewhere, textbooks teach Turkish students that deportations actually sought to protect Armenians from radical-militant Armenian groups, that agricultural opportunities were prepared for resettled Armenians, and that police stations were set up at the places of destination to protect them from violence. The relative size of victimization, as well, deviates gravely from that identified by mainstream scholarship: "[B]ased on figures from unbiased researchers, 300,000 Armenians lost their lives due to war and sickness. . . . [Yet,] according to official Russian records . . . Armenians killed around 600,000 Turks in just Erzurum, Erzincan, Trabzon, Bitlis, and Van and forced 500,000 . . . to migrate" (textbook quoted in Akçam 2014).[5]

In short, Turkish textbooks describe much suffering, manifold deaths, and displacement of populations. Yet the victims are primarily Turks and those Armenians who did not heed the call of their radical brethren to kill Turks. Responsible for the violence are either Armenians generally, radical Armenian organizations, or foreign powers. At times, textbooks present Armenians as internal enemies who betrayed their own country (the Ottoman Empire) to foreign powers. The basic structure of Turkish textbook narratives is thus consistent with that identified for memoirs and media. As is common in textbooks, the narrative is simplified. The contours are yet more starkly recognizable than in the other types of documents. Turks as a carrier group, with the Turkish state as a powerful knowledge entrepreneur, thus recharge sedimented knowledge to transmit it to new generations.

COMPARATIVE PERSPECTIVES: ARMENIANS, TURKS, AND THE USHMM

Karl Mannheim, one of the founders of the sociology of knowledge, believed that the examination of knowledge carried by collectivities with different positions in social life, and thus with different viewpoints, could help scholars approximate that which constitutes truth. Contemporary scholarship no longer shares his hope. Today, the sociology of knowledge limits itself to analyzing and explaining varying and potentially clashing sets of knowledge, and possibly to examining their consequences. The truth about the Armenian genocide thus does not lie somewhere between Armenian and Turkish knowledge. Nor do we arrive at a more objective truth if we add yet other perspectives that are not carried by the adversarial groups.

Nevertheless, comparing Armenian and Turkish depictions of history, and juxtaposing them with knowledge generated by other actors and in the realm of scholarship, holds some analytic benefit. At the least, it alerts us to ways in which each—Armenian knowledge and Turkish knowledge—varies not just from the other, but also from outsider knowledge, generated under conditions that differ from those characteristic of the worlds of Armenians and Turks.

Armenians dominate among those who curate exhibits and establish memorials to the Armenian genocide. The Tsitsernakaberd Memorial Complex in Yerevan and the 2015 exhibit at the Shoah Memorial in Paris are but two examples (chapter 4). While the latter did not take place in an Armenian institution, the curators were prominent Armenian scholars. How does knowledge communicated at these two sites compare with that provided by institutions not associated with Armenians? I select a detailed entry from the website of the United States Holocaust Memorial Museum (USHMM) as a point of comparison.[6] I ask simultaneously how knowledge transmitted by this site compares to Turkish knowledge.

An extended quotation from the USHMM site's entry on the Armenian genocide indicates that the narrative bears close similarity to, but also noticeable distinctions from, the Armenian representations we encountered above, and that—by implication—it radically clashes with Turkish knowledge. The USHMM site states: "The Armenian genocide refers to the physical annihilation of ethnic Armenian Christian people living in the Ottoman Empire from spring 1915 through autumn 1916. There were approximately 1.5 million Armenians living in the Empire. At least 664,000 and possibly as many as 1.2 million died during the genocide. Armenians call these events *Medz Yeghern* (the great crime) or *Aghet* (catastrophe)." Following this quantification of victimhood and sections with historical background information, the narrative continues thus:

> Taking orders from the central government in Constantinople, regional officials implemented mass shootings and deportations, assisted by local civilians.[7] Ottoman military and security organs and their collaborators murdered the majority of Armenian men of fighting age, as well as thousands of women and children. During forced marches through the desert, convoys of surviving elderly men, women, and children were exposed to arbitrary attacks from local officials, nomadic bands, criminal gangs, and civilians. This violence included robbery (e.g., stripping victims naked to take their clothing and conducting body cavity searches for valuables), rape, abduction of young women and girls, extortion, torture, and murder. . . . Although the term *genocide* was not coined until 1944, most scholars agree that the mass murder of Armenians fits this definition.

TABLE 1 Comparison of Three Repertoires of Knowledge along Analytic Dimensions
(based on memoirs, media reports, exhibits, textbooks, speeches)

Dimension of Violence	Three Sets of Knowledge		
	Armenian	Turkish	USHMM
Suffering	perished; massacred; tragic and violent dispersion; first genocide of the 20th century; concentration camps; akin to Holocaust; Deir ez-Zor predecessor to Auschwitz	*Initial:* flood of disaster and death; theft and plunder; houses burned down; deported, drowned; illness and death during transportation *Soon:* millions killed	physical annihilation; genocide; murder; robbery; rape; extortion; torture; abduction of women and girls; forced marches; death from starvation, dehydration, exposure, disease; holding camps
Victims	1.5 million Armenians; Armenian populations; the Armenian people	*Early:* Armenians and Turks *Later:* Turks, 600,000 killed in five cities alone; 500,000 displaced	ethnic Armenians in Ottoman Empire, majority of Armenian men of fighting age; thousands of women and children; Armenian population in Anatolia; 664,000 to 1.2 million Armenians
Responsible actors	Turkish government; Turks, the Turks	*Early:* Armenian revolutionary Committee Dashnak *Later:* Armenians; radical-militant Armenian groups	CUP government, ruling circle, leadership (specific names); Ottoman military and security organs; Special Organization; regional and local officials; civilians; nomadic bands; criminal groups
Time frame	1915–1923	[not specified]	1915; spring 1915 to autumn 1916

Having thus identified responsible actors and types of victimization, including its identification as genocide, the page specifies the stages of death: "Hundreds of thousands of Armenians died before reaching the designated holding camps. Many were killed or abducted, others committed suicide, and vast numbers died of starvation, dehydration, exposure, or disease en route. While some civilians sought to assist the Armenian deportees, many more killed or tormented the people in the convoys."[8]

The narrative of the USHMM closely resembles that of the Tsitsernakaberd Memorial Complex and, yet more closely, the exhibit at the Shoah Memorial in Paris. Noticeable departures are reflected in the somewhat more cautious death estimate, in the limitation to the 1915–16 period, and in the use of the term *holding camps*—"concentration camps" in the other exhibits. Yet we find analogical bridging from the Holocaust to the Armenian genocide by the USHMM and a confirmation that the term *genocide* applies in the judgment of most scholars.

Table 1 juxtaposes the Armenian, Turkish, and USHMM perspectives along a set of analytic dimensions. These dimensions overlap with the categories Jeffrey Alexander (2004) spells out as preconditions of cultural trauma.

Under the label of "suffering," the USHMM describes all forms we typically read about in scholarly literature: physical annihilation, genocide, the Armenian words that mean "great crime" and "catastrophe," murder, robbery (including via strip searches), rape, abduction of young girls and women, forced marches, arbitrary attacks, killing, death by starvation, dehydration, exposure, and disease. This is in line with terms we find in Armenian exhibits.

Comparing both Armenian memorial depictions and the USHMM text to accounts of suffering in Turkish documents, memorials, media reports, and textbooks requires differentiation between early and later sources. The earliest Turkish sources use similar vocabulary to describe the suffering of Armenians: flood of disaster and death, theft and plunder, houses burnt down, people deported, drowned, illness and death during deportations. Yet, when later Turkish documents cite millions of innocents killed, six hundred thousand in just five cities, and five hundred thousand displaced, the victims are Turks. These sources reference "only" three hundred thousand Armenian deaths, which they attribute not to purposeful violence, but to war and sickness.

Armenian sources identify victims as Armenians, Armenian populations, or the Armenian people. The USHMM site writes similarly about the majority of Armenian men of fighting age as well as thousands of women and children murdered. Yet it also specifies ethnic Armenians in the Ottoman Empire and the Armenian population of Anatolia. It further estimates the death toll more cautiously: 664,000 to 1.2 million, contrasting with the 1.5 million estimated in some Armenian sources.

References to responsible actors also show a stark difference between the Armenian and USHMM sites on the one hand and Turkish depictions on the other. In Turkish sources, we find early references to Armenians and the revolutionary committee Dashnak, and later references to Armenians and to militant Armenian groups. This depiction is in line with the identification of Turks as the primary victims of violence. In line with the summary thus far, the Turkish representation of responsible actors differs sharply from those in Armenian and USHMM sources. Armenian representations typically refer to Turks, the Turks, or the Turkish government. Here, too, the USHMM is more specific. We read about the CUP government, CUP ruling circle, and CUP leadership, and we find references to four specific leaders of the Young Turk regime. Other references are to the central government in Constantinople, the Special Organization, Ottoman military and security organs and their collaborators, regional and local officials, nomadic bands, criminal groups, and civilians.

Finally, periodization varies across the different sets of knowledge. Many Armenian sources refer to the years 1915 to 1923 as the era of the genocide, thereby implicating the new Turkish republic, while most other sources refer to the events of 1915 or 1915 to 1916, or—in the more specific demarcation by the USHMM— spring 1915 to autumn 1916.

In short, the structure of Turkish knowledge regarding forms of suffering, types and numbers of victims, and responsible actors differs radically from those in Armenian sources or the USHMM website. We simultaneously find finer differences between Armenian sources and the USHMM representation. This should not be surprising, given that group identification and partisanship promote clear-cut depictions of social reality. In addition, even if historians played a central role in the construction of Armenian knowledge, Armenian knowledge additionally carries features of collective memory as a ritually reinforced and affectively loaded expression of knowledge about the past. Collective memory differs in this respect from historical knowledge. While not independent of the social location of historians, historical knowledge is shaped less by affective and ritual reaffirmation. It is thus not surprising that the USHMM depiction is closest to historical scholarly knowledge about the Armenian genocide. Historians, after all, agree on the core features of the genocide, even if different schools of historiography variably emphasize as conditions for genocide religion and continuity (Vahram Dadrian), nationalism (Richard G. Hovannisian), demographic engineering (Fuat Dündar, Uğur Ümit Üngör, Taner Akçam), cumulative policy radicalization (Donald Bloxham), or state imperialism and contingency (Ronald Grigor Suny) (for a comparative analysis of these positions, see Der Matossian 2015).

Chapter 4 identified conditions that contributed to the shaping of Armenian knowledge repertoires. In the Turkish case, the decisive mnemonic entrepreneur—the centralized and often authoritarian Turkish state—has been in the most powerful institutional position to spread a narrative of Turkish victimization. Importantly, the motivation of the Turkish state remained strong, as continuities from the Young Turk regime and the violence of the early Turkish republic put the glorious foundation myth of the new Turkey at risk. Finally, Turkish society constituted an ideal sounding board in that Turks too had experienced massive death, suffering, displacement, and humiliation during World War I and preceding wars. Sensitivities were heightened further by Turkey's outsider status in a predominantly Western alliance with Christian roots.

International comparison holds potential for further insights. Turkish denial resembles that of the United States, which also displays massive domestic resistance to facing the evil associated with its foundation (Savelsberg and King 2011, 2015). As in Turkey, where mass violence against ethnic minorities extended into the origins of the new republic, the foundation of the United States was associated with the near extinction of the Native American peoples, settler colonialism, and slavery. Mass violence associated with the creation of countries, however, does not sit well in national foundation myths in the modern era.

In contrast to Turkey and the United States, post–World War II (Federal Republic of) Germany cultivated the memory of evil, albeit with delay. Unlike Turkey, Germany was occupied entirely after the end of the war. The occupying powers held major criminal trials against leading perpetrators. Germany eventually gained its independence through economic development and integration into a community of nations, not through armed struggle and in relative isolation as did Turkey. Germany, finally, did not hold the same strong bargaining chip as Turkey, whose military cooperation was crucial to a Western alliance confronted with the instabilities of the Middle East. Western countries thus hesitated for many decades to challenge Turkey's insistence on innocence. A comparative analysis obviously suggests conditions for the motivation and ability of governments to advance revisionist knowledge repertoires about episodes of mass atrocities for which their countries bear prime responsibility.

CONCLUSIONS

Linking back to the conceptual and theoretical tools laid out in chapter 3, social knowledge about the Armenian genocide is a property of collectivities in which it is confirmed and reinforced—ethnic Armenians in one case, Turks in the other. Yet carriers of such knowledge are not a monolithic mass. Some dissent, while others act as entrepreneurs who spread and reinforce representations and narratives with particular efficacy. Under specific post–World War I conditions, even criminal trials against some of the perpetrators did not display the knowledge-generating power known from many other cases.

Organizational actors, especially states, are strong knowledge entrepreneurs. As their interests shift, they introduce new elements into repertoires of knowledge. Chapter 4 showed, for the Armenian case, how the transition from Soviet Armenia to the new independent Republic and the intensification of the Nagorno-Karabakh conflict resulted in mutations of knowledge. In the Turkish case, the state acted as a powerful knowledge entrepreneur, continuously interested in denial, but under shifting circumstances. Its integration into NATO, Armenian terrorism of the 1970s and 1980s, and Armenian independence in 1991 initiated some, albeit modest, modifications of knowledge. These observations provide cautious support for Maurice Halbwachs's argument about the presentism of collective memory.

Yet, just as some basic features of Armenian memory remain constant, firmly sedimented and reinforced in everyday interactions, the stability of Turkish knowledge is pronounced. It settled in soon after the immediate post–World War I years. The highly centralized, at times authoritarian, state with a strong ideological mission is the core source of denialism, and the history of Turkish suffering generated receptivity in the population. Cracks in the body of Turkish knowledge have appeared only in recent decades, especially among intellectuals. Scholarship cited prominently in this chapter illustrates them clearly, and authors such as Taner Akçam, Seyhan Bayraktar, and Fatma Müge Göçek are but examples, all of Turkish descent, albeit now living outside their country of origin.[9]

The stage is now set for part III of this book. Part I explored how knowledge repertoires evolve and how they are negotiated in everyday interactions. Part II showed how they solidify and become sedimented. We also saw how knowledge entrepreneurs intervened in these processes and how different collectivities develop distinct, at times contradictory, sets of ideas about the same event. What Armenians and Turks know about the mass violence carried out in the Ottoman Empire in 1915 and subsequent years presents an astounding example of such contradictions.

Contradictions are likely to erupt in conflict and struggle when collectivities face others with very different knowledge repertoires, especially if that knowledge is central to their identity. How do collectivities act in such situations? Again, sociological traditions provide us with helpful guidance. Some strands of scholarship point to strategies directed at the in-group that do not require conflictual engagement with the antagonist. The Durkheimian tradition alerts us to rituals that tie a community together and reaffirm shared values, norms, and ways of understanding the world. Other scholarly traditions highlight direct confrontation with the antagonist in conflictual processes. Examples, short of the threat of violence, are legislative efforts to acknowledge, and thereby privilege, one set of knowledge over others. Legislation may even aim at the regulation of speech by criminalizing articulations that others perceive as offensive. Law courts may (or may not) apply such laws. In doing so, they respond to concrete disputes between antagonists in struggles over appropriate knowledge or permitted speech.

Both rituals and conflictual engagement with the other are thus crucial in struggles over conflicting knowledge. While scholars typically associate rituals with culture and political conflict with power, cultural strategies and power strategies are certainly not mutually exclusive. Cultural practices, including rituals, involve actors with interests and power, while political and judicial struggles make use of cultural repertoires and mechanisms.

Part III therefore examines conflict and power struggles. We will see that it matters in which social field such struggles are being carried out. Each social field, such as politics or law, is governed by its own rules of the game. Actors in each field have acquired a specific habitus that corresponds with its rules. This habitus includes an immersion in the logic of the institutions that are prominent within each field. Yet there is also room for discretion and improvisation, for a flexible application of the rules of the game. Finally, institutions, nested within fields, take on different shapes across countries. The law works differently in the United States than elsewhere, and politics operate differently in France than in other countries. These particularities are likely to affect the shapes and outcomes of struggles, even in a globalized world.

First, however, I turn to rituals: Durkheimian moments that affirm identities and knowledge repertoires among both Armenians and Turks. Who initiates such rituals? What shape do they take, and what are their consequences?

PART III

Rituals, Epistemic Power, and Conflict over Genocide Knowledge

6

Affirming Genocide Knowledge
through Rituals

Parts I and II of this book examined the emergence of repertoires of knowledge regarding the Armenian genocide through social interaction, objectified thought processes, bearing witness, and the involvement of knowledge entrepreneurs. We saw how knowledge generated through these processes took radically different shapes as it became sedimented within each of two distinct carrier groups, Armenians and Turks. Oppositional worldviews and associated knowledge repertoires are not unique to this case, of course. We find them, for example, when those who recognize the role of human action in global warming encounter others who see a Chinese conspiracy at work, aimed at harming the U.S. economy. Or again, when those who know that liberal or social democracy will secure a prosperous and secure future disagree with followers of populist authoritarian leaders and parties. The question arises of how each collectivity deals with the challenges posed by the other side.

Now, in part III, we encounter two strategies commonly deployed in struggles over knowledge. While chapters 7 and 8 address conflictual engagement with the opposing side in the realms of politics and law, and chapter 9 explores counterproductive effects of denial in an age of human rights hegemony, the present chapter examines the use of elaborate public rituals toward the reaffirmation of genocide knowledge within each of the contending collectivities.

We owe early social-scientific insights into the role of rituals in social life to Émile Durkheim. In his book *The Elementary Forms of Religious Life*, Durkheim ([1912] 2001) tells us about the ability of rituals to sanctify objects and charge symbols that represent them with a special energy. Rituals also generate collective effervescence—a sense of shared excitement and, in consequence, of groupness and belonging among those who partake in them. Durkheim's student Maurice Halbwachs (1992), who coined the term *collective memory*, applied these ideas to strategies through which actors achieve knowledge about past events. Contemporary sociologists recognize that rituals take place in all spheres of life, while that which they sanctify varies. The latter may include otherworldly entities in the sphere of religion; claims of truth in scholarship; justice in law; health in medicine; or the nation and its protection in the military.

RITUALS AND THEIR CONSEQUENCES: A WEALTH OF RESEARCH AND CRITIQUES

Some current scholarship provides clear, almost operational, conceptions of rituals and their consequences. Randall Collins (2005:48), for example, spells out these ingredients: "1. Two or more people are physically assembled in the same place, so that they affect each other by their bodily presence, whether it is in the foreground of their conscious attention or not. 2. There are boundaries to outsiders so that participants have a sense of who is taking part and who is excluded. 3. People focus their attention upon a common object or activity, and by communicating this focus to each other become mutually aware of each other's focus of attention. 4. They share a common mood or emotional experience." The copresence of these elements generates the collective effervescence and its consequences about which Durkheim wrote. We know manifold examples of such rituals from our own experience. Consider, in the secular realm, a graduation ceremony or Fourth of July celebration; or, in religious life, an Easter mass, a Friday prayer during Ramadan, or a Yom Kippur service.

Today, in our mass-mediated societies, physical copresence is still highly effective, but it may no longer be a necessary precondition for the mobilization of emotional energy. In fact, concrete embodied rituals themselves may become enduring symbols that carry the ritual charge through time. Filmed depictions of events are one mechanism (Dayan and Katz 1992), and the analysis below will reference both embodied rituals and their depictions in film.

Rituals work especially well when the symbols they sanctify align with some preexisting belief system. Alexander Riley (2008) provides a powerful illustration when he examines symbols used in the memorialization of victims of United Airlines flight 93. That flight—hijacked by a group of terrorists intending to destroy the U.S. Capitol Building or the White House—crashed in a field in rural Pennsylvania on September 11, 2001. Those who designed the memorial sought to celebrate the passengers as heroes, a first line of defense in the nation's new fight against international terrorism. They stacked the memorial with symbols that speak to larger themes in the nation's history and (closely allied) in Christianity. An initial, improvised memorial featured a forty-foot steel fence, one foot for each passenger killed; a cross, marking the area as sacred ground; and "angels of freedom," one for each passenger, who were thereby depicted as saintly figures. A "thunder flag" displayed four stars, each representing one site of destruction, and three bars: one blue, symbolizing the heavens; one white, representing the purity of the heroes; and one red for the earth of America. Constructed later as a place of commemoration, a "Thunder on the Mountain Chapel" featured an altar resembling the Capitol Building in Washington, D.C., and thus representing the nation, and an eagle as a symbol of deliverance, pointing upward.

A wealth of scholarship has built on Durkheimian thought about rituals and their effects on knowledge. Mary Douglas (1966) explored how rituals separate humans and their dignity from polluting matters—degrading substances, utterances, or actions. Edward Shils (1981) observed how civic rituals celebrate the sacred even in secular life; with Michael Young, he depicted the coronation of Queen Elizabeth II as a ritual that generated national communion within the United Kingdom, thereby supporting shared moral values (Shils and Young 1953). Robert Bellah (1970) relatedly wrote about civil religion—practices that connect the American nation with God and that sanctify persons, places, and events such as George Washington, Abraham Lincoln, John F. Kennedy, or Gettysburg. Through that sanctification, American civil religion provides the American people with a sense of meaning and direction.

Rituals are especially powerful in times of crisis, as Kai Erikson ([1966] 2004) showed in his famous study on punishment in the Massachusetts Bay Colony. Describing three "crime waves," Erikson demonstrates how during these periods, not actually marked by increased criminal behavior, people experienced a perceived threat to the unity of the colony. Perceptions of threat resulted from the arrival of new, less religiously dogmatic immigrants, a loss of political autonomy, and internal discord. They advanced three waves of ritual punishment, of which the Salem witch hunt is best known. Erikson interprets the outcome of these penal campaigns as the redrawing of boundaries around the community and the strengthening of its inner coherence and normative commitment. This benefit came at a price, however, that had to be paid dearly by those defined as responsible for social crises and insecurity.

Rituals and Conflict

Powerful as this body of Durkheimian scholarship is, it nevertheless faces criticism (Smith and Riley 2009). Many studies on rituals assume that consensus and social integration are the only outcome. That assumption, however, may not always hold true, and even when rituals achieve such outcomes, the mechanisms remain obscure. Critics further charge that work in the Durkheimian tradition is idealistic, that it fails to recognize agency, intent, conflict, force, and power (e.g., Goody 1977; Lukes 1975; Turner 1969).

Scholars have argued, and the following will prove them right, that we can take these criticisms seriously and still hold on to the insights a theory of ritual has to offer us. In fact, the explanatory power of Durkheimian theories increases if we incorporate the possibility of discord and the role of power and authority. Yes, rituals may indeed produce consensus, but they may also generate conflict. At times, conflict intensifies exactly as a result of the integrative force of rituals, which is easy to see where intergroup conflict is concerned. By strengthening a sense of belonging and shared ideas within one group, say Turks or Armenians, rituals draw the boundaries to the outside group ever more starkly (see also Simmel [1955] 1964; Coser 1956). Consequently, intergroup conflict is likely to intensify.

Rituals may even generate conflict within a collectivity. Consider a group of Turkish intellectuals gathering for a set of lectures and symposia that seek to challenge the dominant Turkish discourse on the violence of 1915. Exactly this happened in the early 2000s, when a network of journalists and scholars, including many Turks, created a "Workshop for Armenian Turkish Scholarship." A March 2000 conference at the University of Chicago was followed by others in Michigan (2002), Minnesota (2003), Salzburg (2005), New York (2006), and Geneva (2008) (Bayraktar 2010:185–186). These gatherings, conceived of as scholarly rituals, helped sanctify a truth claim about the Armenian genocide that generated conflict within the Turkish context while generating collective effervescence and intensified relationships among participating scholars. Through the latter, it laid the foundation for future scholarship in opposition to dominant Turkish repertoires of knowledge.

We gain further explanatory power, linking back to Randall Collins's ingredients of rituals, when we ask who has the resources, power, and influence to bring together many human beings in one place. Who draws boundaries to the outside world, deciding who partakes in the ritual and its products and who is excluded? Or: Who is capable of transmitting rituals to a broader public via modern media of communication? Further, given the variable content of rituals, who determines which actors say and do what during the ritual, and what objects are offered for sanctification? Finally, what motivates those organizers of rituals, and what power potential or other tools help them achieve their goals?

Rituals, Interests, and Power

Actors, their motivations, and the tools they use to initiate and structure rituals are crucial for their courses and consequences. Consider struggles over the initiation and content of rituals that explicitly aim at the construction and preservation of specific collective memories. Alejandro Baer (2011) describes how Spain, during the Franco regime, repressed engagement with Holocaust history, not surprising in light of the Hitler-Franco alliance dating back to the Spanish Civil War. Spain began to engage with these dark chapters of history only after the transition to democracy of the 1970s. This engagement eventually culminated in the country joining the Stockholm International Forum on the Holocaust (2000), initiated by the Swedish government and seeking to secure the memory of genocides.

In Spain, democratization thus provided Jewish organizations with new opportunities. They successfully suggested an official commemoration, and an initial commemorative ceremony took place on May 3, 2000, in the Madrid Assembly, the seat of the regional government. The ceremony culminated in the lighting of six candles, echoing a practice from Yad Vashem, Israel's official Holocaust memorial center, each candle representing one million of the six million Jewish victims of the Shoah. The election of a socialist government in 2004 opened further opportunities, resulting in the first ceremony officially sponsored by the national government in Madrid. Yet the proposed structure of the ritual provoked conflict. The organizers invited representatives of other victim groups to participate, but only in the candle lighting ceremony; they were not invited to deliver speeches. Republican associations, representing those who had fought the Franco regime in the Spanish Civil War, protested. When the organizers eventually included one of their representatives, Enric Marco, presumably a former inmate of the Mauthausen concentration camp, in the list of speakers, new conflict erupted. Marco referenced Guantanamo Bay and "camps in Palestine," generating intense resentment among Jewish attendees. In response, later ceremonies went through a series of modifications, each of which resulted in new struggles (Baer 2011).

The example of Holocaust commemorations in Spain illustrates how conflict, interest, and power accompany the introduction and structuration of commemorative rituals. Each year's event reflects a new political situation resulting in the incorporation of new memories, in line with Halbwachs's (1992) argument about presentism of memory. Yet we cannot understand these commemorations without considering the previous years' events and the sensitivities they evoked. Memory is thus also path dependent, in line with arguments Jeffrey Olick developed when analyzing series of contested German May 8 commemorations of capitulation at the end of World War II (Olick 1999, 2016). Each of these commemorations gravitated between the notions of Germany's liberation versus its defeat, with their respective sensitivities. The story of Holocaust commemorations in Spain also confirms insights by Francesca Polletta (1998), who examined how interactions between power holders and challengers result in shifting modes of public commemoration and protest repertoires, including the creation of new holidays.[1]

In short, rituals play an important role in social life. They are suited to sanctifying moral standards and sets of knowledge, including memories of difficult pasts. They are typically initiated and structured by powerful and motivated actors, representatives of collectivities, with the intent to generate solidarity and a shared perception of reality. What role, then, do rituals play in solidifying knowledge about the mass violence of 1915 and subsequent years in Armenian life, and in Turkish life, when each group faces challenges from the other side?

ARMENIAN RITUALS AND THE SOLIDIFICATION OF ARMENIAN KNOWLEDGE REPERTOIRES

The Tsitsernakaberd Memorial Complex, high on a hill overlooking Armenia's capital city of Yerevan, consists of three main buildings: the Memorial Wall, the Sanctuary of Eternity (Memorial Hall and Eternal Flame), and the Memorial

Column, entitled "The Reborn Armenia" (see chapter 4). As a memorial made of stone, it represents collective memory. The description on the memorial's website testifies to the meaning inscribed in the hard stone with its seemingly eternal message. Yet that text itself was written in a particular historical situation, and current uses of the memorial continue to express the meaning Armenians bestow on it, especially on special ritual occasions such as the April 24 Armenian Genocide Commemoration Days. The following sections examine three events that took place in Yerevan on April 23 and 24, 2016, one of them at the memorial itself. Based on documents and participant observation, I interpret these events as rituals, and I consider their consequences for the reaffirmation and shape of repertoires of genocide knowledge.

The Commemorative Ritual at Tsitsernakaberd

On April 24, 2016, an early-morning bus took a group of international visitors, including this author, to the memorial. Along the way, the bus passed a steady procession of people who walked up the hill to lay down carnations in a circle around the eternal flame that burns at the center of the "Sanctuary of Eternity."[2] Up on the hill, these visitors joined a crowd of foreign dignitaries, ambassadors, foreign ministers and representatives of various legislatures from around the world, who were gathering at the end of the Memorial Wall. It was a beautiful spring day. The sun was intense. Looking south, our eyes met snow-capped Mount Ararat and its smaller twin peak, sacred to the Armenians but just across the border in neighboring Turkey. Mount Aragats towered in the north. When Armenia's president, Serzh Sargsyan, arrived, he was accompanied by his cabinet, the Catholicos of the Armenian Church, and several guests of honor, including prominent members of the Armenian expatriate community, survivors of the genocides in Cambodia and Rwanda, and celebrities such as actor and activist George Clooney. Slowly the crowd moved along the Memorial Wall, toward the Memorial Hall with the Eternal Flame. The procession came to a halt when the dignitaries had reached the end of the wall closest to the hall. Prayers were said, a choir sang religious and patriotic songs, and military honors were performed. President Sargsyan laid down a wreath, and then, followed by the crowd, slowly descended the steps into the memorial. The carnations that the president, the guests of honor, and members of international delegations laid down in a circle around the flame added to an already meter-high wall of flowers deposited by those who had moved in procession up the hill earlier in the day (see figure 5). When returning to the hill in the late afternoon, a similarly dense procession of Armenians still made its way up the hill, commemorating the genocide and paying respect to those whose lives had been destroyed.

The April 24 event at the Tsitsernakaberd Memorial Complex certainly fulfills the criteria of a ritual. Many people were physically assembled; the Memorial Wall and other architectural elements constituted boundaries to outsiders;

FIGURE 5. A procession bearing flowers descends into the Memorial Hall, where the Eternal Flame is located, at Tsitsernakaberd Memorial Complex, Yerevan. Photo by Andreas Rentz/Getty Images for 100 Lives.

people directed their attention to a common object or activity, and became mutually aware of each other's focus of attention; they finally shared a common somber mood. Those in attendance were reminded of the history of the genocide and its centrality to the identity of the Armenian people. They experienced a sense of collective effervescence, a sentiment of solidarity, of the sacredness of the place and the occasion.

The structure of the event and the identity of those who participated carefully displayed several messages. The presence of the country's president and the Catholicos; their words, prayers, and rites; and the combination of religious and patriotic songs demonstrated the intimate relationship between the state and the Armenian Church. Participation by ambassadors and other representatives of many governments around the globe reflected the growing international recognition of the genocide and solidarity with the Armenian people. Finally, the presence of survivors of other, more recent genocides, globally defined as such, supported the labeling of the violence of 1915 as a genocide, while simultaneously expressing Armenian solidarity with other victimized peoples.

Central organs of the Armenian state and church organized the event, determining the initiation and structuration of this ritual. The power and authority of these entrepreneurs of knowledge and memory were crucial. Simultaneously, however, the mass procession up the hill by tens of thousands of ordinary

Armenians attested to the shared memory, the result of manifold day-to-day inter-actions, of the telling of stories across generations. Documents indicate that the commemorative event of 2015, on the one hundredth anniversary of the genocide, was organized similarly, even if the presence of several heads of state, including the presidents of Russia and France, underlined the special significance of the centennial (Mkrtchyan 2015).

As powerful as the ritual at Tsitsernakaberd was in its own right, we will understand its meaning better if we consider it in context. Sociologist Theodore Caplow (2004) used the term *festival cycle*, exploring how the meaning of a holiday reveals itself most powerfully when we see it in the context of other holidays. In this spirit, I examine two other events that surrounded the commemorative ritual at Tsitsernakaberd. The first, a Global Forum Against the Crime of Genocide, was held on the day preceding the memorial ceremony. The final event, concluding the cycle, was an award ceremony on the evening of the day of commemoration, several hours after the ritual at the memorial. It celebrated the newly created Aurora Prize for Awakening Humanity. Both events took place in Yerevan's massive sports and convention center, sited on the same hill as the genocide memorial.

Global Forum Against the Crime of Genocide

On Saturday, April 23, 2016, a Global Forum Against the Crime of Genocide was held, organized by the Ministry of Foreign Affairs and the National Assembly of the Republic of Armenia. Also involved was a "State Committee for Coordination of the Events Dedicated to the Centennial of the Armenian Genocide." The organizers titled the forum "Living Witnesses of Genocide." The event took place in a large hall in front of an audience of some eight hundred participants, including diplomats and other representatives of foreign governments, members of the Armenian legislature, a small group of survivors of genocides, and scholars. An image of Mount Ararat provided the backdrop behind the speakers (see figure 6).

The Foreign Ministry's concept note describes the meaning of the event:

> During the Global Forum 2016, entitled "Living Witnesses of Genocide", leading politicians, parliamentarians, scholars, media, civil society representatives, and other stakeholders from around the world will address genocide-caused refugee crises, ramifications of protection mechanisms, and, in general, genocide consequences.
>
> The Forum will focus on the protection of people who became refugees because of genocide or its threat. The purpose of genocide perpetrators is to annihilate the representatives and culture of the targeted ethnic group, and as long as they succeed, it is impossible to break the vicious circle of genocidal acts.
>
> For that very reason, the international community should be able to save lives of people subjected to genocide, their property, cultural and public institutions, create favorable conditions for their return, and provide rapid compensation for the destruction through international mechanisms of accountability.

FIGURE 6. Discussion after a panel at the Global Forum Against the Crime of Genocide, Yerevan, 2016, with an image of Mount Ararat as backdrop. Photo courtesy of Ministry of Foreign Affairs, Republic of Armenia.

By organizing the forum in this universalistic spirit, the government of Armenia not only expresses solidarity with other victims of genocide. In addition—and in combination with the commemorative event of the following day ("festival cycle," à la Caplow)—it also pleads for the saving of lives "of people subjected to genocide, their property, cultural and public institutions." It demands that the international community create "favorable conditions for their return, and provide rapid compensation for the destruction through international mechanisms of accountability." The last set of demands is still applicable, in principle, to the violence experienced by the Armenian people, even if the text does not make that explicit.

We gain more insights by examining specifics of the unfolding forum. The event was opened at 10 a.m. with a speech by President Sargsyan, followed by a "High-level Dialogue" moderated by David Ignatius, a self-identified Armenian American and a columnist and associate editor for the *Washington Post*. This dialogue included statements by President Sargsyan; Andrew Woolford, president of the International Association of Genocide Scholars; George Clooney, UN peace envoy and cofounder of Not On Our Watch, a nonprofit organization;[3] Joe Verhoeven, judge ad hoc of the International Court of Justice; and Vartan Gregorian, president of the Carnegie Corporation of New York. Clearly, such a panel demonstrates the country's ability to align behind its agenda diverse sectors of international law, scholarship, and civil society.

The Ministry of Foreign Affairs' concept paper entitles the subsequent Panel Number 1 "Genocide and Displacement: Identifying Genocide from the Perspective of Forced Displacements and Relocation." It describes the panel's charge: "Genocide is an extreme form of identity-based violence. . . . This Panel will concentrate on different stages of genocide in the context of displacement by trying to address the following issues: The common patterns of displacement and relocation in the planning and perpetrating [of] genocide. Displacement as an indicator of the intent to destroy particular groups in part or in its [sic] entirety."

Presenters included professors of international law, philosophy, history, and Jewish studies; a scholar in Russian and Eurasian studies; and human rights activists from a variety of countries, including Germany, the United Kingdom, the United States, Switzerland, and Turkey. Support for the notion of justice against perpetrators of mass atrocities was a common denominator of the presentations. Panel 2, entitled "Preventing Genocide and Protecting Refugees: Contemporary Challenges," featured a sociologist, an anthropologist, a historian, and international lawyers from Italy, the United States, and Sweden. It concluded with a speech by Hayk Demoyan, director of the Armenian Genocide Museum-Institute.

Bringing together an international and interdisciplinary group of scholars in Yerevan to elaborate on issues of genocide on the day before the official Armenian genocide commemoration, the global forum added legitimacy to the identification as genocide of the mass violence against Armenians during World War I. Indirectly, it validated moral and legal claims that today are associated with the notion of genocide.

Artak Zakaryan, chairman of the Standing Committee on Foreign Relations of the National Assembly of the Republic of Armenia, and Garen Nazarian, deputy minister of foreign affairs of the Republic of Armenia, cochaired the closing session. It included presentations by the Speaker of the National Assembly of the Republic of Armenia, and testimonies of genocide survivors. Addresses by guests and delegates followed, mostly ambassadors and representatives of legislatures or administrations of numerous countries. The final speaker was Edward Nalbandian, minister of foreign affairs of the Republic of Armenia, who bridged events and speeches of the day to Armenian claims in the conflict with Azerbaijan over the Nagorno-Karabakh region. In this most political of all the panels, the foreign minister significantly attached contemporary foreign policy claims to an event that had addressed consequences of genocide, on the night preceding the Armenian genocide commemoration. Unsurprisingly, a commemoration organized by a foreign ministry does not unfold in neutral political space. Memory and politics in such settings are intertwined.

In short, we can conceive of the Global Forum Against the Crime of Genocide as a ritual, marked by physical copresence, boundaries to the outside, a shared focus of attention, mutual awareness, and a common mood. It generated an understanding of genocide and its horrors, agreement on the inappropriateness of impunity

FIGURE 7. Aurora Prize Ceremony, Yerevan, 2016. Photo courtesy of Ministry of Foreign Affairs, Republic of Armenia.

for those who initiate, execute, or sanction genocide, and an identification with knowledge, ideas, and symbols that the proceedings had sanctified. The inclusion of genocide scholars from various disciplines and countries added legitimacy for the use of the genocide label and associated claims. Finally, the inclusion of survivors of recognized genocides reaffirmed the validity of the categorization of the mass violence against the Armenians during World War I as genocide.

The event allowed for an expression of solidarity and explicit acknowledgment, for which the ritual at the memorial at Tsitsernakaberd could not provide space. In preceding the commemorative rite, the forum's statements carried over into the gathering at the memorial on the following morning. Adding cognitive content to the affectively charged ritual at the memorial, it reaffirmed basic elements of repertoires of knowledge about the Armenian genocide.

Aurora Prize Ceremony: Dance, Stories, and the Power of Oneness in Ritual Performance

A third event completed the cycle of rituals held in Yerevan in 2016. On the evening of Sunday, April 24, following the morning's wreath laying ceremony at the Armenian Genocide Memorial, a profoundly moving event took place in a large theater that is part of the sports and convention complex on the hill overlooking Yerevan. The occasion was the first Aurora Prize Ceremony (figure 7). An estimated two thousand people attended. The organizers' concept note describes the prize and the event:

The Aurora Prize for Awakening Humanity is a new global award that will be given annually to people who put themselves at risk to enable others to survive. Recipients will be recognized for the exceptional impact their actions have made on preserving human life and advancing humanitarian causes, having overcome significant challenges along the way. Every year the winners will be honored with a $100,000 award as well as the unique ability to continue the cycle of giving by nominating an organization, which inspired their work and is consistent with the spirit of the Prize, for a $1,000,000 grant. The Aurora Prize is designed to further the causes that motivate people to risk their health, freedom, reputation or livelihood by voluntarily carrying out acts that enable others to survive and thrive.

The program note then lists the members of the Aurora Prize Selection Committee as follows:

- George Clooney, Co-founder, Not On Our Watch, humanitarian, performer and filmmaker;
- Elie Wiesel, President of the Elie Wiesel Foundation for Humanity, Nobel Laureate;
- Hina Jilani, Former UN Special Representative of the Secretary-General on Human Rights Defenders;
- Vartan Gregorian, Co-Founder, 100 LIVES, President of the Carnegie Corporation of New York;
- Gareth Evans, Former President Emeritus of the International Crisis Group, Former Australian Foreign Minister;
- Mary Robinson, Former UN High Commissioner for Human Rights; Former President of Ireland;
- Óscar Arias, Two-time President of Costa Rica, Nobel Laureate;
- Shirin Ebadi, Human Rights Lawyer and Iran's first female judge, Nobel Laureate;
- Leymah Gbowee, Executive Director of the Women, Peace and Security Network (WIPSEN-Africa), Nobel Laureate.

The committee thus included four Nobel laureates and others in high positions in international non-governmental organizations and other international organizations. Participation by these persons displays solidarity with the Armenian people and its history of suffering, indirectly and directly confirming knowledge claims regarding the Armenian genocide.

As the event unfolded, capping the cycle of April 2016 commemorations, it displayed all the features of a ritual and conveyed a clear message about the Armenian genocide. I rely on a video recording[4] and on my own observations and detailed note taking at and around the event in the Yerevan convention center.

The award ceremony opened with a five-minute animated film by Armenian filmmaker Eric Nazarian, a true masterpiece in condensation of national memory. The film shows a crane, flying over vast areas of land, imposing mountains, rolling green hills, towns, and churches. The narrator tells about an "ancient civilization" underneath the bird's wing, the "Land of Noah," about its millennia of building and survival, and its inhabitants' contribution to humankind. He tells of the "1.5 million who perished in 1915 together with their culture" and reaffirms Armenian genocide knowledge: "This was a genocide, perpetrated by the Ottoman Empire against its own citizens."

The voice further tells about the many refugees, including seventeen-year-old Aurora Mardiganian, the star of *Ravaged Armenia*, the first Hollywood film about the genocide. This silent movie was made in 1919, based on Aurora's 1918 autobiography. We learn that the film was, at the time, premiered and viewed by large audiences all over the United States, the United Kingdom, France, and Australia, and that the book sold one hundred thousand copies. Interspersed throughout the animated film is footage from *Ravaged Armenia*, including gruesome but fictional images of crucified young women. Historical photographs show death marches and survivors of the mass killings. The voice continues: "To this day, Aurora remains a testament to the living memory of the genocide and the gratitude of the Armenian people to their saviors. Aurora became a symbol of light and hope to an entire generation."

Approaching the conclusion of the film, the message shifts from despair to hope. The voice tells us about survivors in countries around the world. Images show the Statue of Liberty in New York and the Eiffel Tower in Paris, symbols of the two countries in which most Armenian refugees found a new home. The narrator speaks about refugees rebuilding their lives, with dignity, "ever grateful to those who rescued their families," who "put their own lives at risk to save survivors." Concluding images shift to present-day refugees, linking the film with the central theme of the 2016 global forum. The voice speaks about victims of today's man-made disasters. A globe appears on the screen, and the narrator summarizes the central message: "On behalf of the survivors of the Armenian genocide and in gratitude to their saviors, the Aurora Prize for Awakening Humanity honors the power of the human spirit that compels action in the face of adversity." The screen shows faces from around the world, and, finally, again, that of Aurora Mardiganian.

The film clearly connects the Aurora Prize Ceremony to the preceding two events, completing the cycle of commemoration. It reinforces the labeling of the mass violence against Armenians as a genocide and the count of those killed as 1.5 million. The film further pleads for solidarity with other peoples who suffered from mass violence and expresses gratitude and appreciation of those who aided survivors. Mindful of the *power of oneness* (Schwartz 2009), and in line with the title the founders had selected for the prize, the filmmaker introduces Aurora as a representative of the survivors of the Armenian genocide and of the survivors of mass atrocities generally.

A ballet, danced to music performed by the State Youth Orchestra of Armenia, is the second item on the evening program. Ten dancers of Foundation Ballet 2021 appear on the mist-covered stage, in front of four saintly figures woven into a large curtain behind the stage. The dancers' movements are abrupt, signifying struggle, but the scene changes when the mist disappears and a single dancer enters the stage from the left, holding high a bronze sculpture, made up of three branches growing out of a common root. Each branch shows varying numbers of human figures, vertically on top of each other, rising upward, as though they are moving out of ashes into a new life. The sculpture, entitled *To the Eternity*, is a creation of the Armenian artist Manvel Matevosyan and was a prizewinner of a 2015 anniversary contest, "A Message 100 Years Later." A postcard with its image describes it as "12 figures symbolizing Western Armenia going up, to the eternity and the idea of canonization of the Great Genocide victims." The dancer carries the statue to the center of the stage and the curtain in the back of the stage rises, opening the view to a pedestal. The dancer places the statue on top of the pedestal and then raises his arms, like a priest sanctifying a sacred object. The other dancers, no longer in wild motion, stand still symmetrically to both sides of the sanctified sculpture. Exiting from the stage, they leave behind the emblem that from here on represents the Aurora Prize for the Awakening of Humanity. In future years, copies of the statue will be handed to the finalists and recipient of the Aurora Prize.

Following this ritual sanctification of the new emblem, introductory comments by two masters of ceremonies (MCs)[5] reinforce the messages of the film and of the dance performance. They highlight that the inauguration ceremony takes place on Armenian soil on the anniversary of the "genocide" that took the lives of "1.5 million people." They introduce separate awards[6] preceding the core of the event. Eventually, the awarding of the Aurora Prize unfolds in four types of delicately interwoven segments: musical performances, parables told by the MCs, video messages from absent members of the award committee, and the introduction of the Aurora Prize finalists by members of the committee. It culminates in the announcement of the recipient. A few words on each element shed further light on the emotions evoked and the knowledge confirmed through the ritual of the award ceremony.

Auschwitz survivor and Nobel laureate Elie Wiesel speaks—via video, accompanied by pictures of 1915—to the importance of solidarity in the face of atrocity. His appearance establishes a link between the Holocaust and the Armenian genocide, a particular form of analogical bridging. Other video messages come from Mary Robinson, former Irish prime minister and UN high commissioner for human rights, and from Óscar Arias, former president of Costa Rica, who received the Nobel Peace Prize in 1987 for his efforts to end the bloody civil wars of Central America. Again, the structure of the ceremony embeds the history of the Armenian genocide within the worldwide struggle for human rights, and links it to other episodes of mass violence.

Three parables told by the MCs all entail the same message: that giving and supporting those in need is the greatest gain humans can attain, possibly a condition for their own survival. One example must suffice, told by David Ignatius: God shows the questioner two images of people sitting in front of delicious food, holding spoons attached to long handles. Those in one picture, depicting Hell, look emaciated, desperate; those in the other, showing Heaven, appear content, in fact happy. The questioner initially does not understand until he sees that those in Heaven use their spoons successfully by feeding each other. Those in Hell attempt to feed only themselves, but the long handle does not allow them to reach their mouths. The moral is in line with the spirit of the Aurora Prize, given to those who do extraordinary things to save others. In a Durkheimian move, the MCs juxtapose universal solidarity (the sacred) with individual-orientation and selfishness (the profane), confirming the epistemic power of narrative facility (Rydgren 2007).

The stage is thus set for the climax of the ceremony. Award cofounder Vartan Gregorian of the Carnegie Foundation and Liberian peace activist and Nobel laureate Leymah Gbowee tell the audience about the 186 nominees from twenty-seven countries, the selection committee, and its procedures. They and other committee members introduce the finalists, each introduction accompanied by an emotional video depicting their projects.[7] Eventually, Marguerite Barankitse, founder of the Maison Shalom in Burundi, is announced as the award recipient; her actions "saved the lives of 30,000 Rwandan children" who had lost their parents during the genocide in neighboring Rwanda.

Orchestral music intensifies the emotionality of the event. Pieces include the finale of (Soviet-) Armenian composer Aram Khachaturian's Symphony of Bells; a famous Armenian lullaby, sung by Hasmik Papian, the co-MC; and a hymn to Armenia for orchestra and choir, performed in the presence of its composer, the French-Armenian chansonnier Charles Aznavour (born Shahnour Vaghinag Aznavourian). At the end of the ceremony, which has lasted for two hours and twenty minutes, the audience is released with images of Armenia and the appeal to shake off victimization and embrace a shared humanity.

Multiple conversations in the lobby immediately following the award ceremony confirmed its emotional impact. Collective effervescence was the outcome of a ritual that had brought many people together, attentive to the same unfolding events on the stage of the hall, aware of each other's focus of attention, and sharing a common mood. Intense emotions supported the cognitive message.

What Theodore Caplow called the festival cycle had thus concluded. A conference, a ceremony at the genocide memorial, and an award ceremony mutually reinforced and supplemented each other's messages. They instilled and reinforced knowledge the event had repeatedly communicated to the audiences: that the 1915 violence against the Armenians, committed by the Ottoman Empire, indeed constitutes a genocide; that 1.5 million Armenians lost their lives; that the suffering of Armenians links them to victims of other genocides; that all of these groups share a sense of solidarity; that liberators from suffering are to be celebrated as heroes; and that victimized peoples must overcome their victim identity, as helpers and practitioners of solidarity with others who suffer today. Durkheimian ideas about the emotional and cognitive power of rituals find support. Viewers of the video-recorded award ceremony will share some of the experience that moved those who were physically present.

Local rituals supplement grand national events. In Yerevan, they include a reading of "unanswered letters" from the time of the genocide in the Armenian Museum of Arts and Literature[8] and a celebration of commemorative art.[9] In the diaspora, communities around the globe organize commemorations. In 2015, for example, on the centennial of the genocide, Minnesotans held a memorial service in the Armenian Saint Sahag Church, welcoming, under the guidance of its pastor Tadeos Barseghyan, speakers such as U.S. Senator Amy Klobuchar, members of the U.S. House of Representatives, and members of the state legislature. Academic events at the University of Minnesota supplemented commemorations.[10]

In short, in Armenia's capital city of Yerevan and in the diaspora, April 24, the day of commemoration of the Armenian genocide, provides an opportunity for powerful rituals. These rituals evoke emotions and simultaneously acknowledge and reinforce Armenian knowledge repertoires. They strengthen Armenian communities and identity, and they spread the message to broader audiences around the globe.

TURKISH RITUALS AND THE SOLIDIFICATION OF TURKISH KNOWLEDGE REPERTOIRES

Rituals can acknowledge evil and suffering, but by selectively highlighting the glorious history of a collectivity, they can also contribute to denial of evil, to the drowning out of utterances that risk polluting both the sanctified past and a current-day identity built on that past (Vinitzky-Seroussi and Teeger 2010). This indeed is the situation of Turkey.

Celebratory and Purifying Rituals: Reaffirming the Ottoman Past

It is again a young Turkish scholar, sociologist Yağmur Karakaya, who—joining the likes of Taner Akçam, Seyhan Bayraktar, and Fatma Müge Göçek—reflects critically on Turkish practices. In recent work, Karakaya (2018) analyzed a ritual in Istanbul that commemorates the conquest of Constantinople on May 29, 1453, under the command of Ottoman Sultan Mehmed II (also known as Fatih), and with it the final defeat of the Eastern Roman Empire.

Organized by the AKP, the Justice and Development Party headed by President Recep Tayyip Erdoğan, the event cultivates nostalgia for Ottoman Islamic civilization as a source of Turkish heritage. Note that this same civilization also brought the near destruction of the Armenian people and great suffering to Ottoman Greeks, Assyrians, and other minorities. Not accidentally, such nostalgia—connecting a people with an imagined past, creating a sense of collective identity and a wholesome future—coincides with a period of authoritarian populist politics.

In 2016, the same year in which the Armenian events in Yerevan described above took place, one to two millions Turks gathered in Istanbul, and tens of millions across the country joined the nationally televised ritual in front of TV screens. Karakaya describes the event as a "massive rally—one of many throughout the year—[which] combined the latest technology, such as laser light shows and high volume bombastic music through loudspeakers, with Ottoman elements, such as the military marching band [563 strong, equaling the number of years since the conquest], marching to beats that had long ago inspired the Ottoman troops, and virtual neighing and galloping horses, to create a carnivalesque political scene" (Karakaya 2018:126).

Karakaya observes how, in line with the myth of Fatih entering into Istanbul riding a white horse, Erdoğan arrived on the rally ground in a white helicopter. The "announcer declared his arrival like a town crier . . . Istanbul! Here comes the protector of the oppressed, hope of the poor, the strong voice of the underdogs, child of the nation, here comes the fearless advocate of the just cause, grandson of Fatih, apple of the ummah's eye, architect of new Turkey, servant of the nation, president of the republic!" (Karakaya 2018:135). In his speech, Erdoğan referred to the crowd as "the grandchildren of Mehmed the Conqueror" (Karakaya 2018:135). He posed a series of rhetorical questions, each asking for a milestone of economic or development success, and the crowd, in unison, answered "Yes!" Erdoğan appealed to the *ummah*, solidarity with—and Turkish leadership of—the Muslim world. Appearing as a messianic figure, Erdoğan in fact mobilized religious sentiments.

Binaries abounded. The world is one of "winners and losers, oppressors and the oppressed, West vs. East, friends vs. enemies, us vs. them, strong vs. weak, and the dog-whistle Islam vs. Christianity" (Karakaya 2018:137), and the assembled crowd repeated after its leader: "One nation, one flag, one fatherland, one state" (Karakaya 2018:139). The organizers of the ritual further intensified collective effervescence through the event's mise-en-scène, incorporating uplifting music, famous actors from a state-sponsored Ottoman-themed film series reading emotion-laden poems, and jet planes roaring over the crowd. Visual effects, produced by a high-tech light show, repeatedly simulated the breach of the city's fortifications in 1453. Clearly, physical copresence, a shared focus of attention, a shared mood, and mutual awareness provided the event with the quality of a ritual. In addition, and in line with Dayan and Katz's (1992) arguments, the millions watching in front of their television screens, far away from Istanbul, also tanked up on emotional energy.

Emotions (to contradict a widely held belief) do not exclude cognition and knowledge. Karakaya observes correctly how participants feel a need to attribute meaning to their emotional state, in the form of knowledge about the greatness of the nation and the wickedness of its enemies. Repudiating Mustafa Kemal Atatürk and his model for the secular Turkish Republic he founded in 1923, the new script favors a glorious image of Ottoman history. The collective memory associated with this image, the knowledge repertoire it fosters, excludes dark chapters of Ottoman history, including knowledge of genocide committed in the name of the nation. Even if Karakaya's interviewees from different parts of Turkey do not wholeheartedly support the spectacle of the Conquest ritual, all believe in the sanctity of the Ottoman past.

Karakaya's analysis supports arguments about the epistemic power of memory entrepreneurs. They initiated and structured the elements of the Conquest ritual, supplied the audiovisual backdrop, and determined the content of speeches. Turkey's president was the central figure, and the ritual reflected the spirit and practice of his rule. Crucial for our purposes, the ritual reaffirmed a knowledge repertoire that leaves no space for engagement with the Armenian genocide.

Opposition Rituals: Challenging the Dominant Narrative

Yet official Turkish knowledge construction is not without challengers among Turks, and these challengers, too, put rituals to use. Egemen Özbek (2016), for example, describes in vivid detail Turkish-Armenian genocide commemorations in Istanbul. Organized by the Human Rights Association (İnsan Hakları Derneği, or IHD) on April 24, 2010, in front of the Haydarpaşa Train Station, a commemorative event attracted some fifty participants. The gathering culminated with Eren Keskin,[11] a lawyer and human rights activist, reading a press release:

> NEVER AGAIN! On April 24, 1915, 220 Armenian intellectuals, who were among the most productive members of the Ottoman artistic, literary and intellectual world, were arrested. First, they were taken to Mehterhane, which was used as central prison, the next day they were taken to Sarayburnu to board on a boat that would take them to the Haydarpasa train station. From there they began their journey towards Anatolia. They were not informed about where they were taken. One group headed to Ayas and the other to Çankiri. 58 of 70 people who were sent to Ayas and 81 of 150 who were sent to Çankiri were killed. Among the killed were leading intellectuals of the time. . . . Yes, we invite all to be conscientious in line with this convention [Convention for the Prevention and Punishment of the Crime of Genocide] and to properly name the events of 1915. As human rights defenders we say once again that GENOCIDE IS A CRIME AGAINST HUMANITY and NEVER AGAIN—IHD Istanbul Branch. The Commission Against Racism and Discrimination. (quoted in Özbek 2016:414–415)

The IHD repeated similar ceremonies in 2011, 2012, and 2013. The site was either the train station, symbol of the deportation process, or the front of the building in which the Armenian intellectuals were initially kept after the roundup of April 24, 1915.

Özbek (2016:419–427) similarly describes the ritual quality of a gathering of hundreds on Taksim Square in Istanbul, organized by an organization named DurDe, a "European Grassroots Antiracist Movement." A banner printed in Turkish, Armenian, and English read, "This is OUR pain. This is a mourning for ALL OF US." The event's emblem, a pomegranate, symbol of Armenian culture—as celebrated by Sergei Parajanov's famous film *The Color of Pomegranates*—but with a deep cut, symbolized the annihilation of the Armenians. Like the IHD, the organizers had chosen a symbol-rich location, across from the Republic Monument memorializing the military victory of the Turkish national struggle and the establishment of the republic under Mustafa Kemal Atatürk's leadership. By 2012, the number of attendees had grown to two thousand, and the event had expanded to other Turkish cities (Özbek 2016:427).

In short, small and courageous groups of Turkish activists and intellectuals challenge the official silencing of the Armenian genocide. They use rituals and powerful symbols to express solidarity with Armenians and to challenge denial. By contrast, the official commemoration of the Conquest of Constantinople establishes a new link to a past regime under which the genocide against the Armenians and mass atrocities against other minorities were committed. The new model, its self-celebratory excess, and its boundary drawing to outgroups (defined as enemies of the people and the sacred nation) do not bode well for a constructive engagement with the genocide.

CONCLUSIONS

We have seen that rituals are strong mechanisms for the reaffirmation of knowledge repertoires, here knowledge about the Armenian genocide on the side of Armenians, in their own country and in the diaspora, and the evasion of problematic aspects of Ottoman history on the Turkish side. In line with classical (Durkheim [1912] 2001) and modern work (Bellah 1970; Collins 2005; Douglas 1966; Shils 1981), rituals sanctify the nation, strengthen communities, and reaffirm knowledge. Strategic actors, entrepreneurs with substantial resources at hand, initiate and structure these rituals (see also Baer 2011; Karakaya and Baer 2019). They display great epistemic power. In line with Riley's (2008) insights, linking rituals to ancient symbols increases their effectiveness. References to Mount Ararat on the Armenian side and Mehmet the Conqueror on the Turkish side are but examples. The Armenian case further illustrated that we should examine rituals in the spirit of Caplow's (2004) festival cycle (here, a commemoration cycle), where the meaning of one ritual reveals itself fully only in combination with other rituals. Finally, in line with Erikson's ([1966] 2004) insights, rituals play an especially powerful role in times of crisis. They do so particularly when deeply held knowledge repertoires of one group profoundly challenge those of another.

Yet, despite the power of rituals in reaffirming communities and validating knowledge repertoires, challenges from the outside at times provoke direct conflictual engagement with the other, a theme to which the following chapters are dedicated.

Epistemic Struggles in the Political Field—Mobilization and Legislation in France

Collectivities struggling for their understanding of history do not just seek to reaffirm knowledge through rituals such as those discussed in chapter 6. They also engage the other side in conflict, carried out in various social fields, politics and law prominent among them. In this and the following chapters, I am interested in conflicts over genocide knowledge in the two countries with the largest Armenian diasporas besides Russia: France and the United States. The relative weight of politics and law as fields of conflict resolution varies between them. In the United States, law has historically been the central stage on which conflicting parties sought to reach binding decisions. This is not accidental, given that the country, far into the nineteenth century, had no strong central government to regulate domestic affairs. Despite changes in the course of the twentieth century, law continues to be the preeminent field of conflict resolution, as the exceptionally high rate of lawyers per population illustrates (Abel and Lewis 1989). By contrast, in France the political field has historically been the primary realm in which conflicting groups carried out societal conflicts. I examine legal struggles over genocide claims in the United States in chapter 8. In this chapter, after a few observations on broader trends, I address political conflict over knowledge regarding the Armenian genocide in France.

Today, faced with intense mnemonic struggles between Armenian communities on one side and Turkey and its ally Azerbaijan on the other, many countries and organizations around the globe face the choice of recognizing the Armenian genocide or abstaining from official acknowledgment. In this conflict between allegiances to human rights principles and interest in a country that holds a crucial geopolitical position in the conflict-ridden Middle East, human rights principles have increasingly prevailed in recent decades. Actors that have recognized

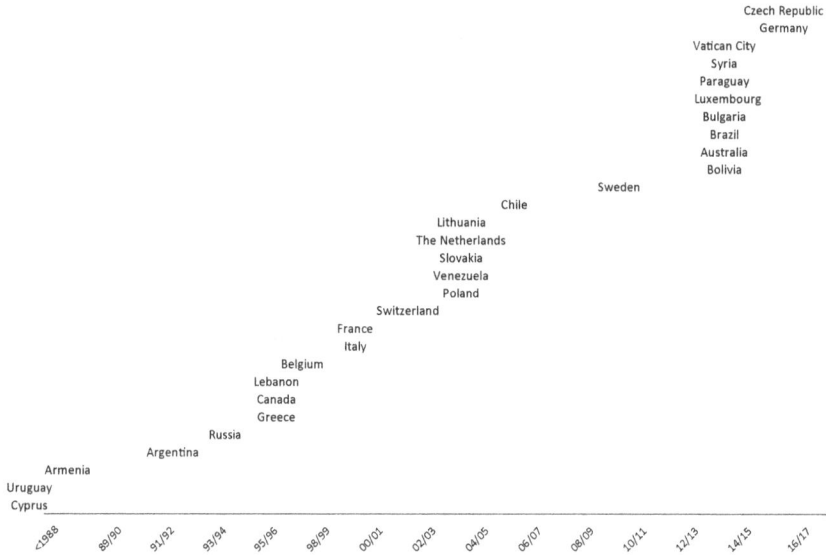

FIGURE 8. Recognition of the Armenian genocide by countries over time.

the Armenian genocide include the UN, with its Genocide Report (or "Whitaker Report," 1985), the International Association of Genocide Scholars (1998), the International Center for Transitional Justice (2002), the Council of Europe (2011), the Catholic Church (2015), the European Parliament (2015), and several European political parties. Many Jewish organizations, their members traumatized by the memory of the Shoah, joined in this chorus of recognizers, including the Union for Reformed Judaism (1989), the Anti-Defamation League (2007), the American Jewish Committee (2014), the Jewish Council for Public Affairs (2015), and the Central Council of Jews in Germany (2015).

Nation-states, as well, took a stance in growing numbers. While they have recognized the Armenian genocide in different forms and through different decision-making bodies, the following overview can at least provide an orientation (see figure 8). Countries that have traditionally had tense relationships with Turkey, such as Cyprus and Greece, started the trend; Cyprus recognized the genocide in 1975, Greece in 1996. Armenia, not surprisingly, declared its recognition on its way toward independence, in 1988. Russia, its allied superpower in the region, followed suit in 1995. By that year, two other countries had recognized the genocide (Uruguay in 1965, Argentina in 1993). Twelve countries followed in the subsequent decade, bringing the total to seventeen by the end of 2005 (Greece and Canada in 1996; Lebanon in 1997; Belgium in 1998; Italy in 2000; France in 2001; Switzerland in 2003; the Netherlands and Slovakia in 2004; and Lithuania, Poland, and Venezuela in 2005). The next decade brought little change, but Chile (2007) and Sweden (2010) joined the group of recognizers. Only in 2015, the year of the genocide's centennial, did seven additional countries fall in line (Australia, Brazil, Bulgaria, Luxembourg, Paraguay, Syria, and Vatican City), immediately following Bolivia (2014), with Germany (2016) and the Czech Republic (2017) in close pursuit. In 2019, both chambers of the U.S. Congress recognized the Armenian genocide, even if the presidential administration has not followed suit. Notably, almost all of these countries are European or Latin American.[1]

Recognition of the mass violence against the Ottoman Armenians as genocide seems to fit into a world in which ever more heads of state express apologies on behalf of their countries for atrocities committed in the course of history (Bilder 2006). It also aligns with Minow's (1998) observation about the increasing willingness of countries and the international community to take steps in response to, or as preventive means against, mass violence. We might finally expect a growing inclination to recognize past atrocities, including that against the Armenians, in an era in which Sikkink (2011) identifies a "justice cascade." Clearly, world polity theorists would recognize in the spread of recognition a global human rights script at work that diffuses to the level of nation-states (Meyer et al. 1992; Boyle 2002; Frank et al. 2000; Tsutsui 2017). Others might speak about a *human rights hegemony*, a term to which I return below.

Yet a view of global trends hides as much as it reveals. If thirty-one countries recognized the Armenian genocide, why did the remaining more than 150 counties not do so, and why is recognition limited almost exclusively to European and Latin American countries? Further, what kinds of recognition did the thirty-one countries choose? Which branches of government made the decisions? Why did some countries publicly recognize the Armenian genocide but no other genocides, except for the Holocaust?

Finally, what domestic processes unfold in the mnemonic struggle over recognition? Who favors recognition, and who challenges it? What types of power do the competing sides bring to bear and with what epistemic consequences? Even if we accept the notion of human rights hegemony, such hegemony is not absolute. It still encounters resistance. Under its umbrella play out nation-level power struggles. Here I examine these questions for the case of France.

The French case lends itself to a close examination for several reasons. First, a remarkable political process culminated in legislation that recognized the Armenian genocide in 2001 and criminalized its denial in 2012. To complicate things, France's Constitutional Council (Conseil constitutionnel) ruled the latter law unconstitutional on free speech grounds. We will learn about the process in detail and about its embeddedness in other French "memory laws." Second, France is home to the largest Armenian ethnic community (per capita) in the diaspora. This is not accidental in light of the long and complex history of French-Armenian relations (below, I present a brief overview of that history). Third, France is obviously part of a broader trend, but it displays both particularities and commonalities with other (democratic) countries. Particularities include unusually close ties between the political field on the one hand and the fields of scholarship and (constitutional) law on the other. Without consideration of such particularities, we cannot understand the political processes that unfold when a country faces the question of recognition of (the Armenian) genocide.

WHAT HAPPENED? FRENCH MEMORY LAWS AND RECOGNITION OF THE ARMENIAN GENOCIDE

Around the turn of the century, French legislators made several crucial decisions regarding the recognition of the Armenian genocide.[2] That story, however, can only be understood as part of a broader trend within the French nation, marking a new era of French engagement with dark chapters of history (Michel 2010). Below, I briefly describe both legislation pertaining to the Armenian genocide and the broader context of French "memory laws," and then suggest explanations.

Laws Pertaining to the Armenian Genocide

On May 29, 1998, the lower house of the French Parliament, the Assemblée nationale (National Assembly), passed a resolution in a legislative act stating in brief and simple words: "France publicly recognizes the Armenian genocide of 1915." Barely two years later, on November 7, 2000, the Senate followed suit, adopting the bill that recognizes the Armenian genocide. On January 29, 2001, President Jacques Chirac signed that bill into law (loi 2001-70). Obviously, this is but a declaration, symbolic law, and cautiously worded at that. It neither spells out responsible actors nor suggests positive or negative sanctions.

Yet the story does not end here. Mnemonic entrepreneurs in the political field soon began to work toward a law that would criminalize denial of the Armenian genocide. On May 18, 2006, the effort seemed to be defeated, facing substantial opposition in the National Assembly, which indefinitely postponed voting on such a bill. Only half a year later, however, supporters had gathered enough votes, and on October 12, 2006, the Assembly approved the bill to criminalize denial of the Armenian genocide.

Opposition in the Senate was substantial, and proponents modified the bill's wording to increase its acceptability. No longer specifying the Armenian genocide, representatives instead introduced a bill to criminalize denial of all genocides recognized by French law. In light of French law at the time, this would have included only the Shoah and the Armenian genocide. Nonetheless, on May 4, 2011, the Senate voted to reject the bill. Now members of the National Assembly adopted the more general wording and, a good one-and-a-half years later—on December 22, 2011—the Assembly passed a bill to criminalize denial of genocides recognized by French law. On January 23, 2012, the Senate changed course, voting 127 to 86 in favor of this bill. It was named the Boyer law (loi Boyer) after Valérie Boyer, a

young representative from Marseille who played a leading role in its promulgation. It threatened a term of imprisonment of one year and a fine of 45,000 euros.
Yet opposition was still fierce, and a group of legislators referred the law to the
Constitutional Council (CC) to have its constitutionality examined—and the law
defeated. They succeeded. On February 28, 2012, the CC struck down the law, an
event to which I return below.

In the Context of Memory Laws—A New Era

We would misunderstand the legislation pertaining to the Armenian genocide
if we failed to recognize broader contexts. We might be tempted, for example,
to attribute it to motivations and social forces that are unique to the Armenian
case. Instead, this legislation is part of a broader pattern of so-called *memory
laws*, a term that some have used polemically (see Adjemian 2012), but by which
I simply mean quite diverse laws that explicitly address the memory of historical
events. The story begins in 1971, when France ratified the International Convention on the Elimination of All Forms of Racial Discrimination. This ratification
required an adaptation of domestic law, which the legislature enacted on July 1,
1972. Named the Pleuven Act, the law prohibits incitement to hatred, discrimination, slander, and racial insults. Not a memory law in its own right, it is an
early predecessor.

The first of a quartet of memory laws followed almost two decades later. On July
13, 1990, the French legislature passed the Gayssot Act, which prohibits any rac-
ist, anti-Semitic, or xenophobic activities, including Holocaust denial. Introduced
by the Communist representative Jean-Claude Gayssot, this law criminalizes the
questioning of the existence or gravity of the category of crimes against humanity
as defined in the London Charter of 1945, based on which the International Military Tribunal at Nuremberg convicted Nazi leaders in 1945–46 (Article 9).[3] This
law constitutes a legislative recognition of the Shoah *and* it penalizes denial.

The timing was not accidental. The 1980s, after all, witnessed the rise of the
Front National, the country's new radical right-wing party, and the growing prominence of its leader, Jean-Marie Le Pen, an outspoken anti-Semite. The decade also
saw the first French trial involving charges of crimes against humanity, specifically
the 1987 trial of Klaus Barbie, who was responsible for mass deportations of Jews
from the city of Lyon into the German death camps. In the same year, Claude
Lanzmann's powerful documentary film *Shoah* appeared—a masterwork with a
running time of more than ten hours, based on interviews with surviving victims,
perpetrators, and bystanders.

All of these events and the passing of the Gayssot Act accelerated public engagement with the time of German occupation, French collaboration, and the Vichy
regime. One highlight was President Chirac's 1995 official recognition of the 1942
"Vel d'Hiv Roundup" (Rafle du Vélodrome d'Hiver) of Parisian Jews, their arrests
and encampment in the Winter Velodrome and subsequent deportation into the

A LA MÉMOIRE DES PETITS ENFANTS
DE CETTE ÉCOLE MATERNELLE
DÉPORTÉS DE 1942 À 1944
PARCE QU'ILS ÉTAIENT NÉS JUIFS,
VICTIMES INNOCENTES
DE LA BARBARIE NAZIE
AVEC LA COMPLICITÉ ACTIVE
DU GOUVERNEMENT DE VICHY.

ILS FURENT EXTERMINÉS
DANS LES CAMPS DE LA MORT.

2 octobre 2004   NE LES OUBLIONS JAMAIS

FIGURE 9. Commemorative plaque at a school building on the Île Saint-Louis, Paris, mounted in 2004. Photo by the author.

death camps. In 1997–98 followed the trial of Maurice Papon, a prominent police leader during the 1940s and into the 1960s, decorated with high honors by President Charles de Gaulle for his repression of militant Algerian activism, and later a long-term representative and minister of the French Republic. The court found Papon guilty on charges of crimes against humanity for his role in the deportation of more than sixteen hundred Jews from the Bordeaux region to Auschwitz, via the Drancy camp just north of Paris. Plaques mounted on the walls of Parisian buildings in the early 2000s today implicate the Vichy regime, something missing from plaques of earlier decades (see figure 9).[4]

In this heated atmosphere, engagement with past wrongs began to reach beyond the Shoah. The 2001 legislative recognition of the Armenian genocide was a first step. Just a few months later, the French legislature passed the Taubira law (loi Taubira), recognizing slavery as a crime against humanity. The law, which went into effect on May 21, 2001, was named after Christiane Taubira, then a representative to the French National Assembly for French Guiana (Guyane) and a member of the Socialist faction (she would later be minister of justice under President François Hollande). This law targets the practice of slavery beginning in the fifteenth century as directed against African, American Indian, Malagasy, and Indian populations. It also encourages scholarly engagement with the history of slavery. Later, in 2006, President Chirac declared May 10, the date on which the law passed, a day dedicated to the memory of slavery and its abolition (Michel 2016).

While the political Left had promoted the Taubira law on the recognition of slavery as a crime against humanity, the Right soon followed with its own initiative. On February 23, 2005, the French legislature passed a law on the memory of French colonialism and the status of former fighters in the Algerian War (1954–62). The Mekachera law (loi Mekachera)—named after Hamlaoui Mekachera, a former military officer and, at the time, minister for ex-combatants—sought, in the minds of its proponents, "recognition of the Nation and national contribution in favor of the French repatriates." These repatriates were some nine hundred thousand French colonialists in Algeria, the so-called *pieds-noirs*, who returned to France at the end of the war in 1962, and "Harkis," some ninety thousand Algerians who, having closely collaborated with the French military, fled to France at that time. This law was in part a response to the National Assembly's 1999 recognition of the Algerian War—a war characterized by massive brutalities and resulting in the end of French colonial rule in Algeria. Previously, France had labeled the conflict a "public order operation."

Among other specifications, the Mekachera law of 2005 obliged high school (*lycée*) teachers to instruct their students about the "positive values" of colonialism (article 4, paragraph 2). The law generated intense public debate and massive opposition, especially from the Left. Teachers and prominent historians charged historical revisionism, and more than ten thousand signed a petition against the law. In 2006, President Chirac, through his prime minister and an appeal to the CC, secured a repeal of article 4, paragraph 2. The other parts of the law remained on the books.

At this point, the history of memory laws ended, at least for the time being. Four such laws remained on the books: the Gayssot Act of 1990, the recognition of the Armenian genocide of 2001 (loi 2001-70), the Taubira law of 2001, and the Mekachera law of 2005.

Clearly, this brief history shows that recognition of genocide is not a simple "dummy variable" that can be coded "yes" or "no." The quality of recognition varies substantially. Furthermore, recognition involves intense political struggles, and, finally, context matters. The recognition of the Armenian genocide is part of a larger trend, an engagement with dark chapters of national history, embedded in global concerns with human rights and their violation.

TOWARD EXPLANATION: THE POLITICAL FIELD, ARMENIAN-FRENCH RELATIONS, AND MOBILIZATION

Despite their embeddedness in new mnemonic practices, the laws pertaining to the recognition of the Armenian genocide are not quasi-automatic accompaniments of other memory legislation. In the absence of legislative decisions that recognize other genocides, with the exception of the Shoah, we have to ask what prompted the special treatment of the Armenian case. In answering that question, we must pay attention to the complex interplay between institutional particularities of the political field in France, the history of French-Armenian relations, the mobilization of French Armenian civil society, and the roles of academia (especially historical scholarship), foreign relations, and the CC. Below, and in chapter 9, I address each of these forces in turn. We will see that the unfolding legislative drama and the political and epistemic outcomes it yielded illustrate interactions between action-based power, played out in concrete legislative struggles on the one hand and human rights hegemony on the other.

The French Political Field in Context

In France, as elsewhere, state actors operate with substantial amounts of material, social, symbolic, and cultural capital. They make binding decisions, in this case decisions to recognize historical events on behalf of the French nation. In Bourdieu's terms, "the state is to produce and impose . . . categories of thought that we spontaneously apply to all things of the social world" (1994:1)—issues of mass violence and genocide included. In other words, the state holds significant epistemic power.

Yet the state does not operate in isolation. In France, it exists in close vicinity to the academic field, and this closeness matters for the convertibility of resources, including academic and political capital, across fields. This particularity results from the high level of centralization of French society and state and from the concentration of politics and intellectual life in Paris, a pattern to which scholars from Norbert Elias ([1939] 2000) to Pierre Bourdieu (1988) have alerted us.

The French political field has another close neighbor that plays a crucial role in the unfolding story of memory legislation: the field of constitutional law, especially its central institution, the Constitutional Council, the French equivalent of a constitutional court. The CC, while part of the judicial branch of government, closely overlaps with the political sector through recruitment mechanisms and the character of its membership (to which I will return below).

Finally, as in all Western democracies, the political field and its neighbors are surrounded by civil society, made up by social movements and organizations that bundle and communicate interests. Ethnic groups and their organizations, cultural associations, schools, and religious institutions are crucial in the case of memory legislation.

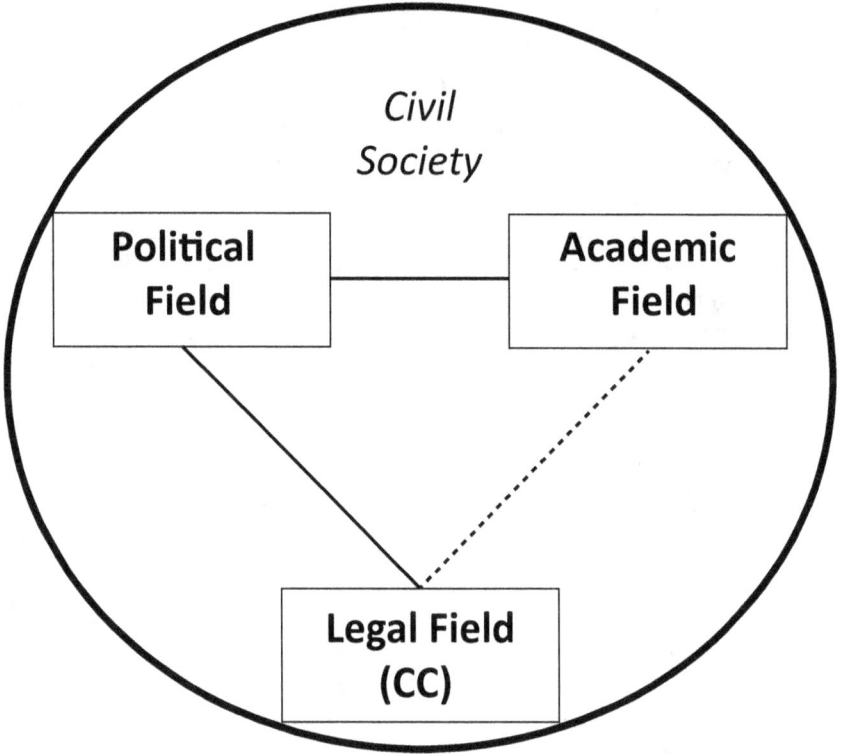

FIGURE 10. The "French triangle": Politics, scholarship, and constitutional law within civil society.

Figure 10 represents the position of the political field vis-à-vis other social fields. At the center is what I call the "French triangle," made up of the closely related political, academic, and constitutional law fields. The strongest connections are symbolized by thick connecting lines, while the dotted line indicates the relatively weaker link between the academic and legal fields. The circle around this triangle symbolizes civil society, in which all three social fields are nested. The depiction in figure 10 is not complete, of course, given that nation-states are embedded in international relations. In our case, relations between France and Turkey play a significant role, as do relationships to the global field of human rights, as a generator of human rights scripts. All of these forces come into play in the unfolding story of legislation pertaining to the recognition of the Armenian genocide.

French Armenian Civil Society: Mobilization and Epistemic Effects

Historical roots lead up to contemporary civil society mobilization of French Armenians without which the laws of 2001 and 2012 would not have been promulgated and passed.

Historical root 1: A sense of guilt.   In his massive volume *La France face au géno-cide des Arméniens* (France facing the genocide of the Armenians), historian Vincent Duclert (2015) traces the history of the relationship between the French state and French intellectuals vis-à-vis the fate of the Armenian people. He spells out the guilt (*culpabilité*) of the victors of World War I, who—after the defeat of the Axis powers—did not ensure that the Ottoman rulers be held accountable and that the Armenians be protected and, to the degree possible, compensated. This aban-donment carries special weight in light of the Allies' declaration of May 24, 1915, that accused the responsible actors of "crimes against humanity and civilization" (Duclert 2015:205–208). Duclert here does for France what Samantha Power (2002) did for the United States in *A Problem from Hell*, accusing his country of repeat-edly standing by even in the face of the gravest atrocities. In Duclert's words, "The French position toward the extermination of the Ottoman Armenians illustrates, in the long run, the attitude of the Great Powers toward abandoning that persecuted minority and their renouncement of principles on which are based their repeated promises to protect its threatened existence" (Duclert 2015:35, translated).[5]

Yet Duclert also describes another France, one that spoke up on behalf of the Armenian people of the Ottoman Empire at the time of the Hamidian massacres (1894–96) under the reign of Sultan Abdülhamid II, which took the lives of up to three hundred thousand Armenians. While the French government joined Russia to block any intervention, prominent representatives made their voices heard in the legislature, and renowned intellectuals backed them up. For example, on November 3, 1896, the historian and Catholic Denys Cochin and the philosopher and socialist Jean Jaurès, both members of the National Assembly, spoke force-fully on behalf of the Armenians, an event that Marcel Proust describes in his first major novel, *Jean Santeuil*. Historian Raymond Kévorkian, author of a massive volume on the Armenian genocide, reconstructs this event and its consequences: "The Parisian newspapers, each of which knows that they receive generous subsi-dies from agents of the Ottoman sultan, now change their tone" (Duclert 2015:46, translated). The new movement overlapped with the defenders of Alfred Dreyfus, the French officer who, in 1894, was falsely accused and convicted of spying for the German military, a prosecution motivated by anti-Semitism. Once born, this Armenophile movement grew impressively, especially after 1900, organized around the newly founded magazine *Pro Armenia*.

The new Armenophiles again urged intervention in 1915. Prominently, writer Anatole France spoke up powerfully on behalf of the Armenians throughout World War I. Yet activists did not convince their government to intervene until the end of the war, when the French Navy saved the lives of Armenian villagers who had defended themselves, on the mountain Musa Dagh (Mount Moses), against the onslaught of the Ottoman army. Jewish Austrian writer Franz Werfel described this event, famously and dramatically, in his 1933 novel on the Armenian genocide, *The Forty Days of Musa Dagh*.

Mass immigration of survivors of the Armenian genocide to France followed the end of World War I, partly owing to French domination of many of the territories that housed the survivors, partly encouraged by an intense labor shortage in France after the war. Yet civil society engagement subsided in the 1920s and 1930s, and the years of Nazi Germany's occupation and the Vichy regime obviously were ill suited to revive the memory of Armenian suffering.

A revival of civil society engagement would not occur until six decades later. In March 1979, a large group of prominent French intellectuals and academics issued a new plea for genocide recognition, this time to the United Nations and its Human Rights Commission. They included prominent jurists such as Robert Badinter; social scientists, including Raymond Aron and Roland Barthes; Nobel laureate François Jacob; philosopher Jacques Derrida; physicians such as Bernard Kouchner (cofounder of Médecins Sans Frontières); and famous writers, including Simone de Beauvoir. Just five years later, on April 13–16, 1984, in Paris, the Permanent Peoples' Tribunal—an international opinion tribunal founded in Bologna, Italy, in 1979—dedicated its session to the Armenian genocide. On the basis of historical documents and legal doctrine, the tribunal concluded that "the extermination of the Armenian populations by way of deportation and massacre constitutes a crime of genocide, not subject to statutory limitations as defined by the Convention of 9 December 1948 for the prevention and punishment of the Crime of Genocide" (in Duclert 2015:57, translated).

This historical trajectory of genocide recognition interacted with changes in the nature of French Armenian civil society to which I turn now. Together, both trends formed the foundation without which we cannot understand the later civil society mobilization and legislative initiatives toward Armenian genocide recognition.

Historical root 2: The path from discrimination to recognized social force. Following the years of violence in the Ottoman Empire, hundreds of thousands of surviving Armenians sought refuge either in Armenia—the small, newly independent country, soon to be absorbed by the Soviet Union—or in the diaspora. The United States and France were privileged destinations. In France, many settled in the cities of Marseille, Lyon, and Paris and in surrounding departments. Yet their legal status initially was tenuous. They gained citizenship only after World War II. Like other victimized peoples—and maybe more so, given their marginal status—those who had survived the killings did not easily remember and pass on their knowledge to their children and grandchildren. (Chapter 1 provides evidence for patterns of silencing in the biographies of French Armenians, albeit with some important exceptions of acknowledgment.)

Significant public events paralleled the biographical patterns described above. For example, after decades of silence, Armenian voices made themselves heard on the fiftieth anniversary of the genocide. In France as elsewhere, "demonstrations are organized, brochures published, appeals issued to save the genocide from forgetting. In Paris, a great mass brings together thousands of Armenians in the

Pleyel Auditorium" (Duclert 2015:339, translated). The first French historical study of the Armenian genocide, entitled *Un Génocide exemplaire, Arménie 1915* and authored by Jean-Marie Carzou, appeared in 1975, a decade after the commemoration of the fiftieth anniversary (Carzou [1975] 2006). Plans for a first memorial, to be set up in an Armenian church in Marseille, were about to materialize in 1973. Yet French government action, prompted by Turkish intervention, initially prevented the realization of this project. Terrorist actions by militant Armenian groups in the 1970s and 1980s, while causing a backlash against the Armenian cause in Turkey and elsewhere, were violent proof that the history of the genocide had caught up with young Armenians.

Today, the desire to spread knowledge about the genocide and the longing for recognition continue unabated, but they no longer translate into violence. Stopping over at Charles de Gaulle Airport on a journey to attend an April 24 genocide commemoration in Yerevan, the traveler may observe groups of children with T-shirts identifying them as Armenians. Similarly, in the American diaspora, Armenian churches offer summer trips to Armenia for young Armenian Americans (see chapter 4). Large crowds attend commemorative events in Armenia and in the diaspora (chapter 6). In intellectual life, we observed new interest, for example, when historian Claire Mouradian and Anaïd Donabédian recreated and reoriented, in 1992, the Société des Études Arméniennes. Only one year later, a group of academics founded an allied association with a complementary journal, the *Revue du Monde Arménien moderne et contemporain* (Duclert 2015:356–357).

In short, delays to the recognition of the Armenian genocide, even among Armenians, reflect period and cohort effects known from multiple cases of memory formation. Today, however, genocide knowledge is firmly sedimented. It is hard to imagine the legislative initiatives in support of the recognition of the Armenian genocide without the changes unfolding in the Armenian community of France. Yet ethnic consciousness does not suffice. Civil society mobilization is another necessary component in the transmission of popular will into legislative action, as the following section demonstrates.

Political Debate and Contemporary Armenian Mobilization: Epistemic Efficacy

Six of the seven sessions in the National Assembly and in the Senate in which legislators deliberated on laws concerning the Armenian genocide are well documented.[6] Together with my research assistants, I identified all speakers in these debates, their political party affiliations, the regions or departments they represented, their positions for or against the law under debate, and the types of arguments they articulated.

As an illustration, consider the last debate by the French Senate, in January 2012, about the Boyer law pertaining to the criminalization of denial of the Armenian genocide. Patterns of statements by senators reveal that the facticity of the genocide is one of the most frequently raised themes (table 2). Other

TABLE 2 Arguments Presented by French Senators, January 23, 2012, during Debate over the Boyer Law

Senator	Position	Party[b]	1	2	3	4	5	6	7	8	9	10	11	12	13
								Issue Discussed[a]							
Patrick Ollier	In favor	UMP		X	X			X				X	X		X
Jean-Pierre Sueur	Against	Committee	X	X	X				X						X
Isabelle Pasquet	Against	CRC						X		X		X	X		
Jacques Mézard	Against	Radical Left		X	X		X		X	X					
Roger Karoutchi	In favor	UMP		X								X	X		
Esther Benbassa	Against	Env.		X						X			X		
Hervé Marseille	In favor	UDI	X	X	X							X	X		X
Philippe Kaltenbach	In favor	Socialist	X	X	X		X					X	X		
Luc Carvounas	In favor	Socialist	X	X				X				X	X		
Bruno Giles	In favor	UMP	X	X								X	X		
Jean-Vincent Place	Against	Env.	X	X	X	X		X							
Nathalie Goulet	Against	UDI	X	X				X							
Bernard Piras	In favor	Socialist	X	X				X	X			X			X
Ambroise Dupont	Against	UMP		X	X		X	X							
Sophie Joissains	In favor	UDI	X	X								X	X		X
Nicolas Alfonsi	Against	RDSE	X	X	X										
Nicole Borvo	In favor	CRC	X	X								X	X		
Jean-Jacques Pignard	Against	CRU		X	X										
Jean-Michel Baylet	Against	RDSE	X	X	X	X	X						X		
Natacha Bouchart	In favor	UMP	X				X					X	X		
Anne-Marie Escoffier	Against	Radical Left		X	X					X					
Yannick Vaugrenard	In favor	Socialist		X	X			X				X	X		X
Christian Poncelet	Against	UMP		X	X			X							X
Robert Hue	Against	RDSE		X	X										
Catherine Tasca	Against	Socialist	X	X	X	X	X	X		X					
Jean-René Lecerf	Against	UMP		X	X					X					
Jean-Noel Guerini	In favor	Socialist	X	X								X	X		
Gaëtan Gorce	Against	Socialist	X										X		
Gérard Larcher	Against	UMP		X	X										
Jean-Claude Gaudin	In favor	UMP		X											

[a]Code for issues discussed: 1 = Existence of the Armenian genocide; 2 = Role of Parliament in writing history; 3 = Constitutionality; 4 = Prospects for Turkey's joining the EU; 5 = Armenian-Turkish relations; 6 = French-Turkish relations; 7 = Recognition of other genocides; 8 = Political maneuvering; 9 = French atrocities in Algeria; 10 = Insufficiency of 2001 law; 11 = Comparison to Gayssot Act; 12 = Pleven Act; 13 = Aligning French law with European law.

[b]Political party affiliations: Committee = Law Committee of the Senate; CRC = Communist, Republican, and Citizen; Env. = Environmentalist; UDI = Union of Democrats and Independents; RDSE = European Democratic and Social Rally; CRU = Centrist Republican Union.

prominent topics include the role of the legislature in the writing of history, the constitutionality of the bill, the quality of French-Turkish relations, the sufficiency of the 2001 law of genocide recognition (loi 2001-70), and the discrepancy between the 1990 Gayssot Act, which had criminalized denial of the Shoah, and the 2001 law, which did not reinforce recognition with the threat of sanctions. While positions on most themes are divided and in line with the senators' utterances in favor of or against the legislation, they are almost unanimous, and in the affirmative, in statements about the facticity of the genocide.

Some details illustrate the spirit of deliberations. The Senate debate of January 23, 2012, opened with a statement by Patrick Ollier, minister for relations with Parliament. Ollier, speaking in support of the Boyer law, quoted philosopher George Santayana's words that are engraved on many memorials: "Those who forget the past are condemned to repeat it."[7] He insisted that the law under consideration simply sought to fill a legal vacuum in providing consistency with the Gayssot Act. He also argued that it would be applied only to cases of outrageous denial, to be punished by one-year imprisonment and a fine of 45,000 euros. Ollier further insisted that the government support the law even though it was aware of potential repercussions for French-Turkish relations.[8]

Several speeches by senators echoed his comments. Some underlined their supportive position by establishing links to the Shoah and its recognition by French law. Senator Roger Karoutchi, of the center-right UMP (Union pour un mouvement populaire) faction, stressed the need for France to be consistent in its enforcement of memory laws. Given that the French Parliament had passed laws recognizing both the Holocaust and the Armenian genocide, he argued, the denial of both genocides should be sanctioned in the same way. The drawing of such parallels, however, sparked vocal protests.[9] Senator Esther Benbassa, a French-Turkish-Israeli historian and politician and a member of the Green Party, opposed the legislation. She drew a clear distinction between the Shoah (followed by the Nuremberg trials) on the one hand and the Armenian genocide on the other. She reminded the Senate that the latter was not declared criminal by an international court. Her comments drew applause from the environmentalist group and from some members of the Socialist faction.[10]

Importantly, however, even opponents of the criminalization of denial explicitly and strongly recognized the Armenian genocide. Prominent among them was Jean-Pierre Sueur, rapporteur and president of the Constitutional Law Commission (La commission des lois constitutionnelles, de législation, du suffrage universel, du règlement et d'administration générale). Sueur spoke in clear opposition to the criminalization of Armenian genocide denial. He clarified that he did not speak on behalf of his political party (the Socialist Party), but on behalf of the commission (equivalent to a committee in the U.S. Congress). He insisted that the legislation was at high risk of constitutional censureship, citing (fellow) Socialist Catherine Tasca, who had stressed in committee that allowing the law to rule on historical facts violates the principle of separation of powers. Additionally, the commission believed, according to Sueur, that the bill violated the principle of freedom of opinion and expression, as well as the principle of legality of offenses and penalties.[11] Sueur's arguments are reflected in the commission report submitted to the Senate before the debate: "Condemning all forms of denialism, which constitutes despicable harm to the memory of the disappeared and the dignity of the victims, and reiterating its infinite respect for the Armenian people and the terrible hardship it had to endure, [the commission] has examined the legitimacy of legislative intervention in the field of history—concluding that the adoption of resolutions and the organization of commemorations probably are better means to express the Nation's solidarity with the suffering endured by the victims" (p. 5, translated).[12]

The body of the report spells out (and I paraphrase its wording) the suffering of the Armenians under Young Turk rule, the decision of deportation after an uprising by Armenians in the city of Van in April 1915, the arrest and killing of 650 Armenian notables in Constantinople on April 24, 1915, and the loss of some 800,000–1,250,000 Armenian lives. The report also applies the term "génocide de 1915" (p. 9) to the violence. In short, even opponents of the bill that sought to criminalize denial of the Armenian genocide documented and reinforced a knowledge repertoire that strongly overlaps with that of Armenians as described in chapter 4. Armenian mobilization was one social force that enhanced this documentation of genocide knowledge, and empirical support is about to follow. A broader human rights culture may have contributed, but it would not explain why exactly the Armenian genocide received this recognition while other genocides are not subject to legislative affirmation.

We were able to relate positions taken in the Assembly and Senate debates by departments (départements) to data on the density of Armenian cultural associations in those jurisdictions. Patterns reveal substantial variation across departments of the French Republic, with concentrations in Paris and the Ile de France region surrounding the capital, and in Marseille (bouche du Rhone) and Lyon (Rhone) and their environs.[13] A selection of departments illustrates such uneven distribution (see table 3).

Descriptive analyses indeed show a link between the concentration of Armenian cultural associations and the positions legislators took in debates regarding the Armenian genocide between 1998 and 2012.[14] Table 4 demonstrates that senators and representatives from departments with larger numbers of Armenian cultural associations were much more likely to intervene in favor of each of the legislative projects concerning the Armenian genocide, even if the difference diminishes somewhat in debates on the criminalization law. It comes to full display again, however, in the final vote.

Descriptive statistics always warrant caution. For example, some departments are Left leaning, while others gravitate to the political Right, and political position

TABLE 3 Numbers of Armenian Cultural Associations, by Département, 2015

Département	Number of Associations
Aisne	1
Alpes-de-Haute-Provence	1
Hautes-Alpes	1
Alpes-Maritimes	15
Ardèche	1
Bouches-du-Rhône	110
Calvados	1
Pyrénées-Orientales	2
Bas-Rhin	2
Rhône	55
Sarthe	1
Haute-Savoie	1
Paris	130
Seine-Maritime	3
Seine-et-Marne	4
Haute-Vienne	1
Essonne	1
Hauts-de-Seine	43
Seine-Saint-Denis	11
Val-de-Marne	27
Val-d'Oise	6
74 other départements	0

SOURCE: www.acam-france.org/contacts/index_associations_culturelles.php (last viewed on April 12, 2019).

TABLE 4 Average Numbers of Armenian Cultural Associations in Départements of Senators or Representatives Intervening in Favor of and against Armenian Genocide Legislation, by Date

Date	In Favor	Against
2000	43.8	0.6
May 2006	67.8	0.5
October 2006	38	11.5
May 2011	44.8	10
December 2011	40.4	28
2012	62	12.4
Average	**47.3**	**10.5**

TABLE 5 Regression Analysis: Armenian Cultural Associations per Département in Relation to Position Taken in Legislative Debates, by Political Party of Speakers and by Date

	Odds Ratio	Standard Error	z	P > z	95% Confidence Interval	
Number of Associations	1.038	0.01	3.5	0***	1.016	1.059
Socialist Party						
UMP	0.175	0.14	−2.22	0.026*	0.037	0.813
Radical Left	0.172	0.19	−1.61	0.107	0.020	1.459
Centrist/Independent/ Center-Right	0.908	0.86	−0.10	0.919	0.142	5.808
Moderate Left	0.079	0.10	−2.03	0.042*	0.006	0.911
2000						
May 2006	0.478	0.61	−0.58	0.561	0.039	5.751
October 2006	1.032	0.98	0.03	0.973	0.161	6.596
May 2011	0.331	0.33	−1.12	0.264	0.047	2.301
December 2011	3.615	3.79	1.23	0.221	0.462	28.255
2012	0.146	0.13	−2.15	0.031*	0.025	0.841
_Constant	5.014	4.83	1.67	0.094	0.759	33.108

NOTE: *P < 0.05, **P < 0.01, ***P < 0.001.

may well affect interventions in debates and votes on genocide laws. It is also possible that the distribution of participants from various regions in debates varied over time. We thus conducted a regression analysis that controls for potentially distorting factors.

Results displayed in Table 5 confirm the patterns revealed by descriptive statistics. Representatives and senators from departments with many Armenian cultural associations are more likely to speak in favor of legislation pertaining to the Armenian genocide than speakers from other regions, even when we control for time and political party. In other words, Armenian representation was decisive for the patterns of arguments in the legislature and for the outcome of the legislative process.

How, then, does representation translate into political and legislative positions? The strength of the Armenian vote may have been decisive, even if leaders of the French Armenian community insist that there is no Armenian voting bloc, and even if French Armenians count only an estimated three hundred thousand to five hundred thousand people among the sixty-three million French (2010)—and not all French citizens of Armenian descent identify as Armenian. Nevertheless, organizational representation, in addition to (anticipated) voting patterns and civil society mobilization, as manifested by many well-attended demonstrations around the time of legislative debates, appears to have sufficiently impressed

French politicians to adjust their voices, and likely their votes, to the strength of their Armenian constituents.

Electoral politics as a driving force were indeed on the minds of some participants in legislative debates. For example, in the final Senate debate on the bill, Isabelle Pasquet—a member of the Central Revolutionary Committee (CRC), a Marxist-inspired political party—raised questions regarding the politics of the administration of President Nicolas Sarkozy and its supporters in the legislature. Claiming that the president had attempted to gain the votes of five hundred thousand French citizens of Armenian descent by supporting the legislation, she accused legislators from his party, the center-right UMP faction, of changing their position for political reasons. Pasquet rejected the bill, concluding that it would lead to more outrage from Turkish protesters.[15]

Indeed, presidential elections were approaching fast when the 2012 bill came to a vote. Importantly, also in support of the legislation was Sarkozy's challenger, the Socialist François Hollande, a long-term friend of French Armenian leader Mourad Papazian, copresident of the Coordination Council of Armenian Organizations.

In short, building on a long-term process of identity formation, French Armenians mobilized successfully to enhance the chances of the recognition laws. Legislators, it seems, heard their voices well. Yet French Armenians are not the only constituents in these debates, and neither the quality of deliberations nor the final decision-making outcome can be understood without considering the role of three other types of actors: historians, the Turkish government, and the CC.

Epistemic Politics and Academia: Legislation and the Historians

The "French triangle" (figure 10) indicates the close relationship between the political and academic fields in France. This closeness is due to the concentration of the country's political and academic elites in Paris (Elias [1939] 2000), the often shared educational experience of political and academic leaders in the same elite institutions (Bourdieu 1988), and media practices, whereby prominent academics frequently articulate their positions in debates over political issues. Geographic proximity, network ties, and academic access to civil society via prominent media allow for a comparatively easy conversion of political capital (power, votes) into academic capital and vice versa. Historians obviously matter, especially in the context of memory laws. Their utterances register with the French political field far more than in other countries, especially the United States.

Political mobilization of scholarship.   Given the weight of scholarly interventions in the political field, political actors seek to mobilize scholarly contributions to public debates. The numerous historians' commissions initiated by the French state include one, for example, that President Emmanuel Macron established in spring 2019 to examine the role of France in the Rwandan genocide.[16] Another commission, under the leadership of historian Vincent Duclert and also sponsored by the French government, produced a broader report on conditions of genocide.

The interest of political actors in the work of historians manifests itself, especially and not surprisingly, in the history of memory laws. Two such laws explicitly appeal to research and instruction. Article 2 of the Taubira law of 2001, addressing the legacy of slavery, states: "Educational and research programs in history and the human sciences accord to the treatment of people of African descent and to slavery the weight they deserve. Cooperation should be encouraged and favored that allows for synergy between archival sources in Europe and oral sources as well as archaeological knowledge accumulated in Africa, the Americas, the Caribbean and in all the other territories that knew slavery" (translated).[17] Note, however, that this is symbolic law. The legislature attached neither positive nor negative sanctions to scholarship that does or does not follow its plea. It also does not specify the content of scholarship it expects historians to produce, even if the qualification of slavery as a crime against humanity in the same law speaks to the legislature's reading of history.

The law of 2005 pertaining to those repatriated from the North African colonies uses similar wording. Article 4 states: "Research programs in universities grant the deserved place to the history of the French presence overseas, especially in North Africa. The law encourages cooperation that allows for mutual engagement of oral and written sources available in France and abroad" (translated). Here, as in the Taubira law, the law entails neither positive nor negative sanctions. It also does not prescribe the content of research or instruction. It is worth remembering, however, that the current wording is a modification of the original text. The original text had required history teachers to cover the "positive impact" of colonialism in their instruction (article 4, paragraph 2). After the legislature had initially passed the entire act, this part of the law was later overruled.

The only memory law that threatens criminal sanctions is the 1990 Gayssot Act against genocide denial. Article 9 indeed modifies the criminal code and adapts the media law (loi de la presse) of 1881 that guarantees freedom of the press.[18] Yet this law does not specifically address scholarship and instruction.

In sum, the French state seeks to mobilize, and thereby at times to regulate, scholarship and education. With the exception of the Gayssot Act, it does not threaten penalties for denialist utterances, but it occasionally encourages or demands—as in the laws regarding slavery and colonialism—consideration of specific subjects in research and education. The 2001 law recognizing the Armenian genocide (loi 2001-70) does not pose demands on research or education, nor does it threaten penalties. The 2012 Boyer law, by criminalizing denial of the Armenian genocide, sought to correct this omission. Yet the CC overruled this law.

The agency of (divided) historians vis-à-vis the political field.   Historians were not just targets in this unfolding legislative history. Instead, they displayed substantial agency. They entered the stage early on, in response to the Gayssot Act, which criminalized Holocaust denial. Prominently, historian Madeline Rebérioux (1990) published an article in the November issue of the journal *L'Histoire* that criticized the new law. She stressed that earlier law had already allowed for a civil court condemnation, on grounds of public defamation, of Holocaust denier Robert Faurisson in 1981, without necessitating that the courts cast judgment on historical truth. She found herself in the good company of renowned historian Pierre Vidal-Naquet, an outspoken challenger of denialist claims.

While these powerful but isolated scholarly voices in response to the early memory law found little echo in the political field, the situation would change radically a good decade later. Three events prepared fertile ground for an uprising among historians against laws that regulate articulations about history. First, in June 21, 1995, Princeton historian of the Middle East Bernard Lewis was convicted in a Parisian civil court. Lewis—although he had written about the "Holocaust against the Armenians" in publications decades before—had referred, in an interview with *Le Monde*, to the mass killings of Armenians in 1915 as "la version arménienne de cette histoire" (the Armenian version of this story). He was sentenced to the payment of one (symbolic) franc to the state, 10,000 francs to the Forum des associations arméniennes de France, and 4,000 francs to the Ligue internationale contre le racism et l'antisémitisme. Lewis subsequently softened his language but continued to insist on his rejection of the term *genocide*, claiming that the Young Turk government had no deliberate plan to exterminate the Armenian people.[19]

The second event that shook the scholarly field occurred in 1998: the election of Ottomanist historian Gilles Veinstein to the Collège de France almost failed over an article he had published three years earlier in *l'Histoire*, for which he was accused of denialism, a charge other prominent historians such as Pierre Vidal-Naquet forcefully challenged. The third event occurred in 2005, when a group called the Collectif des Antillais, Guyanais, Réunionnais (representing peoples of French overseas territories) filed a complaint, later withdrawn, against Olivier Pétré-Grenouilleau, a historian of slavery who—in an interview with the newspaper *Le Journal du Dimanche* on June 12, 2005—refused to apply the term *genocide* to the history of slavery. Hundreds of academics turned out to support Pétré-Grenouilleau.

It was against this background that scholars reacted to the memory laws initiated and/or passed after 2005 with an intensity not known in the context of the Gayssot Act of 1990. On March 25, 2005, historian Claude Liauzu and several colleagues published an article in the daily *Le Monde* in response to the Mekachera law. They demanded, "Non à l'enseignement d'une histoire officielle" (No to the teaching of an official history). Their statement was supported by the Ligue des droits de l'homme (Human Rights League) and by several teachers' unions. The initiative soon took organizational form, when members of this group of historians, later in spring 2005, founded the Comité de vigilance face aux usages publics de l'histoire (Committee of vigilance against the public uses of history).[20]

Similarly, and soon after the March 25 article in *Le Monde*, the Comité national de l'Association des Professeurs d'Histoire et de Géographie (National Committee of the Association of Teachers of History and Geography) took action against article 4, paragraph 2 of the Mekachera law (May 22, 2015). They demanded that the legislature "must end practices that constitute an instrumentalization of history curricula in the service of memory obligations" (translated). They further insisted "that the content of history and geography curricula must be based on the state of scientific research for which the university and the National Center for Scientific Research (CNRS) should be sufficient means" (translated). Yet the majority of the legislature remained unimpressed, and thus, in early December 2005, the Ligue des droits de l'homme and a collective of historians issued a petition under the title "We Shall Not Apply Article 4 of the Law of February 23, according to which school curricula must acknowledge the positive role of Colonialism" (translated). Within a month, the petition gathered more than 1,120 signatures, including 572 provided by historians and history teachers.

The historians' opposition, specifically against the law's demand to teach the benefits of colonialism, finally yielded political results. On December 9, 2005, President Chirac declared that "in the Republic, there is no official history. It is not the role of the law to write history. The writing of history is the task of historians" (translated). Presidential intervention no doubt augmented the weight of subsequent actions on the part of historians.

The next such action followed soon, when—on December 12, 2005—nineteen renowned academics and intellectuals signed a new declaration, entitled "Liberté pour l'histoire" (Liberty for history) and founded an association with the same name. In their declaration, they demanded an end to legislative dispositions unworthy of a democratic regime ("dispositions législatives indignes d'un regime démocratique"). They directed their attack broadly against what they called "memory laws," with a derogatory intent, subsuming under this category laws as diverse as the Gayssot Act (aiming at the Shoah and threatening criminal sanctions), the 2001 Armenian genocide recognition law (simply recognizing the genocide), and the Mekachera and the Taubira laws (not threatening criminal sanctions while, however, demanding instructional and research programs). These historians accused the four laws of having restrained the liberty of historians ("restraint la liberté de l'historien") and of having instructed them, under the threat of sanctions ("sous peine de sanctions"), what to do research on and what to find. This was different from previous declarations, in that these intellectuals claimed to speak for all historians.

Yet many historians challenged such claims. Prominent among them, Marcel Dorigny expressed his regret about the shocking amalgam ("amalgam choquant") of laws that the signatories had attacked. Others charged this new group of historians with political bias, demonstrating that members of the group themselves did not stick to their historiographic work, but instead took political positions in divisive public debates. Boris Adjemian quotes Pierre Nora to show that keeping the law out of the task of history writing was certainly not the only objective of the "Liberté pour l'histoire" activists: "Two thousand years of Christian culpability against human rights have been reinvested . . . in broad accusations and radical disqualification of the French nation. And public schooling was sucked into the rupture, with zeal, as it, favoring multiculturalism, found a new mission in national repentance and masochism. Historically the tug boat of humanism, France now became the avant-garde of the universal bad conscience" (Pierre Nora quoted in Adjemian 2012:18, translated).

Other signatories of the declaration expressed concerns about a fractioning ("fragilization") of French society because of a "multiplication of memory laws," and about minorities imposing on the entire nation their particular memories. In short, the "Liberté pour l'histoire" signatories and their spokespersons were not just concerned with the independence of scholarship, but also with an identity of French society, reflected in some of the memory laws, that they did not embrace.

When President Chirac expressed his opposition to article 4, paragraph 2 of the Mekachera law, in response to the earlier and more narrowly conceived objections by historians and teachers, its revocation was almost certainly not the result of the "Liberté pour l'histoire" group, even if the removal followed shortly after their proclamation. Six years later, however, the group's rhetoric did color the political debate over the Boyer law, passed in January 2012, criminalizing denial of the genocide against the Armenians. Its members expressed their opposition to the law in the strongest possible terms, speaking about a civil memory war ("une guerre civile des mémoires"; Nora in Adjemian 2012:23). This language aligns with previous objections against repentance ("contre la repentance") and the victim claims of insufficiently assimilated minorities ("victimisme" des "communautés imparfaitement assimilées"). The new law, Nora argued further, prohibits "all historical research dedicated to one of the first great tragedies of the twentieth century" (translated). He in fact wrote about the risk of a sovietization of history ("risque de soviétisation de l'histoire").

In short, historians made their voices heard in struggles over the appropriate form of memorializing mass atrocity crimes, including the Armenian genocide. The intensity and character of their positions changed over time. Individual interventions turned into collective action. Initially cautious articulations gave way to strong statements driven by political agendas of different sorts, prominent among them concerns with the purification of Western, Christian, and specifically French history.

Our analysis of legislative debates suggests that historians' critiques and legislative voices reinforced each other. Concerns with the role of the legislature in writing history certainly featured prominently in Assembly and Senate deliberations. In the November 2001 Senate debate, twelve out of nineteen interventions raised the issue of legislative history writing. The respective numbers for subsequent sessions are, for the Assembly debate of May 2006, six out of eight; for the Assembly debate of October 2006, thirteen out of twenty-one; for the Senate debate of May 2011, nine out of sixteen; and for the Assembly debate of December 2011, eleven out of twenty. Finally, and topping all others, in the January 2012 Senate debate, twenty-seven out of thirty interventions raised the issue of legislative history writing. Not all of these came from challengers. Yet, in this concluding debate, the majority of legislators who addressed the issue were in opposition to the bill (fifteen opposed and twelve in favor).

In general, the "role of the legislature in the writing of history" and the "constitutionality" of legislative interventions are among the most frequently raised themes in the final Senate debate on the Boyer law, the attempted criminalization of denial of the Armenian genocide (table 2). Senators who raised the issue and opposed the Armenian memory laws clearly aligned with the skepticism articulated by influential historians. This alignment shows in a speech Jean-Pierre Sueur, rapporteur and chair of the Constitutional Law Commission, delivered in the Senate. Senator Sueur had spoken—as we saw earlier—in opposition to the law. Here, he partly repeats the reasoning in the commission's report:

> The Commission inquired into the legitimacy of the legislative intervention in the field of history . . . considering that the adoption of resolutions and the organization of commemorations probably constitute more appropriate methods to express the Nation's solidarity with the suffering endured by the victims. It has further reasoned that the creation of a criminal offense of the challenge and the outrageous minimization of genocides recognized by the law would constitute a substantial risk of offending against several principles of our Constitution—especially the principle of legality of criminalization and penalties [*nullum crimen, nulla poena sine lege*], the principle of the freedom of speech and the principle of the liberty of research. (p. 5, translated)

In an interview I conducted with Senator Sueur, he confirmed his strong identification with some of the "Liberté pour l'histoire" positions. He referred particularly to the arguments of Pierre Nora, one of the main drivers of this movement. Clearly, a conversion of scientific into political capital was at work when close ties between politics and academia played out in this legislative drama concerning memory laws. This affected, especially, laws concerning the recognition of the Armenian genocide and the criminalization of its denial. Scholarly interventions colored debates on the Senate floor, and they may have motivated referral of the Boyer law to the CC.

Epistemic Politics and Foreign Policy: The Turkish State and the French Legislative Process

Attempts to intervene in legislation concerning the Armenian genocide did not just originate within the French Republic and French society. Most noteworthy,

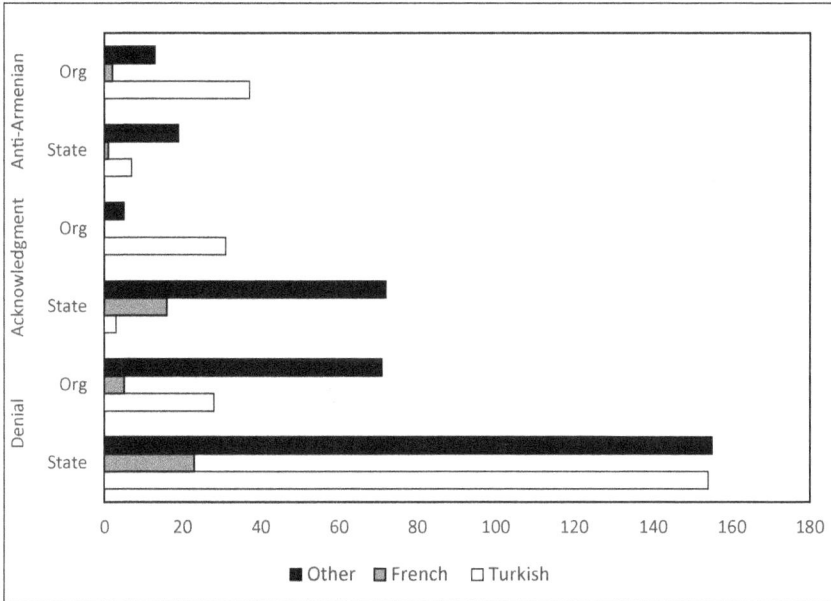

FIGURE 11. Frequency of types of actions and actors identified by Collectif VAN (sample of every third entry) between 2006 and 2016.

the Turkish state intensely sought to affect the outcome of the legislative process, as indicated by an analysis of data on denialist acts collected by a civil society group, Collectif VAN (Vigilance Arménienne contre le Négationnisme), since 2006.

Figure 11 shows that the vast majority of actions measured by Collectif VAN are denialist actions, as opposed to either statements of recognition or anti-Armenian actions such as vandalism of memorials and hate crimes. This is not surprising, given that the movement names itself "vigilance against denialism." Further, most denials result from state action, and almost half of these are statements articulated by the Turkish state and its representatives. Note that the more than 150 Turkish actions documented here tell only part of the story, because figure 11 is based on a random sample of one-third of the incidents recorded by Collectif VAN. The actual number of known denialist interventions by the Turkish state in the ten-year period is thus likely to be closer to 450.

Numbers alone never tell the full story, and a few examples suffice to illustrate the prominence of Turkish actors and the character of their statements:

- The passing of the recognition law by the National Assembly in May 1998 prompted protest letters from the Turkish president (Süleyman Demirel), prime minister (Mesut Yilmaz), foreign minister (İsmail Cem Ipekci), and parliamentary Speaker (Hikmet Çetin). In addition, Turkey suspended the purchase of missiles from France, and it canceled a previously scheduled high-level meeting between officials of both countries.

- In response, some French officials expressed hope that the resolution would die in the Senate. That response only partially calmed the concerns of Turkish government representatives. They sought the actual defeat of the bill. They expressed concerns that the adoption of a genocide resolution in France could set an example for other parliaments in Europe and elsewhere. Some argued publicly that such a bill might encourage Armenian militants like the gunmen who killed thirty-four Turkish diplomats and their relatives in the 1970s and 1980s.

- After attempts in May 2006 by the National Assembly to criminalize denial of the Armenian genocide, Turkish officials warned France of "irreparable damage" to bilateral ties if the bill passed. Turkey temporarily recalled its ambassador to France and suspended military collaboration.

- After the National Assembly actually passed a bill to criminalize denial of all genocides recognized by French law, interventions intensified. Turkey halted diplomatic consultations and military cooperation. Turkish lawmakers joined their government to denounce the bill and called on France to investigate its own atrocities in Algeria and Rwanda. Turkish Foreign Minister Ahmet Davutoğlu stated that the bill violated the spirit of the French Revolution and of European principles like that of free speech. Prime Minister Recep Tayyip Erdoğan (later president) recalled Turkey's ambassador and canceled the annually issued permission for French military planes to use Turkish airspace and for French naval vessels to enter Turkish harbors. The French air force now had to apply for permission for each flight. Turkey finally refused to cooperate with France in joint European Union projects and declined to participate in an economic summit meeting scheduled to take place in Paris in January of 2012.

We do not know if these objections and actions affected the French government and the outcome of the legislative process. We do know, however, that legislators worried that Armenian memory laws might harm French-Turkish relations. Their concerns permeated all legislative sessions on the laws pertaining to the memory of the Armenian genocide. In a corpus of 113 speeches given in six sessions, thirty-two representatives, senators, or ministers addressed Turkish-French relations. Seventy-four arguments pertained to international relations more broadly, including Armenian-Turkish relations and complications for a potential admission of Turkey to the European Union.

Again, examples must suffice. During the Senate session of November 7, 2000, Senator Jacques-Richard Delong, of the conservative Rally for the Republic, argued that the benefit of genocide recognition would not outweigh an almost certain backlash from Turkey and a complication of French-Turkish relations.[21] Jean-Jack

Queyranne, minister for relations with Parliament, expressed similar concerns in the same session. He stressed that France had worked for years to bring Turkey closer to Europe, and he argued that the passage of the bill could reverse such improvements. He referred to Dominique de Villepin, at the time chief of staff for President Chirac and later foreign minister, who—according to Queyranne— was concerned that the recognition bill, if passed, would damage France's relationship with Turkey.[22] Philippe Douste-Blazy, minister of foreign affairs, similarly intervened to speak against the bill. He, too, argued that France could easily anger Turkey with the legislation.[23]

Ministers and representatives expressed similar concerns during the National Assembly deliberation on the criminalization bill of October 12, 2006. Catherine Colona, minister for European affairs, spoke against the bill on behalf of the government. One of three reasons she cited was the government's concern that its passing could have detrimental effects on France's relationship with Turkey.[24] Socialist Charles Gautier expressed similar objections and received applause from a few members of the Socialist Party and from most of the center-right UMP.[25] Senator Bruno Giles, a proponent of the law, and thus in a minority position within his UMP faction, contended that most constitutional arguments were actually rooted in economic worries that Turkey could act against French business interests.[26] Concerns about French-Turkish foreign and economic relations indeed permeated the legislative debates until their final stages. During the Senate session of January 23, 2012, Isabelle Pasquet, member of the left-wing CRC, further contemplated that foreign policy complications could spill over into domestic unrest, pointing at the risk of intensified outrage from Turkish protesters.[27]

Yet Turkish threats did not impress all legislators. Some doubted that Turkish protestations would actually translate into deteriorating international or economic ties. For example, during the National Assembly session of December 22, 2011, Representative François Pupponi, a member of the left-wing SRC (Socialiste, républicain et citoyen), used his speaking time to summarize five reasons to vote for the proposed bill. They included his belief that it is not productive to continue a relationship, in fact a strong partnership, with Turkey, based on taboos and false pretenses.[28] During the Senate session of January 23, 2012, Socialist Luc Carvounas pointed out that in 2002, a year after the passing of the recognition act had evoked Turkish outrage, trade between the two countries actually increased by 22 percent. He concluded that foreign policy considerations should not preclude a vote for the bill. Legislators should instead focus on remembering the genocide.[29]

Yet others were willing to accept negative foreign policy outcomes should they in fact materialize. At this point, with the Sarkozy government favoring the bill, the minister in attendance also pleaded for a "yes" vote. Patrick Ollier, minister for relations with Parliament, concluded his introductory remarks to the Senate by stating that the government was aware of potential implications the legislation could have in regard to French-Turkish relations, but the government was still in support.[30]

In short, many French legislators across party lines did indeed take Turkish threats and concerns about French-Turkish political, economic, and military relations seriously. Further, actors responsible for foreign policy dominated among those who expressed concerns. Many had not only French-Turkish relations in mind, but also relations between Armenia and Turkey and between Turkey and the European Union. The latter relationship was a special concern for the Left, which had worked with particular intensity for Turkish admission to the EU. Prominently, Daniel Cohn-Bendit of the Green Party, leader of the 1968 student movement and son of survivors of the Shoah, opposed the criminalizing bill, motivated, he argued, by the desire to advance Turkey's EU admission.

More broadly, we observe a tension between human rights principles on the one hand, including the desire to represent and remember mass atrocities as crimes, and the foreign policy field on the other. The tension results in part from the concern of foreign policy makers with diplomatic capital, built through networks of international collaboration. It is intensified by a desire to achieve substantive outcomes that often collides with the process orientation of human rights law and the values focus of its supporters. Previous studies have demonstrated such tension in debates surrounding human rights violations in the former Yugoslavia (Hagan 2003) and in Darfur (Savelsberg 2015).

Again, foreign policy concerns may have impeded, but did not derail, the French legislative projects pertaining to the memory of the Armenian genocide. Yet the CC had not yet spoken. I now turn to that final and decisive stage of the French story of Armenian memory legislation.

The Constitutional Council, the Political Field, and Armenian Genocide Laws

The final act regarding the Boyer law, which had criminalized denial of the Armenian genocide, was the Constitutional Council decision that declared the law unconstitutional. The CC made this decision on February 28, 2012—just one month after a majority of the Senate had passed the law. It proceeded most economically, addressing only one of several grievances expressed by the legislators: the charge of an unconstitutional limitation on the freedom of expression and communication. In the words of the CC:

> Article 1 of the law referred punishes the denial or minimization of the existence of one or more crimes of genocide recognized as such under French law; that in thereby punishing the denial of the existence and the legal classification of crimes which Parliament itself has recognized and classified as such, Parliament has imposed an unconstitutional limitation on the exercise of freedom of expression and communication; that accordingly, without any requirement to examine the other grounds

for challenge, Article 1 of the law referred must be ruled unconstitutional; that Article 2, which is inseparably linked to it, must also be ruled unconstitutional. (Conseil Constitutionnel—Décision n° 2012–647 DC du 28 février 2012)

We do not know if considerations of constitutionality alone informed this decision, as suggested by the formal reasoning and the above quotation. Might political dynamics have played a role? Might CC members have been more concerned with power, with direct or mediated pressure from the academy and/or the Turkish Republic, than with norms? Might constitutional arguments only have disguised political intent?

Two members of the CC whom I was able to interview articulated their conviction that indeed, constitutional concerns were decisive. One expressed his dismay at Turkish news media's interpretation of the decision as a victory for the Turkish cause and a confirmation of the denial of genocide. He added credibility to his account by his familiarity with the history of the genocide and the centennial exhibits—seemingly supporting his identification with the Armenian cause.

This constitutionality position is supported further by the description of the CC by its (sole and former) sociologist member, Dominique Schnapper (2010). Schnapper, after concluding her term, published a book in which she highlights the central role of a staff of highly trained jurists who prepare the CC's decisions. The book's core message seeks to instill confidence in the institution. It speaks to the continuity of the CC's actions, the core role of the general secretariat, and the weight of professional jurists who prepare the dossiers for its members. Professional and highly competent jurists, Schnapper argues, make sure that decisions are rationally founded on reference to jurisprudence and precedent.

Others insist, instead, that political rationales played a central role in the CC's decision regarding the Boyer law. Leading French Armenians, especially, strongly believe that the articulation of constitutional concerns are mere rationalizations, a formal façade behind which are hidden political motives. Several members of Armenian civil society pointed, in interviews, to close ties between a high-level Turkish official and a prominent member of the CC. Information circulating within French Armenian circles suggests that the decisive communication between these two actors occurred just days before the CC overturned the Boyer law. I can neither confirm nor reject this position. To understand the impact of power politics on the CC, we need a sociology of the CC that, to my knowledge, does not exist to date. Its construction, summarized on the CC's own website, certainly suggests close ties with the political field: "The Constitutional Council was established by the Constitution of the Fifth Republic adopted on 4 October 1958. It is a court vested with various powers, including in particular the review of the constitutionality of legislation. . . . The Constitutional Council is comprised of nine members who are appointed for nine-year terms. The members are appointed by the President of the Republic and the presidents of each of the Houses of Parliament (National Assembly and Senate)."[31]

The staffing of the CC is, not surprisingly, highly political, which is reflected in its membership. Almost all members at the time of the Boyer law decision had been appointed after successful political or administrative careers. Jean-Louis Debré, then president of the CC, had previously served as president of the National Assembly (2002–7). He had been minister of the interior from 1995 to 1997, during the presidency of Jacques Chirac. Jacques Barrot had previously occupied several ministerial positions, including those of minister of health, minister of trade, and minister of labor. Claire Bazy Malaurie had held high-level administrative posts in the ministries for transportation and health. Michel Joseph Charasse is a career politician, holding the position of a senator before President Sarkozy appointed him to the CC. Renaud Denoix de Saint Marc is a lawyer who had served as head of the Conseil d'État before his appointment to the CC. Jacqueline de Guillenchmidt had been a member of a national council that regulates electronic media. Hubert Haenel was a career politician and senator before Senate President Gerard Lercher appointed him to the CC. Finally, Pierre Steinmetz had pursued a high-level government administrative career, previously serving as chief of staff of Prime Minister Jean-Pierre Raffarin. Guy Canivet is the only exception. He joined the CC following a career as a judge. The background of the CC's members thus differs radically from that of members of the U.S. Supreme Court, for example, or the German Verfassungsgericht, where successful judicial careers pave the way to membership. The CC's constitution confirms the strong tie with the political field marked in the depiction of the "French triangle" (figure 10).

In short, a politically oriented CC, albeit supported by a professional and well-trained staff of lawyers, decided on the Boyer law in a highly politicized environment. On one side, civil society organizations, especially Armenian ethnic organizations, pleaded for the law. On the other side, the Turkish state and its representatives exerted substantial pressure, threatening complications to political, military, and trade relations between Turkey and the French Republic. Were these, or the critical sentiments historians had expressed, on the minds of CC members? They certainly were aware of them, given their high visibility in public debates and reflection in legislative sessions. Yet, as the CC decided to declare the law unconstitutional, it referred neither to Turkish interests nor to the concerns of historians. The explicit reasoning backing the legal decision follows purely formal and constitutional arguments. We will encounter formal reasoning again when examining court disputes in chapter 8, and there, too, massive substantive battles over genocide knowledge turn out to be driving forces. Further, in both the legislative and the judicial cases, the impact of formal decisions was substantive and political, in unexpected ways, a finding to which I turn in chapter 9.

CONCLUSIONS: BATTLES IN THE FRENCH POLITICAL FIELD AND EPISTEMIC OUTCOMES

Increased recognition of the Armenian genocide may be indicative of the weight of global human rights scripts in the current era. This in-depth study of the French case has shown us, however, that recognition can mean different things, and that— even in an era of human rights hegemony—struggles over knowledge pervade the political field before a decision on recognition is reached and partially defeated. The French case shows further that ethnic representation and civil society mobilization likely affect the outcome of epistemic struggles in the political field, not surprising in a democratic context. The analysis teaches us further that specifics of epistemic struggles in the political field, their unfolding and outcome, depend on the relationship between the political and neighboring fields. In the French context, the academic field has particular weight. Similarly, the realm of constitutional law aligns closely with the political field. In the end, the legislative process— advanced by civil society mobilization but constrained by what I call the French triangle and by foreign policy pressure—resulted in the formal recognition of the Armenian genocide and legislation criminalizing denial of this genocide, as well as a successful challenge of the criminalizing law by a sizable group of legislators before the Constitutional Council. France thus partakes in the global trend toward recognition, but recognition here takes a specific shape in light of the particular institutional arrangements and conditions of the political field.

Epistemic Struggles in the Legal Field— Speech Rights, Memory, and Genocide Curricula before an American Court

by Joachim J. Savelsberg and Brooke B. Chambers

Epistemic struggles unfold not only in the political field, but also in courts of law. Particularly in the United States, the legal field serves as a frequent battle-ground when questions of knowledge and denial are at stake. In line with the neo-Durkheimian tradition discussed in chapter 6, such battles take the form of rituals, suited to impress on the public a sense of shared norms and facts, right and wrong (Smith 2008).

Struggles between denialist intent and the desire to recognize genocide unfolded in several legal disputes. Prominent among them was *Griswold v. Driscoll*, a court case carried out in Massachusetts between 2005 and 2010. At stake were guidelines for teaching about the Armenian genocide issued by the Massachusetts Department of Education. The case pitted actors who self-defined as free speech advocates, but were considered denialists by their opponents, against the Department of Education. While several actors on the side of the State agreed that this was a case about free speech, many simultaneously expressed concern with memory and values, considering *Griswold v. Driscoll* a fight for recognition of the violence against the Ottoman Armenians as genocide. Examining this case, we discovered fascinating mechanisms. First, a subterranean engagement with substantive concerns took place under the cover of formal arguments. Second, a form of decoupling separated "front stage" actors organized around free speech rights from "back stage" actors concerned with denial of the genocide.

While this chapter builds on a long tradition of work on the cultural effects of prosecutions and criminal trials of perpetrators of mass violence (Marrus 2008; Pendas 2006; Hagan 2003; Savelsberg and King 2007, 2011; Savelsberg 2015; Savelsberg and Nyseth Brehm 2015), it goes beyond previous work in three ways. First, it shifts attention from trials of suspected perpetrators to court cases that explicitly address the generation and dissemination of knowledge about mass atrocity and genocide. Second, it highlights the strategic use of trials and their cultural potential by powerful actors who explicitly seek to affect knowledge about the past. Third, while taking the rules of the legal game and the institutional logic of formal law seriously, this chapter also investigates cultural effects of trials that result from informal aspects of legal proceedings, their initiation, their unfolding, and their use as platforms from which to talk to a broader public during and after the trial. Participants use the proceedings as a stage. Some of their arguments, even if not formally relevant, might yet affect court decisions; they certainly do reach various audiences inside and outside of the court.

INSIGHTS FROM PAST SOCIO-LEGAL LITERATURE: RITUALS, LAW, AND KNOWLEDGE

Scholarship has shed light on cultural effects of trials, the role of strategic and powerful actors in legal rituals, formal and substantive concerns in legal proceedings, and tensions between free speech claims and fights against denial. Insights from this literature can help us understand struggles over knowledge concerning the Armenian genocide. It is thus worth diving into this literature before examining a significant judicial fight over genocide versus free speech claims, carried out in a U.S. court, and pitting Turkish denialism against Armenian struggles for recognition: *Griswold v. Driscoll*.

Rituals and Law in the Hands of Powerful and Strategic Actors

Power and culture are mutually constitutive, generally and in the legal field. Trials produce culture—in this case knowledge about genocide—while simultaneously being shaped by interests and power. Consider the International Military Tribunal (IMT) at Nuremberg. Responding to the Nazi crimes by way of a trial was not a foregone conclusion. The victorious powers disagreed about appropriate responses. President Franklin D. Roosevelt eventually agreed to holding trials, "determined that the question of Hitler's guilt—and the guilt of his gangsters—must not be left open to future debate. The whole nauseating matter should be spread out on a permanent record under oath by witnesses and with all the written documents" (according to his confidant Judge Samuel Rosenman, cited in Landsman 2005:6; see also Douglas 2001). One of Roosevelt's goals was to undermine domestic support for American isolationism that had grown during the post–World War I era.

History-writing expectations, paired with anti-isolationist leanings, not only contributed to the initiation of the IMT. They also colored the structure of the trial. Words by Robert Jackson, American chief prosecutor at the IMT, indicate that much: "Unless we write the record of this movement with clarity and precision, we cannot blame the future if in days of peace it finds incredible the accusatory generalities uttered during the war. *We must establish incredible events by credible evidence*" (quoted in Landsman 2005:6–7; our emphasis). More specifically, charging a relatively small number of leading Nazis, the Allies allowed the majority of Germans to be ritually divorced from their past leaders. Cultural sociologist Bernhard Giesen (2004a) calls this a decoupling effect, through which many are (at least judicially) absolved while guilt is attached to a few. In addition, the organizers of the trial selected defendants carefully so that each would represent a major organization of the Nazi state. The expected guilty verdicts thus not only served as degradation ceremonies toward the defendants (Garfinkel 1956) but also delegitimized the organizations they represented, separating them ritually from the majority of the German people.

Such strategizing continued in the subsequent Nuremberg trials, held by the United States in the U.S.-occupied zone of Germany. Each trial was dedicated to a select number of individuals from different professional groups such as lawyers, physicians, and industrialists who had collaborated with the Nazi state. Again, a decoupling effect was to separate the majority of professionals from a small number of perpetrators as historian Michael Marrus (2008) critically documents for the Nuremberg "Doctors' trial."

Identifiable strategic actors in the realms of politics and law thus initiated the post–World War II trials and determined their structure. They sought to generate an image of the past in line with the law, but also in line with their geopolitical interests. These actors depended on power and authority, which the total defeat of the Nazi state and the military occupation of Germany provided.

Actor-driven intent, backed by power and authority, is certainly not unique to the IMT, as documented by political scientists, historians, and sociologists for many other court cases against perpetrators of mass atrocity. A prominent example is the trial of Adolf Eichmann, the organizer of the transportation of Jews to the extermination camps. The Israeli secret service captured and abducted Eichmann from Argentina, his place of refuge, and the Israeli government put him on trial in Jerusalem (Arendt 1963). David Ben-Gurion, Israel's prime minister at the time, was determined to reawaken Israelis' engagement with the Holocaust, especially among the younger generation. In Germany, Fritz Bauer, minister of justice of the state of Hesse, was the driving force toward the initiation of the Frankfurt Auschwitz trial of 1962–63 (Pendas 2006). To break the silence about the

Holocaust that had ruled supreme during the first postwar decades, Bauer wanted a single trial for many defendants, and his efforts bore fruit. All of these initiatives aimed at (re-)awakening memory and shaping knowledge.

Interest-driven strategic actors also drove recent international judicial responses to mass atrocity. In the case of Yugoslavia, they include jurists and prosecutors (Hagan 2003), diplomats (Scheffer 2012), and social movement leaders (Neier 2012). Consider further the UN Security Council's 2005 referral of the situation in Darfur, Sudan, to the International Criminal Court (ICC) (Savelsberg 2015). Without the massive engagement of American civil society groups under the umbrella of the Save Darfur movement, the George W. Bush administration would likely have vetoed a referral of the case to the court to which it stood in opposition. Eventually, ICC intervention substantially colored the representation of the violence of Darfur in prominent news media across the Western world (Savelsberg and Nyseth Brehm 2015).

In short, a study of cultural consequences of human rights trials needs to consider social, political, and legal actors who initiate and structure court cases. We think of these legal actors as knowledge entrepreneurs with strategic interests and varying degrees of power. This is in line with Maurice Halbwachs's (1992) arguments regarding the presentism of collective memory, the notion that interests of today's actors shape memories of past events, even if in a path-dependent fashion (Olick 1999).

From the Legal Field and Its Rules of the Game to Substantivized Law

Once strategic actors decide to pursue the production of knowledge through legal trials, they avail themselves of a potentially powerful tool. Yet they also pay a price by tying themselves to the rules of the law (Thompson 1975). Pierre Bourdieu (1987), examining law as one specific social field within modern societies, highlights that, like actors in all other fields, legal actors seek to advance their own power and status. Yet ways to secure power and status are constrained by each field's particular rules of the game. Socialized into such constraints, actors develop a specific habitus, a set of relatively fixed dispositions that reflect their trajectories and their position within the field (Bourdieu 1987; see also Emirbayer and Johnson 2008). Rules of the legal field prescribe, for example, who can charge a crime, who can speak at a trial, what utterances the judge will allow, and which evidence the jury can consider when deciding on the guilt of defendants. In the adversarial system, the judge acts as an umpire, ensuring that trial participants follow these rules, disqualifying statements and actions that offend against them.

Playing by the rules of the game includes adhering to a specific logic that is inherent to the institutions within the field. In criminal law, for example, a final and binding decision has to be reached regarding the criminal liability of individual defendants. Social structures and larger cultural patterns that enabled a murderous event may interest sociologists, but they are irrelevant for the court. In addition, to secure due process, only some kinds of evidence are admissible in the court of law, different from those a social scientist would consider. Further, a trial's time horizon tends to be limited. Longer historical trajectories, of central interest to historians, are immaterial. Finally, the decision of a criminal court is binary, between guilty and not guilty, disregarding shades of gray that a social psychologist would take seriously. These elements of the institutional logic of criminal law become absorbed into the habitus of lawyers who operate in the context of criminal courts.

Recent scholarship has identified pronounced traces of such logic in the narratives generated through criminal trials. These traces are particularly evident when contrasted with competing narratives, generated in other social fields with different rules of the game (e.g., Savelsberg and King 2011, on the My Lai trial; Pendas 2006, on the Frankfurt Auschwitz trial; Marrus 2008, on the "Doctors' trial").

Yet, while formal law, with its rules of the game and its institutional logic, demands obedience from legal actors, and while it does color legal representations, a sole focus on formal rules misses important aspects of law in action.

First, participants in court proceedings may use the court as a stage to express their understanding of events, even if these accounts do not enter into the court's record or affect its decision. Second, what participants perform, whether it is formally admissible or not, potentially affects perceptions and actions of audiences outside the court. Third, legal decision makers operate with varying degrees of discretion that leave room for extralegal considerations. Discretion varies by type of law and historical time. Some eras celebrate formal features of law, while others open the gates to, in Weberian terms, substantivation of law, an increasing orientation of legal decision making toward extralegal criteria (Savelsberg 1992; Weber 1978; relatedly, see Unger 1976; Nonet and Selznick 1978; Stryker 1989). Such criteria may affect which facts of the case will be considered, and to what degree, in court decisions (e.g., offense versus social context), and they may concern the goals toward which law is oriented (e.g., retribution versus social peace).

The notion of substantivized law is consistent with Bourdieu's view of habitus, which, despite its focus on rules, also leaves room for improvisation. Bourdieu referred to jazz musicians or basketball players for an illustration, but we may extend the argument to lawyers. No matter the discipline, players would be disqualified if they did not follow the rules of their game, but they would be incapable of playing successfully were they not skilled improvisers.

Max Weber (1978) points at three driving forces that are likely to advance substantivation. First, legal clients to whom the notions of formal law are alien seek pragmatic solutions to their problems. Second, social activists seek interpretations of law that reach beyond formal rights to embrace social justice. Third, lawyers resist a law that reduces them, using Weber's terms, to automatons that, after one inserts the facts and the fees, spew out the decision and opinion. Lawyers' social status, after all, depends on the exercise of an appropriate level of discretion. In court cases involving grave human rights violations, each of these three factors weighs strongly against the pursuit of purely formal law. Audiences are especially alert when incidents of mass violence are at stake. Courts, responsive to their sensitivities, encourage public attention. The IMT, for example, removed the back wall of the courtroom to allow for a larger representation of the world's media. Contemporary human rights courts such as the ICC run substantial media departments and set up sophisticated websites.

Public attention intensifies further when movement organizations and NGOs are involved in the mobilization of legal action. Regarding the consideration of extralegal outcomes of trials, stakes tend to be especially high in cases of mass atrocity crimes, even more so when violence is ongoing, or when political or military leaders might easily reignite violence or recede from peace agreements (Savelsberg 2015). Similarly, when historic cases of mass atrocity are at stake and identities of entire national, ethnic, racial, or religious groups are tied to the acknowledgment of past victimization, courts are under substantial pressure to be mindful of their sensitivities. Human rights cases thus bring a variety of issues into the courtroom: emotions and values as well as cultural trauma and collective identities (Alexander et al. 2004).[1]

In short, we take formal law, Bourdieu's rules of the game, law's institutional logic, and the related legal habitus seriously, but we also recognize discretion, room for improvisation, and the consideration of extralegal criteria in court processes. Captured in the Weberian term *substantivation of law* (Savelsberg 1992), conceived of by others as technocratized law (Stryker 1989), responsive law (Nonet and Selznick 1978), or neoliberal law (Unger 1976), we expect these forces to have special weight in court cases that involve issues of human rights and historical responsibility as they clash with free speech claims.

Free Speech Claims and Historical Responsibility in Court: Toward the Armenian Case

Moving beyond court cases against actors charged with mass atrocity crimes, scholars have now begun to examine lawsuits against those charged with misrepresenting past episodes of mass violence. Several factors account for the increase of such cases that typically pit free speech claims against demands for recognition of past violence. First, legal responses to human rights violations are historically new, and they have increased in the post–World War II era. Second, groups that have experienced victimization increasingly demand recognition. African Americans during and after the civil rights movement (and with renewed determination in 2020) and Jews in the post-Shoah era are but examples. Acknowledgment of their suffering reinforced the desire for recognition among those whose suffering had previously been silenced. In this climate, court battles began to erupt against actors who denied victimization and, in reverse, against others whose claims of genocide the alleged perpetrators deemed defamatory.

The case against Princeton historian Bernard Lewis cited in chapter 7 is an early example, and more detail on that case will be helpful here. On May 19, 1985, an advertisement appeared in the *New York Times* and the *Washington Post*, sponsored by the Assembly of Turkish American Associations (ATAA). This ad cast doubt on the identification of the violence against Ottoman Armenians during World War I as genocide. Sixty-nine academics signed the ad, including Lewis, one of America's foremost authorities on the history of the Ottoman Empire. The action sought to discourage members of the U.S. House of Representatives from passing Resolution 192, which would have applied the term *genocide* to the mass killings of Armenians. Eight years later, in 1993, Lewis traveled to France on the occasion of the publication of two of his books in French. In an interview with journalists of the daily *Le Monde*, he praised the Turkish government, argued in favor of Turkey's admission to the European Union, and—when asked about the Armenian genocide—referred to it as "the Armenian version of the story." This interview provoked not only a rejoinder by thirty intellectuals and academics, but also civil law suits brought by the Forum of Armenian Associations of France and by a Committee for the Defense of the Armenian Cause. The latter group simultaneously initiated criminal proceedings, based on the Gayssot Act, passed by the French legislature in 1990, aimed at Holocaust denial but framed more broadly. The trial was held on October 14, 1994. Lewis offered a partial correction of his position, but he insisted on the absence of explicit orders by Ottoman leaders to exterminate Armenian life, a precondition for the application of the term *genocide* according to the Genocide Convention. The court eventually found Lewis guilty and sentenced him to a symbolic monetary penalty of one franc (Ternon 1999) and to compensating the charging groups for their legal expenses, amounting to 14,000 francs.

Almost two decades later, another European case attracted attention. Doğu Perinçek, a Turkish politician and lawyer, chair of the left-wing nationalist Patriotic Party, had publicly declared—during a visit to Switzerland—that the killing and deportation of Armenians in the context of World War I was a necessary consequence of the war and did not constitute genocide. The Swiss authorities prosecuted Perinçek, and the court convicted him of racial discrimination in March 2007. The judges relied on the official Swiss recognition of the Armenian genocide and on article 261, paragraph 4 of the criminal code that penalizes denial and justification of genocide. After a Swiss appeals court confirmed the decision, Perinçek filed an appeal to the European Court of Human Rights (ECHR). In a five-to-two vote, the ECHR overruled the Swiss decision. It argued that Perinçek's statements did not entail a call for violence, that free speech is legitimate in the search for historical truth, that the qualification of anti-Armenian violence by the Ottoman Empire is still debated, and that it is not up to judges to decide whether the claimant's statements threaten the identity of a people (for details, see Langer 2014). The court also referred to Spanish and French court cases with similar outcomes.

Generally, the position of European courts seems to have shifted, during the 1990s and 2000s, toward a more robust protection of free speech rights, known from U.S. law, and against the legal enforcement of recognition claims by victimized groups.

In light of such developments abroad, how did U.S. courts decide in free speech cases that pertain to the Armenian genocide? Material to answer the question abounds, because claimants—typically involving Turkish lobbying groups—contested the use of the term *genocide* on several occasions. In 2010, for example, the Turkish Coalition of America (TCA) sued the University of Minnesota and its Center for Holocaust and Genocide Studies (CHGS). On its website, the CHGS included the following disclaimer alongside TCA and other Turkish sources: "Warnings should be given to students writing papers that they should not use these sites because of denial, support by an unknown organization, or contents that are a strange mix of fact and opinion" (*Turkish Coalition of America, Inc. v. Bruininks*, 0:10-cv-04760-DWF-FLN [MN District] [2010], Mar. 30, Memorandum and Order:3). The complaint claimed that CHGS engaged in censorship. Though the CHGS later removed the list of unreliable sources and replaced it with a general disclaimer about vigilance in evaluating source credibility, the TCA lost the lawsuit on its censorship claims.

Another instance of litigating discussion of the Armenian genocide unfolded in California in *Movsesian v. Victoria Versicherung AG*. In this case, the legal conflict was initially over insurance claims. In 2000, California passed a law that extended the statute of limitations for insurance claims made by survivors of the Armenian genocide who had lacked the resources to comply with the time limits. The insurance companies claimed that the California law was unconstitutional because the State had used the genocide label, thus interfering with the federal government's foreign policy authority. Remember that the U.S. federal government had not recognized the Armenian genocide. The Ninth Circuit Court of Appeals overturned the initial district court decision that had upheld the extension, ruling that the California law overstepped state authority and violated the foreign affairs doctrine (*Movsesian v. Victoria Versicherung AG*, 07–56722 [U.S. Court of Appeals, 9th Circuit]).

Lawsuits initiated by Turkish or Turkish American organizations, often in alliance with lawyers specializing in free speech cases, do not unfold in a vacuum. Turkish engagement against genocide claims had intensified in the 1970s, partially in response to the first modern historical studies by Armenian American scholars such as Richard Hovannisian (2002) and V. N. Dadrian (2002) and the consideration by Congress of recognizing the Armenian genocide (Zarifian 2014, 2018). In 1975, Turkey hired the public relations firm Manning Selvage & Lee, and later it hired additional firms, including Hill & Knowlton (which had earlier served the tobacco industry against claims that smoking constituted a health risk) (Mamigonian 2015). Mustafa Şükrü Elekdağ, Turkey's new ambassador to Washington, played a major role. Furthermore, 1982 witnessed the foundation of an Institute for Turkish Studies at Georgetown University, established with a grant by the Turkish government and directed by Ottoman scholar Heath Lowry. Additional funding came from the defense industry, with an interest in weapons exports to Turkey. In 1985, Lowry crafted statements for advertisements in the *New York Times* and the *Washington Post*, cited above, that challenged the genocide claim. Lowry also wrote critical reviews on scholarship that acknowledged the Armenian genocide and sent them to the Turkish ambassador in Washington, who almost literally used these reviews in letters to prominent scholars, encouraging them to adopt his (or Lowry's) critical arguments for future publications (Smith, Markussen, and Lifton 1999). In 2009, the TCA funded the establishment of a Turkish Studies Project under the leadership of Hakan Yavuz at the University of Utah. The project was to become the source for numerous denialist claims and attacks on genocide scholars such as Hans-Lukas Kieser. Developments culminated in the 2008 claim by ATAA president Ergün Kirlikovali that "The Turks are the new Jews. Genocide crowds are the new KKK" (quoted in Mamigonian 2015:76). Plaintiffs in *Griswold v. Driscoll* (and similar cases) cited publications of these institutions as authoritative sources of knowledge from which they drew in forming legal arguments.

In short, in a politically and affectively charged atmosphere, strategic actors seek to mobilize law in battles over recognition of mass violence as genocide, here in regard to the Ottoman Armenians. In epistemic struggles, actors use formal arguments, drawing on free speech rights and substantive claims involving historical truth and issues of dignity and identity.

A COURT CASE AND ITS CONTEXT: *GRISWOLD V. DRISCOLL*

The *Griswold v. Driscoll* case, regarding guidelines issued by the Massachusetts Department of Education for teaching about the Armenian genocide, lends itself to a sociological exploration of epistemic struggles over genocide recognition in legal contexts and their mobilizing force. Massachusetts is home to one of the largest Armenian American communities in the United States. Watertown, a suburb of Boston, is the site of both the Armenian Museum of America and the *Armenian Weekly*, a publication focused on issues of interest to Armenian Americans. Neighboring Belmont is the seat of the National Association for Armenian Studies and Research. It is thus not surprising that Massachusetts has a long history of supporting Armenian Americans, for example through regular April 24 gubernatorial proclamations and legislative resolutions, beginning in 1965, that recognize the Armenian genocide.

Below, we introduce the main actors and basic features of the case, describe our data, and subsequently juxtapose a formal account of the legal proceedings with a substantivized, value-driven alternative understanding of the case's initiation, unfolding, and audience reception.

Basics of the Case

In August 1998, the Massachusetts General Court approved chapter 276 of the annual Acts and Resolves, legislating that the Massachusetts Board of Education create a document to provide curricular guidelines on the teaching of genocide and human rights in the state's schools. The court called for the board to include discussion of the slave trade, the Holocaust, and the Armenian genocide, among other cases it might see fit to include in the document. On January 15, 1999, the board released an initial draft of this curriculum guide for public feedback. "The Massachusetts Guide to Choosing and Using Curricular Materials on Genocide and Human Rights Issues" provided brief summaries of historical human rights abuses accompanied by lists of suggested sources for teachers to utilize in their classrooms. Within the initial review process, individuals or groups were invited to provide the Board of Education with suggested changes or additional sources.

Over the subsequent years, the content of this guide was contested in federal court in the *Griswold v. Driscoll* case, at both the district and appellate levels. The court case unfolded in four steps. On October 26, 2005, a group of students, parents, teachers, and the ATAA filed a lawsuit against the Department of Education and other actors before the U.S. District Court, District of Massachusetts. On June 19, 2009, the court ruled against the claimants. On August 11, 2010, the First Circuit Court of Appeals upheld the ruling. Finally, on January 19, 2011, the U.S. Supreme Court declined to hear an appeal.

The plaintiffs, made up of local students and teachers, as well as a Turkish American community organization, sued the Massachusetts Board of Education in regard to "contra-genocide" content they had asked the board to include in the guide. This content challenged the application of the genocide label to the mass violence directed against Ottoman Armenians in the context of World War I. The debate over the guide's content dealt with themes of genocide denial and memory, free speech and censorship, and the intersections of politics, ethics, and law. These contestations provided the stage for both formal legal debate and negotiations of memory in the courtroom and beyond.

*Uncovering the Logic of a Trial through Court Documents
and Interviews*

Our analysis of the case is based on two data sources: court documents and interviews. Using two legal databases, Bloomberg Law and Westlaw, we were able to access over a thousand pages of court documents from both the district and appellate cases. After accessing these remotely, a visit to the Massachusetts courthouse and use of onsite court records confirmed that we have access to the complete docket for each case. We reviewed these documents to chart general arguments from the plaintiffs, defense, amicus brief authors, and judges. We then coded interviews and key documents for themes about denial and free speech, as well as extrajudicial content.

In addition to the analysis of court documents, we conducted in-depth interviews with several actors involved in the case. We interviewed members of the defense and plaintiffs, including lawyers, activists, a teacher, and a student. In general, plaintiffs expressed more hesitancy to participate in this study. Several declined to be interviewed. In addition, we spoke with reporters and with members of the current Department of Education to better understand both the perception and the lasting curricular effects of the case. The latter interviews also provide insights into the procedures of guideline promulgation.

Interviews complicate the neat picture painted by the court documents, as we will see. While the documents show finalized arguments, the interviews provide clearer insight into the social processes that enabled their creation, the motivation of actors, and the meaning individuals attributed to their actions. We asked participants about their initial motivations to join the case, including discussion of their previous knowledge about the Armenian genocide and early debates (both legal and extralegal) surrounding the case. We then inquired into their participation throughout the case, including their individual roles, their perceptions of the case, and their interactions and conversations with others as *Griswold v. Driscoll* unfolded. We concluded with an inquiry into lasting effects of the case on personal, legal, and communal dimensions.

Combining insights from the analysis of court documents and interviews provides us with insights into both the formal legal process and the cultural trauma, identity, and values mobilized throughout the unfolding case. It allows us to chart the arguments as they were constructed within and outside of the courtroom, while also accounting for the numerous legal, political, and moral incentives that shaped these proceedings and influenced their effects.

From Administrative Process and Pre-legal Controversies to the Court Case

The Massachusetts Board of Education first circulated a draft of the curriculum guide on January 15, 1999. As part of the review process, the board requested public feedback. Days after the draft was released, the Turkish American Cultural Society of New England (TACS-NE), affiliated with the national ATAA, contacted the Board of Education with a request that additional materials be included. As it stood, the guide's suggested resources all supported the categorization of the violence against the Armenians as genocide. The Turkish organizations instead asked that sources be included that called this labeling into question. The TACS-NE argued that reputable scholars contested the assertion that the Turkish state had advocated a formal genocidal policy, and therefore that the mass killings of Armenians did not meet the legal definition of genocide. The board then incorporated these "contra-genocide" materials in the guide before circulating a second draft for review in March 1999. When local Armenian American organizations got word of this update, they contacted the board to request that the added "denialist" materials be removed from the guide, claiming that these documents negated the historical fact of the Armenian genocide. They argued further that, beyond being inaccurate, these materials caused pain to survivors and the descendants of survivors and victims. The board subsequently removed the Turkish sources in the final version of the curriculum guide, a move that motivated the initiation of the *Griswold v. Driscoll* case.

Griswold v. Driscoll: Initiating the Case

A series of questions arise about the initiation of the case: Who activated the law in this dispute? Who initiated the court case, based on which law? In line with the distinction between formal versus substantivized law, explored above, different answers come to the fore.

A formal perspective.   The formal perspective is well reflected in the name of the case—*Griswold v. Driscoll*, referring to two individual actors: Theodore (Ted) Griswold, a Massachusetts high school student, and David Driscoll, the Commissioner of Education. It seems as though Ted (rather than David) rose against Goliath. Yet names of court cases leave out essentials. The "Complaint and Jury Demand" the plaintiffs filed with the U.S. District Court, District of Massachusetts, on October 26, 2005, lists, on the side of the plaintiffs, Theodore Griswold "and his parent and next friend, Thomas Griswold,"[2] as well as William Schechter (Griswold's social studies teacher), Lawrence Aaronson, another social studies teacher at the same school, and the ATAA. Two additional students and their fathers later joined these plaintiffs. Ted Griswold was represented by attorney Harvey Silverglate, known for his pursuit of free speech cases, especially in educational settings. On the side of the defendants, we find listed "David P. Driscoll, Commissioner of Education, Massachusetts Department of Education, in his official capacity, James A. Peyser, Chairman, Massachusetts Board of Education, in his official capacity, The Department of Education for the Commonwealth of Massachusetts, and the Massachusetts Board of Education." Other defendants later joined the case, including intervenor defendants from the local Armenian American community.

The students and teachers claimed that the removal of materials suggested by Turkish organizations had violated their free speech rights and that the State had censored students' and teachers' access to educational material. The ATAA joined the plaintiffs—they openly did so as the producer of some of the removed sources—but also claimed to represent Turkish parents and students who were, in their view, facing discrimination. The plaintiffs expressed their belief "that the truth of an idea cannot be tested in a marketplace artificially circumscribed by censorship and the imposition of government orthodoxies." They summarized their goal as "a judicial declaration that actions taken by the Massachusetts Department of Education and by the Massachusetts Board of Education to excise academically sound materials from a state human rights curricular guide because of political hostility toward certain viewpoints have violated their rights to free expression and belief guaranteed by the United States Constitution" (*Griswold v. Driscoll*, 1:05-cv-12147-MLW [MA District Court] [2009], Nov. 25, Complaint and Jury Demand: 2).

The remainder of the "Complaint and Jury Demand" takes all the legally required steps. It clarifies the jurisdiction of the court, introduces the parties, and presents the facts of the case, as seen by the plaintiffs. A core passage states: "The [guideline] summary argued that the 'Muslim Turkish Ottoman Empire' was responsible for the deaths of large portions of the Armenian population of the Ottoman Empire around the time of World War I. No resources that mentioned the contra-genocide perspective on this period in history were included in the draft Guide, even though the Guide stated that one of its standards for select-ing instructional materials on genocide and human rights issues was to provide 'differing points of view on controversial issues'" (*Griswold v. Driscoll*, 1:05-cv-12147-MLW [MA District Court] [2009], Nov. 25, Complaint and Jury Demand:8). The document concludes with the legal norms the plaintiffs consider to have been violated, notably the Federal Civil Rights Act, 42 U.S.C., paragraph 1983, and the First and Fourteenth Amendments of the U.S. Constitution.

In the same document, the plaintiffs also cite precedent to back up their con-stitutional claims. They refer to a 1982 case, *Board of Education v. Pico*, in which a local board of education in the state of New York removed several books from a school library, asserting that the removed books were morally unfit. Students in the district then sued, arguing that the board was employing noneducational motivations to censor student access to materials. After the district court ruled in favor of the board of education, the case rose to the U.S. Supreme Court, which affirmed the district court's decision but emphasized the centrality of the board's motivation in their interpretation of the law; the board could remove materials only for educationally legitimate reasons (*Griswold v. Driscoll*, 1:05-cv-12147-MLW [MA District Court] [2009], Nov. 25, Complaint and Jury Demand).

In *Griswold v. Driscoll*, the plaintiffs argued that the Massachusetts Board of Education removed documents from the teaching guidelines, interpreted as a vir-tual library, for political, rather than educational, reasons. Central to this argu-ment, they claimed, is the educational legitimacy of the "contra-genocide" stance. Their arguments proclaimed the existence of a rigorous, two-sided debate about the appropriate labeling of the violence against Ottoman Armenians in 1915–16. The plaintiffs insisted that the State, in preventing such a debate by removing the "contra-genocide" content, had introduced into its educational guidelines politi-cal will. The plaintiffs asserted that this intrusion of politics into the educational sphere could disrupt the education of students as they learn to evaluate and ana-lyze arguments, a position that the American Civil Liberties Union (ACLU) later supported in an amicus brief.

A substantive perspective: actors behind actors, process behind process. While the court files capture the inclusion and removal of the documents and the legal arguments regarding violation, they do not convey the steps that led the plaintiffs to formally initiate the case, and this initiation remains contentious. Though the plaintiffs were outwardly united, they remained isolated behind the scenes. The teachers and students rarely, if ever, interacted with the Turkish lobbying group. All interviews indicate that the lead attorney, Harvey Silverglate, orchestrated the case without facilitating interactions between these groups. Consider the account provided by a former student who played a leading role in the case:

> I became interested in the American Civil Liberties Union when I was in ninth grade in high school. And I think in tenth grade I approached Bill Schechter. . . . He was a history teacher, and he was my journalism teacher at the time. And I threw the idea across his desk, and he was really into it. And we started the club together. It continued through the next three years that I was there, and I think it still existed for a few years afterwards . . . ACLU Club. Like an extracurricular, after school we'd meet—we got involved in a few [issues], we were protesting the Patriot Act, you know, we'd just latch on to, like, certain causes. Gay marriage was a thing at the time in Massachusetts, and we got on board with that, and then Schechter, I think, was approached by Harvey, or he was friends with Harvey or something like that, and he was already a plaintiff as a teacher in the case, and explained to me the whole situation, that they needed a student . . . and I was into the idea, and got involved.

The interview with this student reveals other sources of support, such as peers in the ACLU Club, a recent publication by "a Princeton professor" who had challenged the genocide label for the Armenian case, and a front-page article in the *Wall Street Journal*. As a high school student interested in civil liberties, the student experienced the article as a major thrill; while presenting both sides, it cited him and displayed sympathy for his cause. The driving force, however, according to the student, was attorney Harvey Silverglate, in whose house "four meetings" took place, over dinner, designed to tighten bonds and to strategize. The attorney's role was so central that the student never set foot in the courtroom. Our interview with a social studies teacher who played a central role in the case sheds additional light on the network ties within the group of plaintiffs. Attorney Silverglate approached this teacher through a colleague on the staff of the school. The teacher describes Silverglate as a member of Cambridge progressive circles, mentioning Silverglate's wife and her old friendship with Beat poet Allen Ginsberg.

Also in our interview, the student discussed challenges, including overwhelmingly negative press reactions, the upset of fellow students of Armenian descent, including a friend from the ACLU Club, and—especially—a call from an elderly Armenian woman:

> I remember at one point, people were calling the school. I worked on the school newspaper at the time, and I was working after school. And for some reason the receptionist sent the call to me in that room—and it was a woman who was crying,

because she said her parents had been beheaded in front of her in Armenia back in the day. And I had to talk to her, try to explain what we were doing. And I was just like—I can't do this, I can't really explain. . . . She was just going on and on about how this really happened. That's what she wanted me to hear and acknowledge. And so I was like, I do believe that, believe you, and that's terrible. And I'm sorry—you know, I'm not trying to deny that, or detract from that at all. But I started to try to defend the case the way we did typically. But then I was just like, for this woman, you can't really make some kind of abstract legal argument. So I was just like, I'm really sorry, I don't know very much about this. I'm involved with this case because I think it's important for this reason.

Despite such challenges, and his expressed empathy with a representative of the victim group, the student's excitement about being involved in a big civil liberties case prevailed. The student also confirmed that he continues to feel pride about his role in a case over free speech rights, and that he continues to admire Silverglate: "I still think it's cool that there are people like Harvey who really do know how those things work, and who see an important case—'cause they're always thinking about precedent, that's the whole point, it's not just about this case at all. It's really not, obviously. And—so he saw this as an important thing. . . . And he was doing this work for free."[3] Yet the student also distanced himself from the case, culminating in the statement that he, who never set foot in the court and eventually lost sight of the case as it unfolded over several years, was not upset about the outcome: "And so—ultimately, if we lost, I'm just like, okay . . . yeah, they won. Maybe the people who were upset about it, maybe it makes them feel a little better. I'm alright with that. . . . I don't feel terrible—the Turks probably feel bad about it. But again, that's not why I was involved."

Obviously, the tie between the student and his admired teacher was crucial for their engagement in the case. Like the student, the teacher we spoke with also stressed that his sole interest was in free speech issues, not in a statement about the Armenian genocide. He expressed concern about the political determination of suggested instructional materials, especially in the context of high-stakes standardized testing. He also strongly articulated his belief in the pedagogical value of students being exposed to different sides of a debate, even if one side's arguments might appear outrageous, and for students to have to struggle with disparate positions. While he expressed sympathy with the Turkish position and referred to arguments by historian Bernard Lewis in this context, he stressed that the court proceeding had, in his perception, nothing to do with a statement about history. "Yes, the amicus people came up afterwards and gave their spiel, and it kind of—it had nothing to do with anything, except their deeply felt ideas, and support for the Armenian American community."

The interviews thus provide a sense of some of the plaintiffs, their network ties, and their substantive positions. Some actors were centered on the school setting, but linked with civil libertarian and free speech lawyer Silverglate and progressive-libertarian circles in Cambridge of which Silverglate was a part, and with which some social studies teachers were marginally linked. These plaintiffs were ambivalent regarding the historical question of the Armenian genocide; their focus was on free speech issues. Acting on the trial's "front stage," their network was organized around civil libertarian issues in the school setting.

Yet these plaintiffs did not act alone. They were joined by the ATAA as a co-plaintiff. The network ties between these two sets of plaintiffs are murky. Evidence suggests that the teachers and students did not have ties with the ATAA; multiple interviewees reported that they never interacted with ATAA representatives. The relationship between free speech lawyers and Turkish organizations, however, is more difficult to ascertain. Who was the driving force in this constellation, free speech lawyers or Turkish American organizations? Harvey Silverglate declined to be interviewed. Other participants suggested that the ATAA sought involvement because of the concerns of local Turkish Americans who feared that their children would receive prejudicial treatment in schools, based on the curriculum guidelines. Court documents do reveal that the Turkish American Legal Defense Fund (TALDF) hired at least one attorney as a consultant who had previously been involved in the University of Minnesota case cited above. That attorney later also wrote an amicus curiae brief for the TALDF.

In sum, while not all social ties and motives that lead to the initiation of a case such as *Griswold v. Driscoll* can be identified, our interviews render some of them visible. The pattern that emerges speaks to the difference between what appears through the formal setup of the case and the substantive reality of what drives it. On the one hand, we have progressive, civil libertarian high school teachers and their students. They act on the front stage, as it were. On the other hand, we find a network of free speech lawyers and Turkish and Turkish American organizations who are involved in multiple cases of this nature, but who remain backstage, at least in *Griswold v. Driscoll*. We were not able to ascertain who among the latter dominates in this dyadic relationship. Yet it seems clear that together they are the driving force that seeks out suitable actors, such as civil libertarian–oriented students and their teachers, to initiate cases and to serve as the "poster children" in what is meant to appear as a struggle over civil liberties.

We can depict the social structure of this group of actors in a Simmelian model of overlapping social circles (see figure 12). The first circle consists of civil liberties–engaged high school students, supported by parents and teachers. The second circle, partially overlapping with the first, consists of progressive-libertarian free speech attorneys. Among them, too, civil liberties concerns appear to dominate. The third circle, overlapping with that of the free speech lawyers, consists of Turkish or Turkish American organizations. Some plaintiffs argue that Turkish organizations joined the case at the pleading of local Turkish Americans who expressed concern over discrimination or animosity due to the curriculum guide. Yet, given the massive infringements on civil liberties in Turkey, the imprisonment of

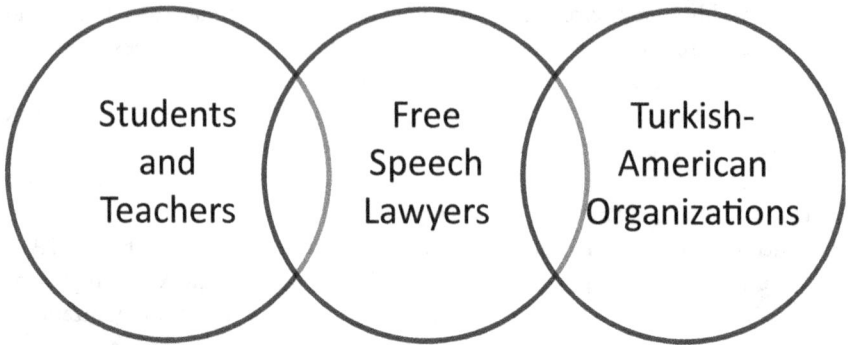

FIGURE 12. Social organization of plaintiffs and their discourses in *Griswold v. Driscoll*.

journalists and academics, and the criminalization of the mere use of the term *genocide* in regard to the mass killings of Armenians—and given, finally, these groups' silence vis-à-vis the repression of free speech in Turkey—it is implausible that free speech concerns in fact drove their actions. Instead, their intervention can only be understood as a new front in the struggle against recognition of the Armenian genocide. Through these interlinked social circles, substantive, extra-legal concerns and their discursive expression hid behind formal free speech claims to motivate the initiation of the *Griswold v. Driscoll* case, even if that initiation was formally based on concerns with legal principles of the U.S. Constitution alone. A decoupling arrangement separated the front stage actors organized around free speech rights from the back stage actors concerned with denial of the genocide.

The initiation of the case by the plaintiffs and their supporters brought many other actors into the legal game. The defendants challenged the plaintiffs' position, various groups supported them through amicus briefs, and the judges deliber-ated and decided. The defendants and their supporters brought arguments into the unfolding trial that appealed to the issue of free speech or First Amendment pro-tections. Yet they also raised issues that the plaintiffs had not formally addressed, but that appear to have motivated their action, at least partially. Central among them was the debate over the appropriateness of the genocide label for the mass violence against the Ottoman Armenians. Formally about free speech rights, the court case also involved a substantive debate about the Armenian genocide. For-mal and substantive discourses in fact interpenetrate, as the following shows.

Deliberation in Griswold v. Driscoll

Over the course of six years, *Griswold v. Driscoll* unfolded in three courts. The majority of the legal disputes, however, took place outside of the courtroom. Plain-tiffs, defendants, and contributors of amicus briefs submitted hundreds of pages of documents to the district and appellate courts, while only two formal hearings were held.

A formal perspective: trial as procedure and the free speech issue.   In September 2006, the U.S. District Court first heard the case. After nearly three years, Judge Mark Wolf ruled in favor of the defense. Speaking to formal matters of the case, he cited the legitimacy of political participation in the process of developing the instructional guide. He also rejected the plaintiffs' claims that censorship had occurred, denying *Board of Education v. Pico* as a precedent. In summarizing his opinion, the judge wrote the following:

> The Complaint and attached exhibits demonstrate that plaintiffs and those who share their viewpoint concerning the treatment of Armenians in the Ottoman Empire are capable of participating fully in the political process, which provides the opportunity to petition the government to alter its policies. The efforts of the ATAA and the others who share its viewpoint evidently caused the inclusion of contra-genocide materials in the Curriculum Guide for a while. If plaintiffs still want those materials included in the Curriculum Guide, they will have to resume their efforts to prevail in the political arena because they are not entitled to relief in federal court. (*Griswold v. Driscoll*, 1:05-cv-12147-MLW [MA District Court] [2009], Jun. 10, Judgment: 30)

The judge did not explicate an opinion on the substantive dispute over the appropriate labeling of the mass violence against the Ottoman Armenians that had motivated major factions among both the plaintiffs and the defendants. We will never know what his position on this matter was or whether that position affected the court's decision.

In a next step, the plaintiffs appealed the district court's decision, taking the case to the appellate court. After a hearing and deliberation, Associate Justice David Souter (retired U.S. Supreme Court justice) confirmed the ruling of the district court. He affirmed that the Massachusetts Board of Education had not violated the First Amendment. Like Judge Wolf, he also denied the plaintiffs' censorship argument: "The revisions to the Guide after its submission to legislative officials, even if made in response to political pressure, did not implicate the First Amendment. The judgment of the district court is affirmed" (*Griswold v. Driscoll*, 09–2002 [MA Court of Appeals] [2010], Aug. 11, Judgment: 15). Again, the reasoning that carries the decision does not engage with the substantive debate over the appropriate labeling of the violence, and again we will never know whether such consideration affected the decision in any way.

Following this defeat, the plaintiffs sought to bring *Griswold v. Driscoll* before the U.S. Supreme Court, which, however, declined to hear the case. Following its notification of this decision on January 19, 2011, the case formally concluded.

In sum, while substantive debates over the genocide label, and associated identity issues, motivated much of the dispute, most clearly among Turkish American and Armenian American organizations, the courts never addressed those concerns. They instead stuck strictly, and in line with a formal legal logic, to constitutional arguments about free speech.

TABLE 6 Formal-Legal and Substantive Arguments in *Griswold v. Driscoll*

	Defendants	Plaintiffs
Free Speech— Formal	(1) State has authority to regulate educational curriculum	(2) State overstepped by censoring educational curriculum
Armenian Genocide— Substantive	(3) Violence against the Armenians constituted genocide, and Turkish lobbying groups sought to include propaganda in the state's educational curriculum	(4) Violence against the Armenians is an unsettled case; both legitimate sides of the historical debate deserve to be heard

From a formal to a substantive perspective: court as stage—history, values, and identities. The previous section showed how both parties in *Griswold v. Driscoll*, while agreeing on what had occurred in the process of educational guideline promulgation, profoundly disagreed on the legality of the Massachusetts Board of Education's actions. The plaintiffs argued that the State had overstepped its authority by censoring the educational curriculum and that, by doing so, it had infringed on free speech rights of students and teachers. The defendants argued instead that the State had the authority to regulate the educational curriculum and that the omission of certain arguments did not constitute an infringement of free speech rights (this legal disagreement is represented in table 6, quadrants 1 and 2).

Yet the formal debate over free speech simultaneously allowed for two substantive arguments to unfold. On one side, a subgroup of plaintiffs, specifically Turkish American associations, argued that debates over the appropriate labeling of the mass violence against the Armenians are unsettled and that both sides of the historical debate are legitimate and need to be included in the curriculum (table 6, quadrant 4). On the other side, the defendants and writers of several amicus curiae briefs unanimously argued that violence against the Armenians constituted genocide, and that Turkish lobbying groups sought to introduce propaganda into the state's educational curriculum (table 6, quadrant 3).

The contending positions manifested themselves in divergent terminologies. Where plaintiffs referred to "wartime conflict materials" or "contra-genocide materials," defendants used the term "denialist materials." Moreover, according to some participants, the mere presence of such contestations within the courtroom gave legitimacy to the contra-genocide perspective. As one Armenian American advocate put it: "To make it into the other side in a debate, you can agree or you can disagree, but if you're talking about it in its terms of being a debate, you're at least recognizing that there are two sides. And that's more than half the battle, in this case."

At times, this juxtaposition, and the simultaneity of formal free speech and substantive genocide arguments, resulted in actors talking past each other. It also resulted in uneasy alliances, managed by way of the interactional distance shown above in the example of civil liberties advocates on the one hand and Turkish American actors on the other, the latter allied with a country that criminalizes slanderous speech about the nation, including the use of the word *genocide* for the violence against the Armenians during World War I.

A very different pattern of relationships emerges on the side of the defense. Armenian American groups, other contributors of amicus briefs, and the State articulated similar arguments, all advocating the appropriateness of the genocide label. State actors differed somewhat, however, in that they prioritized the argument of legitimate governmental power and free speech rights. Accordingly, we observe intense interactions (largely overlapping social and argumentative circles) between Armenian American groups and the Massachusetts Department of Education, much in contrast to the decoupling we identified above on the side of the plaintiffs.

In short, while *Griswold v. Driscoll* was formally about free speech issues, the case also provided a space for a substantive debate about the Armenian genocide. The latter, in fact, was the central motivating force for many participants.

Interpenetration of formal and substantive debates.   Importantly, participants in the legal fight did not just add substantive arguments to formal ones. Instead, the formal and the substantive interpenetrated in *Griswold v. Driscoll*. The topic of free speech specifically provided opportunities for both defendants and plaintiffs to insert substantive debates about the Armenian genocide into formal legal contestations. This insertion is most explicit in arguments over "educational legitimacy," or the existence of scholarly (versus political) support for documents suggested for the curriculum guide. Here substantive concerns were debated in formal rules-of-the-game terms, facilitating debates about the Armenian genocide under the cover of formal legal language. This mechanism enabled actors to interpret the Armenian genocide either as centrally important or as irrelevant for the case. It even allowed actors to hold both interpretations simultaneously. Some interviewees rejected the premise that the Armenian genocide had legal relevance to the case at hand (understanding this as "political" and outside of the legal realm) while concurrently and formally advocating the truth (or untruth) of the Armenian genocide claim. The following paragraphs illustrate how actors on both sides of the case maneuvered this interpenetration within the formal rules of the game.

In the view of the plaintiffs, the State was quieting a viable perspective in response to political pressure. They had to argue that experts supported their contra-genocide position, because the successful argument of free speech violation relied on the educational worthiness of the documents. Their lawyers referenced academic support for this perspective and expanded the importance of recognition to the Turkish American community. In a request for permission to submit an amicus brief, the TALDF, an arm of the TCA, expressed its concern that its "ability to educate the general public about Turkey and Turkish Americans will be impaired if the District Court stands." The text of the request continues: "Most Turkish Americans espouse a viewpoint upon their ancestral homeland that differs in an important respect from that expressed in Ch. 276 of the Massachusetts Sessions laws of 1998. Primarily, they believe that teaching the historical controversy of the Ottoman Armenian tragedy solely within the rubric of the crime of genocide is incorrect and deprives Massachusetts students of crucial context of the devastation inflicted on all civilian populations, Muslims and Christians alike, on the eastern and Caucasus fronts in World War I" (*Griswold v. Driscoll*, 09–2002 [MA Court of Appeals] [2009], Oct. 15, TALDF Amicus Brief:2).

In its actual amicus brief, the organization refers to the guidelines as "propagandistic" and charges anti-Turkish discrimination. Other amicus briefs for the plaintiffs similarly tie together formal free speech arguments with substantive statements about the genocide. The ACLU, for example, writes in its amicus brief: "As submitted to the legislature, the resources included the website of Georgetown University's Institute for Turkish Studies and other organizations with a viewpoint different from those of other scholars and Armenian groups on whether the treatment of the Armenians constituted genocide" (*Griswold v. Driscoll*, 1:05-cv-12147-MLW [MA District Court] [2009], Nov. 4, ACLU Amicus Brief: 19). Here again, the substantive validity of the Turkish stance becomes a key component of the legal debate.

We see similar interpenetrations between formal and substantive arguments in amicus briefs on the side of the defense. One brief, dated March 8, 2006, submitted by attorney Arnold Rosenfeld on behalf of a community of educators, students, and the Armenian Assembly of America, calls the plaintiffs' assertions "historically and educationally unsupported." The brief includes a lengthy argument as to why the events in the Ottoman Empire constituted genocide, supported by legal and scholarly sources. Having made these arguments, aware of substantive motivations held by some plaintiffs, the majority of the brief addresses the plaintiffs' free speech claims, demonstrating attorney Rosenfeld's mindfulness of the formal issues at stake (*Griswold v. Driscoll*, 1:05-cv-12147-MLW [MA District Court] [2006], Mar. 8, AAA Amicus Brief).

Similarly, a brief submitted some days later by the Armenian Bar Association and others provides formal arguments on government speech that are interspersed with commemorative considerations. Here the authors argue that governments have the right to commemorate tragedy and to take a non-neutral stance in the case of such violations. Arguments are enriched with analogical bridging to other events addressed by the educational guidelines, including the Holocaust and Ireland's Great Famine. The authors compare attempts to legitimize pro-Turkish materials to legitimizing the Holocaust and other recognized instances of genocide (*Griswold v. Driscoll*, 09–2002 [MA Court of Appeals] [2009], Oct. 5, Motion to Dismiss, *Griswold v. Driscoll*, 1:05-cv-12147-MLW [MA District Court] [2006], Mar. 8, Defendants' Reply Memorandum of Law in Support of Their Motion to Dismiss).

An amicus brief from the International Association of Genocide Scholars, filed on April 28, 2006, equally supports the government's formal right to select educational material, linking this right with the government's responsibility to train citizens to participate in democracy and to take on national and global responsibilities, resisting indifference. It too, however, simultaneously engages in substantive debate on the appropriateness of the genocide label. It challenges the plaintiffs' position that there are two valid sides to this debate, provides a historical overview of the Armenian genocide, and cites scholarship and widespread international recognition. The authors use the language of genocide denial as the last step in the unfolding of genocide. They engage in extensive analogical bridging to other genocides, referring to the Armenian genocide as the first genocide of the twentieth century, from which Hitler and the Nazis borrowed techniques in orchestrating the Holocaust (*Griswold v. Driscoll*, 1:05-cv-12147-MLW [MA District Court] [2006], Apr. 28, IAGS Amicus Brief).

In short, *Griswold v. Driscoll* shows how free speech debates allow substantive arguments to interpenetrate with formal discourse. Two mechanisms are at work. First, formal debate over speech rights invites arguments over the legitimacy of specific speech acts. It partly necessitates such arguments, given that only some speech is free, especially in an educational context. Formal claims are thus contingent on substantive ones. We refer to this phenomenon as the *substantive contingency of formal claims mechanism* in processes of formal-substantive interpenetration.

Second, legal cases over formal claims open a subterranean realm where coded language allows for substantive debate, hidden behind formal language. Actors may, as in *Griswold v. Driscoll*, claim to fight for free speech and reject the notion that they pursue a denialist agenda, while simultaneously relying on denialist interpretations of material when articulating their legal argument. Those who stress their sole focus on the formal provide space, simultaneously, for the subterranean insertion of the substantive. Such subtle insertion of substantive concerns into formal debate allows participants to engage in double-speak, with one message openly articulated and the other implied. These actors can reject the charge that a case is about genocide denial, while simultaneously acknowledging as legally relevant "propaganda" or "contra-genocide" sources, categorizations informed by their stance on the Armenian genocide. Subtle changes in language allow these actors to shift back and forth, in what they classify as legally valid lines of argument. Perhaps this is why debates over denial often arise in the context of trials over speech. We call this the *subterranean argument device* in processes of formal-substantive interpenetration.

CONCLUSIONS ON GENOCIDE KNOWLEDGE
AND TRIALS: LESSONS FROM *GRISWOLD V. DRISCOLL*

Court cases, even if fought under the guise of formal claims and through formalized procedures, involve substantive claims. Importantly here, they have epistemic consequences. They affect the shape of knowledge and collective memories about events under deliberation, including episodes of mass violence. Neo-Durkheimians have made this point convincingly, for criminal law generally (Smith 2008) and for human rights trials specifically (Alexander 2004). The present chapter has provided further evidence.

This chapter shows, moreover, that the ritual power of legal proceedings can be a tool in the hands of strategic actors who seek to shape the public understanding of history. Durkheimian and conflict perspectives are not mutually exclusive (Garland 1990). This is in line with insights from past work on the cultural effect of court trials of perpetrators of mass atrocity crimes and their initiation by strategic actors (Hagan 2003; Savelsberg 2015). The *Griswold v. Driscoll* case illustrates that strategic actors are also active when the subjects of trials are not atrocities themselves, but claims of denial and demands for recognition. While such court cases may be less dramatic than trials of perpetrators of mass atrocity crimes, they may nevertheless shape narratives and affect the epistemic power of competing collectivities.

Past work has also documented how narratives produced and disseminated to the public by legal proceedings reflect not only the cultural power of trials as rituals and the efficacy of strategic actors, but also the institutional logic of law (Pendas 2006; Marrus 2008; Savelsberg and King 2011). The narratives they produce are constrained by the rules of the legal game. This chapter has shown that these constraints also apply to trials in which cultural production is not a byproduct but is the issue at stake. Yet extralegal considerations also play out, often in subterranean ways, in this case debates over the appropriateness of the genocide label for the mass violence committed against the Ottoman Armenians during World War I.

While formally dealing with free speech claims, judges at the district and appellate court levels were intensely exposed to such substantive pronouncements, but they did not use them when deciding, or at least when justifying their decisions. Instead, they stuck to arguments about free speech. Their line of argument thus suggests that they adhered to the rules of the legal game, to use Pierre Bourdieu's language, or to the principles of formal-rational law in Max Weber's terms.

We cannot know whether the judges' decisions were in any way affected by the substantive debate over the appropriateness of the genocide label and the respective sensitivities and interests of the conflicting groups, and whether they thus constituted substantivized law. We do know, however, that parties concerned with free speech issues on the one hand and genocide arguments on the other engaged in strategic coalitions, presenting a discourse in which formal free speech arguments and substantive genocide debates interpenetrated.

The trial also provided a stage on which the parties could carry out their dispute and present their positions to a broad public. It seems as though the victim side won this contest, not just in formal legal but also in substantive terms. The trial, after all, resulted in the mobilization of Armenian Americans, public resonance, and sympathy for their cause, and in an encouragement of other victim groups to pursue the public acknowledgment of their history in the education system and in the public sphere (see chapter 9).

Finally, our analysis speaks to the fate of recent legal decision making on issues of free speech in the context of genocide debates. It may challenge common expectations that in cases processed in U.S. courts—in a country that, more than other democracies, privileges individual rights—those sides lose their cases that claim free speech rights, while in several European cases—most famously the Perinçek case before the European Court of Human Rights—free speech arguments have prevailed (Langer 2014). Note, however, that Perinçek was initially found criminally guilty and sentenced in a Swiss court. Note also that a French court had earlier found Princeton historian Bernard Lewis guilty for statements he made in interviews regarding the Armenian genocide (Ternon 1999). Note, finally, an important difference in the character of these European cases compared to the U.S. cases mentioned above, including *Griswold v. Driscoll*. While the European trials were held against individuals who had made use of free speech rights, even to the detriment of victimized groups (specifically Armenians), American cases such as *Griswold v. Driscoll* and those involving the University of Minnesota dealt with the right of institutions to practice free speech rights. The decisions in *Griswold v. Driscoll* additionally stated that the Massachusetts Department of Education had not infringed upon the rights of teachers and students to articulate ideas that were not included in curricular guidelines. The varying nature of plaintiffs and defendants adds complexities that future work should address.

In conclusion, a new type of trial pits those who make free speech claims, some of them seeking to advance denial of genocide, against others who represent, or identify with, victimized groups. While initiators of such trials act with strategic intent, the consequences of resulting court cases are cultural, potentially coloring collective memories and knowledge about the past. Throughout the proceedings in *Griswold v. Driscoll*, formal legal arguments interpenetrated with substantive concerns with history, memory, and identity, even if only the former became visible in judicial decisions. Substantive concerns intruded through several hidden mechanisms: the decoupling of back stage actors with denialist intent from front stage actors who pursue civil liberties; the substantive contingency of formal claims; and subterranean insertions of substantive claims in formal legal arguments.

This would be the end of the story if we limited ourselves to a classic decision-making approach. Yet the decision-making process, be it in the field of politics or that of law, unfolds in a larger cultural environment. Chapter 9 therefore addresses unintended, in fact counterproductive, consequences of denialism in the context of an era characterized by a human rights hegemony.

9

Denialism in an Age of Human
Rights Hegemony

Denialism can be effective, especially when powerful and influential actors repress dark chapters of history that the populace already seeks to avoid. Yet denial of mass atrocity and genocide in the context of human rights hegemony is likely to fail. In fact, denialists have to expect counterproductive consequences. Their "successes" turn out to be Pyrrhic victories.

To argue this point, I briefly return to central insights from the two preceding chapters. There I examined epistemic conflicts in the context of legal and political decision-making processes. Both chapters taught us important lessons about the social forces at work, the entrepreneurs of knowledge and carrier groups, the effect that rules of the game have on fights carried out in specific social fields, the limits of those rules when players improvise, and the weight of national contexts in which fields are nested.

Yet focusing on concrete processes of decision making alone leaves out something important. It does not speak to situations in which problems never become issues in the first place, in which they do not enter public consciousness and are absent from the realm of deliberation and decision making. Scholarly debates of the 1960s and 1970s about community power structures can teach us important lessons about such blank spots. These debates initially involved two camps. One camp used a conflict theoretical model inspired by C. Wright Mills and took a reputational approach to measuring power, asking experts or members of local elites about the amount of power held by different actors in the community. The resulting image was that of a steep hierarchy, resembling a pyramid. The other camp used a pluralist model, following political scientist Robert Dahl. Its proponents inquired about specific decision-making issues that came before city councils. They identified involvement of diverse groups and shifting coalitions with variable outcomes, depending on the issues at stake. Findings of this school were in line with a schoolbook model of American democracy and a pluralist notion of American politics.

Both schools, however, overlooked that some problems, often the most funda-mental ones, were never articulated. Peter Bachrach and Morton Baratz (1970), in a groundbreaking study of the city of Baltimore, found that no city leader and no constituent group articulated the issue of poverty, an overwhelming condition for many of its (minority) residents. Nor did any leader or interest group have to intervene to keep the problem of poverty out of public view. Similarly, air pollution never became an issue in some municipalities (but it did in others), and patterns of issue making were independent of the actual concentration of pollutants in the respective cities (Crenson 1972). In other words, hegemonic thought can keep a problem off the radar of public engagement and policy making.

Just as hegemony can keep a problem away from the realm of concrete deci-sion making, it may frustrate efforts of those who seek to hide an issue that hege-monic thought embraces. When actors attempt to initiate and color the outcome of concrete decision-making processes with the intent to deny grave violations of human rights, then they are likely—in the current era of a human rights hegemony—to encounter counterproductive consequences. Both the *Griswold v. Driscoll* court case in Massachusetts and the memory legislation in France serve as examples.

In this concluding chapter, I explore such counterproductive consequences of denialist actions in the context of a human rights hegemony. I do so both for cases analyzed in the preceding chapters and for denialism of the Armenian genocide more broadly, using media reporting and documentary films for data. A brief terminological clarification of human rights hegemony, however, is warranted at the outset.

HUMAN RIGHTS HEGEMONY

By human rights hegemony, I mean the domination of a mode of thought that submits events and phenomena to a specific interpretation, as consistent with, or in violation of, human rights. The term *hegemony* derives from the work of Italian neo-Marxist thinker Antonio Gramsci. While I borrow the term from Gramsci, I do not limit hegemony to class-based hegemony. Instead, I see additional forces at work, invoking their power, including "soft power." I do, however, follow Gramsci's focus on universal acceptance, taken-for-grantedness, and the special attention he pays to the potential role of the state and its ability to "regulate beliefs within civil society" (Smith and Riley 2009:36). In addition to the state as a contribu-tor to hegemony, Gramsci alerts us to "organic intellectuals," including journalists and priests who translate complex themes into everyday language to instill them in the minds of readers and believers. Today, journalism is still a powerful force, but other interpreters—such as filmmakers, social movement actors, and non-governmental organizations (NGOs)—often take on the role previously fulfilled by clerics (Levy and Sznaider 2010; Keck and Sikkink 1998).

Structural and cultural changes, reinforced by historical contingencies, advanced the notion of human rights. Transformations such as global interdependencies and the advancement of human rights NGOs were undergirded by contingencies such as the catastrophes of World War II and the Holocaust to promote a new focus on the dignity of individuals. Human rights hegemony now accepts the rights granted each human being, even if these rights are often underenforced. It is expressed in the Universal Declaration of Human Rights and in the protections promised to members of social categories such as ethnic, racial, religious, and national groups by the Convention on the Prevention and Punishment of the Crime of Genocide and by the Rome Statute of the International Criminal Court. Human rights hegemony challenges actors who seek to deny the recognition of victims of grave violations against human rights norms. Those who bear responsibility for massive human suffering may have been seen as heroes for much of human history, but contemporary institutions increasingly classify them as criminal perpetrators.

Human rights hegemony experiences blowback in times of right-wing populist movements and authoritarian leaders, even in Western democracies such as the United States. Its principles certainly clash with concentration camps, euphemized as reeducation facilities in China; mass killings of "infidels" by militant "Islamists"; murderous campaigns in the name of drug control in the Philippines; arbitrary imprisonment of scholars, journalists, and others in Turkey; and large refugee populations worldwide. Yet none of the above go unnoticed, and perpetrators see reason to hide their deeds or to use coded language. For example, they call torture "enhanced interrogation" and use new torture methods that do not leave traces on the body (Senate Select Committee on Intelligence 2014). They know that their deeds evoke outrage if they reach the eyes of a world public. Their attempts at cover-up only show that today we live with a taken-for-granted notion that humans are carriers of certain unalienable rights. We live in an era of—at least partial—human rights hegemony.

COUNTERPRODUCTIVE CONSEQUENCES OF DENIALISM IN A TIME OF HUMAN RIGHTS HEGEMONY

In a time of human rights hegemony, state actors are tempted more than ever to deny or to neutralize grave violations of human rights. Yet they face challengers, and their denialism generates counterproductive consequences. Both the Massachusetts case and the French legislative story support this thesis.

The Griswold v. Driscoll Court Case

The legal conflict over teaching guidelines pertaining to the Armenian genocide in the state of Massachusetts showed that formal legal processes, constrained by

FIGURE 13. Armenian Heritage Park in Boston. Photo courtesy of the Armenian National Institute.

the logic of law, nevertheless have substantive consequences.[1] While *Griswold v. Driscoll* shaped the law by clarifying the extent of government speech protections in the realm of public education,[2] the court proceedings also provided a stage for the presentation of claims about the Armenian genocide, most noteworthy in various amicus briefs.

Most importantly, the case mobilized Boston's Armenian American community and supporting groups, with detrimental consequences for those who initiated the court case with denialist intent. A lawyer and high-ranking official with the Armenian Association of America reports how, in the midst of *Griswold v. Driscoll*, an Armenian Heritage Foundation was formed with the goal of building a memorial space on the Boston Greenway. Ground was broken a year after the court case concluded (Armenian Weekly 2012). Called the Armenian Heritage Park, the area features green space, a fountain, and seating (see figure 13). It provides information about the Armenian genocide, as well as personalized panels that individuals dedicated to prominent Armenian Americans and Armenians, including those killed in the genocide. The outcome is all the more remarkable in that the Boston Greenway, a mile-long park near the Boston Harbor, was originally mandated to not include culturally specific memorial spaces.[3] Numerous respondents to our study commented on the link between the *Griswold v. Driscoll* case and the creation of the memorial. They tell how efforts toward realization of this project had been stagnant until the case provoked support by local Armenian Americans and the public. They believe that the eventual construction of the Armenian Heritage Park succeeded, at least in part, because of successful fundraising mobilized by the court case.

The court case also mobilized other local groups that live with the cultural trauma of past mass violence. The local branch of the Anti-Defamation League (ADL), a Jewish international NGO, for example, originally took no stance on *Griswold v. Driscoll*. Yet, after neighboring communities threatened to draw out of their Holocaust remembrance campaigns and after pushback from national headquarters, the local ADL began to support Armenian American groups in their legal mission.

Finally, the Armenian success advanced the struggle for recognition of the plight of other groups, for example in 2018, when the Massachusetts Board of Education released a new history and social studies framework. The development of this guide again provided an avenue for public feedback. This time, a group of Ukrainian Americans contacted the Department of Education, requesting that the Holodomor, the Stalinist-induced mass famine in Ukraine, be included in the new document. The updated curriculum guide now lists this famine, depicting it as a Ukrainian genocide. An interviewee from the Board of Education explained the emotionality of this inclusion for her contacts within the Ukrainian American community. Their letters and statements had contributed to the curricular innovation, and the addition "elated" them.

In short, attempts to prevent the inclusion of the Armenian genocide in the Massachusetts curriculum guidelines, or to neutralize them through the inclusion of denialist materials, were defeated in court. Importantly, in the context of human rights hegemony, these attempts contributed to community mobilization that eventually resulted in the strengthening of public acknowledgment of the Armenian genocide and of other occurrences of mass violence. Denialist efforts, in this cultural context, yielded counterproductive consequences for those who engaged in them.

The French Legislative Case

In France, too, despite the Constitutional Council overruling the 2012 criminalization of denial of the Armenian genocide, the consequences of the struggle substantially supported the acknowledgment agenda. Here, too, the legislative

TABLE 7 French Ministry of Education Guidelines Pertaining to the Armenian Genocide

II—GUERRES MONDIALES ET REGIMES TOTALITAIRES (1914–1945)
(environ 25% du temps consacré à l'histoire)

Thème 1– LA PREMIÈRE GUERRE MONDIALE: VERS UNE GUERRE TOTALE (1914–1918)

CONNAISSANCES	DÉMARCHES
La Première Guerre mondiale bouleverse les États et les sociétés: – elle est caractérisée par une violence de masse,	Après la présentation succincte des trois grandes phases de la guerre on étudie deux exemples de la violence de masse: – La guerre des tranchées (Verdun). – Le génocide des Arméniens.
– avec la révolution russe, elle engendre une vague de révolutions en Europe,	L'étude s'appuie sur la présentation de personnages et d'événements significatifs.
– elle se conclut par des traités qui dessinent une nouvelle carte de l'Europe source de tensions.	L'étude de la nouvelle carte de l'Europe met évidence quelques points de tensions particulièrement importants.

CAPACITÉS

Connaître et utiliser les repères suivants
– La Première Guerre mondiale: 1914–1918, la bataille de Verdun : 1916 ; l'armistice : 11 novembre 1918
– La révolution russe : 1917
– La carte de l'Europe au lendemain des traités
Décrire et expliquer la guerre des tranchées et le génocide des Arméniens comme des manifestations de la violence de masse

SOURCE: French Ministry of Education (www.education.gouv.fr).

process—and upset over massive interventions by the Turkish state beginning in the late 1990s—had mobilized ethnic Armenians and their supporters. After the CC struck down the law, mobilization intensified and induced other means to meet substantive demands for recognition.

Already in 2008, the French government had decided that the Armenian genocide should be included in history curricula (see table 7). Guidelines promulgated by the French Ministry of National Education, Higher Education and Research specify subjects to be covered in the French equivalent of ninth grade: "II. WORLD WARS AND TOTALITARIAN REGIMES (1914–1945) (about 25% of time dedicated to history). Theme 1 'THE FIRST WORLD WAR: TOWARD TOTAL WAR (1914–1918). KNOWLEDGE. The First World War shook states and societies: It is characterized by mass violence. . . . PROCEDURE: After the succinct presentation of the three phases of the war, two examples of mass violence are to be studied: trench warfare (Verdun) and the *genocide against the Armenians*. . . . *To describe and to explain* the trench warfare and the *genocide against the Armenians as manifestations of the mass violence*" (Bulletin officiel spécial n° 6 du 28 août 2008, p. 41; translation and emphasis by author).[4]

Further specifications followed the defeat of the 2012 law aimed at the criminalization of genocide denial. These culminated in the April 2015 promulgation of a teaching aid by the Ministry of National Education. Authored by historian Vincent Duclert, the teaching aid is entitled *Le Genocide des Arméniens Ottomans: Mise au point scientifique et pédagogique pour les enseignements* (The genocide against the Ottoman Armenians: scientific and pedagogical focus for instruction). The ministry's introduction states: "The transmission of such knowledge is central to the mission of schools because the Armenian genocide figured prominently in historical programs, especially in mandatory schooling, but also because the necessity to know and the study of a world confronted by such trauma are part of the ambitions of moral and civic education. . . . We also requested that Vincent Duclert, Inspector General of National Education, simultaneously historian and scholar of the Armenian Genocide, propose resources on this subject. He proposes here an easily accessible synthesis that summarizes that history and addresses the challenges of its transmission" (Duclert 2015, translated).

This excerpt states that the highest national authority in the realm of education asked an actor at the intersection of scholarship and political administration to summarize, and provide resources that communicate to teachers, knowledge about the Armenian genocide and sources for instructional purposes. The guidelines' central tenets confirm Armenian knowledge. A brief chapter on the genocide, as the first event of this kind in contemporary history (modified in the text by a recognition of the German genocide in today's Namibia), is followed by a central chapter entitled "1915–1923. The Destruction of the Armenians of the Ottoman

Empire." A history of oppression preceding World War I follows, informing readers about the Armenians as an ancient, faithful, and vulnerable population in the Ottoman Empire. It addresses the "genocidal" massacres under Sultan Abdülhamid II in the years 1894–96; the Young Turk revolution with its hopes for democratization, defeated by nationalist radicalization; total war and the release of exterminationist forces; phases of the genocide; and weak punitive responses in the aftermath of World War I. A final chapter addresses the state of historical research under the title "Scientific progress and struggle against denialism." A brief paragraph shows that the basic contours of knowledge communicated here are in line with sedimented knowledge within Armenian communities and with dominant scholarship, and are detrimentally opposed to Turkish knowledge: "At the heart of the First World War, between 1915 and 1917, the Ottoman Armenians, who formed the most important among the non-Muslim communities of the Empire, endured a programmed destruction, efficiently and effectively executed. Sixty percent of the population, some 1.3 million men, women and children disappeared, were massacred through numerous techniques with a cruelty that surpasses the limits of comprehension and marks a fall into the darkness of inhumanity" (Duclert 2015:4, translated).

Other initiatives in the realm of higher and public education, some state-initiated, others originating in civil society, parallel these educational efforts. The year 2013, for example, witnessed the foundation of a Conseil scientifique international pour l'étude du génocide des Arméniens (an international scientific council for the study of the Armenian genocide), which organized a major international colloquium on the subject in the Grand Amphitéâtre of the Sorbonne University. Furthermore, in 2015, the centennial year of the Armenian genocide, two prominent exhibits on the genocide took place in Paris, one in the Hôtel de Ville (city hall), the other at the Mémorial de la Shoah, the official French Holocaust memorial (see chapter 4). Numerous magazines chose to display the event on their cover pages, prominently visible on kiosks throughout Paris.

A few years later, in February 2019, President Emmanuel Macron lived up to a promise he had made during his election campaign. He issued a decree declaring April 24, the day on which Armenians remember the genocide, an official national memorial day of the French Republic (see box 1). President Macron explained his decision in these words: "France is above all a country, which knows how to look history in the face . . . among the first to denounce the murderous manhunt of the Armenian people in the Ottoman Empire . . . , which—already in 1915—called the genocide for what it was: a crime against humanity, against civilization. Which, in 2001, after a long struggle, recognized it by law, and which—as I promised to do—will make April 24 in the coming weeks a national day of commemoration of the Armenian Genocide" (in *Le Monde*, February 2019, translated).

BOX 1. Decree by President Emmanuel Macron Declaring April 24 an Official French Memorial Day. Source: Legifrance (www.legifrance.gouv.fr).

Décret n° 2019-291 du 10 avril 2019
relatif à la commémoration annuelle du génocide arménien de 1915

NOR : *PRMX1820266D*

Le Président de la République,
Sur le rapport du Premier ministre,
Vu l'article 37 de la Constitution ;
Vu la loi n° 2001-70 du 29 janvier 2001 relative à la reconnaissance du génocide arménien de 1915,
    Décrète :
Art. 1er. – La date de la commémoration annuelle du génocide arménien de 1915 est fixée au 24 avril.
Art. 2. – Chaque année, à cette date, une cérémonie est organisée à Paris.
Une cérémonie analogue peut être organisée dans chaque département à l'initiative du préfet.
Art. 3. – Le Premier ministre est chargé de l'exécution du présent décret, qui sera publié au *Journal officiel* de la République française.

Fait le 10 avril 2019.

EMMANUEL MACRON

    Par le Président de la République :
Le Premier ministre,
EDOUARD PHILIPPE

Observations at the first official commemoration show how a presidential decision translates into practice. On April 24, 2019, a large crowd gathered at the Armenian genocide memorial of Paris, the Komitas statue. This statue is a six-meter-high representation of Father Komitas, a priest and scholar of Armenian music, a survivor of the genocide, and a refugee to France. It stands prominently at the entrance to Yerevan Park (Jardin d'Erevan), at the northern end of the Pont des Invalides and close to the Grand Palais. It serves as a commemorative monument to the Armenian victims of the genocide and to those Armenians who fought and lost their lives in French military service and in the Résistance against Nazi German occupation. The City Council of Paris voted for its establishment on January 29, 2001, the day on which the legislature passed the recognition law, and the inauguration followed in 2003.

On the memorial day of 2019, close to the statue and with its back to the river Seine, stood a temporary stage with the inscription "Commemoration Nationale du Génocide Arménien." Around the stage, a first security perimeter was reserved for dignitaries, ministers, prefects, mayors, legislators, ambassadors, and leaders of the Armenian community. An outer perimeter began to fill with a mostly French Armenian crowd at 5 p.m. Bags and purses were checked at the entry points. By 6 p.m. an estimated two thousand people had gathered, and the official ceremony began half an hour later. Many in the crowd held up posters with the words "Génocide Arménien. 24 Avril. Journée Nationale de Commémoration. 1915–2019. Mémoire et Justice." Others waved French or Armenian flags. The symbolic display, and the ritual itself, demonstrated unity between the Armenian and

FIGURE 14. A crowd gathered in Paris for the first national day of commemoration of the Armenian genocide, April 24, 2019. Photo by the author.

French nations and their joint memory of the genocide against the Armenians of the Ottoman Empire (see figure 14).

The ceremony included the playing of the Armenian and French national anthems, the laying of wreaths at the memorial, and four speeches. Mourad Franck Papazian and Ara Toranian, copresidents of the Coordination Council of Armenian Organizations of France, delivered the first speeches.[5] The event culminated in speeches by Anne Hidalgo, mayor of Paris, and Édouard Philippe, prime minister of France.

All speeches specified the close alliance between Armenians and the French nation. They referred to Armenian immigrants who became heroes in the fight of the Résistance against Nazi Germany's occupation, famous among them Missak Manouchian, and to those who became national treasures in the world of arts such as chansonnier Charles Aznavour. Importantly, all speakers confirmed the Armenian repertoire of knowledge concerning the mass violence against the Armenians in 1915 and subsequent years, as illustrated by a quotation from Prime Minister Philippe:

> Between April 1915 and July 1916, one million Armenians disappeared, their blood shed, burned alive. The massive deportations transformed the Anatolian highways into routes of death. Women and children of all ages were martyred. An industrious people with a millennial history that had contributed much to the prosperity of the Ottoman Empire experienced a methodical and organized attempt at annihilation.
>
> The Armenians were put to death, as a people, because they were "guilty of being children of Armenia." Because they embodied an ethnic and Christian minority, thus a difference. The specificity of genocide is that one is guilty of being oneself.[6] (translated)

Conceding that the 2001 recognition law alone does not do sufficient justice to history, the prime minister stressed the need for this day of commemoration to secure the memory of the Armenian genocide. He challenged denialism, but—different from the two copresidents—he did not explicitly refer to Turkey and its current government as denialists and aggressors. Instead, he offered an olive branch and encouraged cooperation, stating, "For a long time already, ladies and gentlemen, courageous voices engage in the labor of memory and dialogue between Turks and Armenians. This day of commemoration of the Armenian genocide, of that we are convinced, is a day of peace. This day is not being celebrated to the detriment of any people" (translated).

In short, like the Massachusetts court case, the French story shows that massive opposition to genocide recognition, in an age of human rights hegemony, backfires. Acknowledgment of the genocide intensifies and is diffused. The knowledge repertoire of the victimized group enters into the edifice of hegemonic thought.[7] It solidifies and becomes further sedimented. In line with Gramsci's arguments, the state and "organic intellectuals" play key roles in this process. Gramsci's identification of media as another transmitter of hegemonic thought suggested an examination of media reports and documentary films.

Effects of Denialism: Contention in Western Media Reporting

Media reflect and transmit articulations by knowledge entrepreneurs—and the public events they initiate, including rituals and legislative and judicial proceedings—thereby enhancing hegemonic thought and communicating it far into civil society. Simultaneously, media filter articulations and events through their own institutional logic. Pierre Bourdieu characterized journalism as "a microcosm with its own laws, defined both by its position in the world at large and by the attractions and repulsions to which it is subject from other such microcosms" (1998:39). He appropriately depicted these microcosms as relatively independent or autonomous fields, following their own "rules of the game." Journalistic depictions of the world thus cannot be read, for example, as simple reflections of economic interests—even if pursuit of such interests is vital to the operation and survival of a newspaper or TV station.

While highlighting internal rules of the game, Bourdieu's argument is not necessarily contradictory to Gramsci's point about journalism's role in hegemonic thought. The field's rules, after all, are informed by its "position in the world at large" and by "attractions and repulsions from other fields." Bourdieu thus refines Gramsci's argument: news media's rules of the game are themselves affected by the environment in which they operate. Media are only *relatively* autonomous. While they must bolster legitimacy by projecting a sense of procedural fairness, they also depend on markets, thereby securing survival (and profits), and on sources of information.

All of this matters here because media pay attention to the judicial, legislative, and ritual events surrounding struggles over Armenian genocide recognition and denial. Even a simple count of all reports on Armenian issues in U.S. newspapers of record (*New York Times, Washington Post, Wall Street Journal*) and in renowned

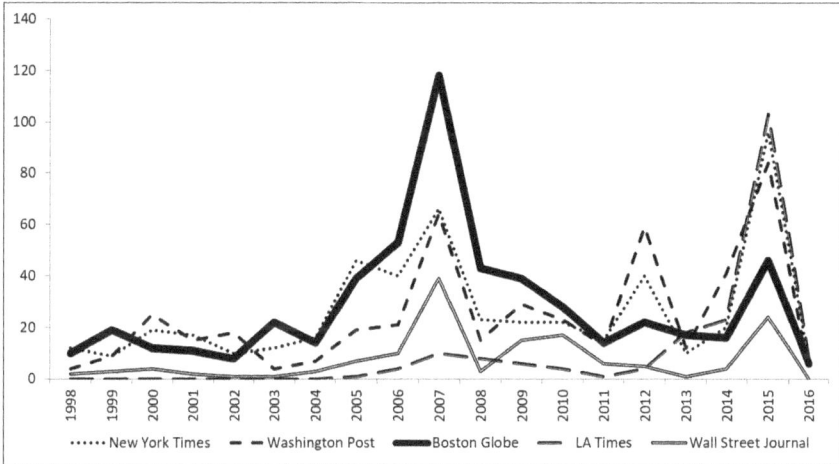

FIGURE 15. Frequency of reporting on Armenian affairs in selected U.S. newspapers.

papers from those regions that are home to the majority of diaspora Armenians (*Los Angeles Times, Boston Globe*) reveals remarkable patterns.

Figure 15 displays, by years, peaks and valleys in the frequency of reporting on Armenian issues. Three peaks stand out: 2007 and surrounding years, 2012 (albeit less pronounced), and 2015. Each peak speaks to an event analyzed in the preceding chapters. The years around 2007 witnessed the unfolding of *Griswold v. Driscoll*. Since that case was about Massachusetts teaching guidelines, it is not surprising that this peak of reporting is especially high for the *Boston Globe*. In 2012, the year of the second peak, the French legislature passed the law criminalizing denial of the Armenian genocide, and France's Constitutional Council overruled that legislative decision. This peak shows that important political events pertaining to the memory of the Armenian genocide register in U.S. reporting, even when they unfold abroad. Finally, 2015 is the centennial of the Armenian genocide, an event commemorated by Armenian communities and their supporters in Armenia and in the diaspora (see chapter 6). Media reported these rituals widely and thereby transformed public events into cultural events, multiplying their effects on collective perceptions (Dayan and Katz 1992).

What, then, do journalists write when they address the Armenian genocide and struggles over its recognition? An analysis of a random sample of 301 articles from English-language newspapers in various countries around the globe and of 265 French media reports provides answers. For the latter, we selected articles published in *Le Monde*, the leading center-left daily newspaper, and in *Le Figaro*, the most prominent center-right paper of record in France. The period included in the analysis is from 1998, just preceding the French legislation recognizing the Armenian genocide, to the beginning of 2016, the year after the centennial commemoration.

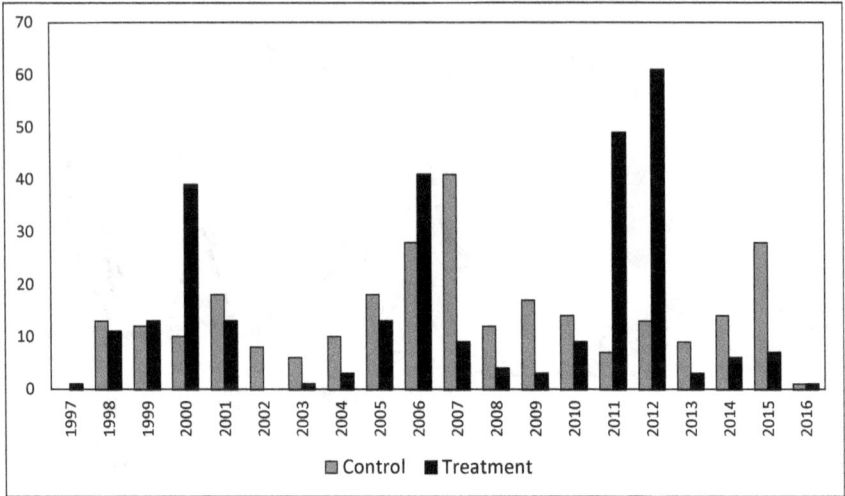

FIGURE 16. Frequency of reports in news media sample, by treatment vs. control group, over time.

Out of the articles we selected, seventy-four English-language pieces and 179 French articles addressed the French legislative process. Twenty-nine articles in English (and no French articles) engaged with the *Griswold v. Driscoll* court case. Given my interest in effects of legislative and legal struggles on knowledge, I refer to these as treatment cases. I refer to other articles that speak directly to the Armenian genocide as control cases.

Figure 16 shows that the distribution of this sample of articles over time is quite similar to that for the population of articles in U.S. newspapers shown above, confirming that the events we are interested in resonate transnationally. In addition, debates over the 2001 French recognition law are reflected in the sample, adding an additional peak in reporting. Figure 16 also shows a noteworthy specification: peaks surrounding major legislative decisions are due to articles that focus on debates over recognition as opposed to articles about the genocide per se. The peak of the 2015 centennial instead results primarily from reporting on the genocide itself. Figure 16 further indicates that political struggles (2000, 2011–12) are less likely than a court case (2006–7) to evoke reports about the genocide as such. At the expense of reporting history of the genocide itself, politics keeps journalistic attention focused on controversies carried out by highly visible political actors, compared to judicial proceedings or memorial events. The following, then, is a significant takeaway from this analysis: Commemorative events, and even court trials, are more likely than political struggles over recognition to direct public attention toward the events of the genocide per se.

Content analysis of the sample of 566 articles reveals the structure of representations of the genocide and of disputes over its recognition, the time and place of publication, and voices cited.[8]

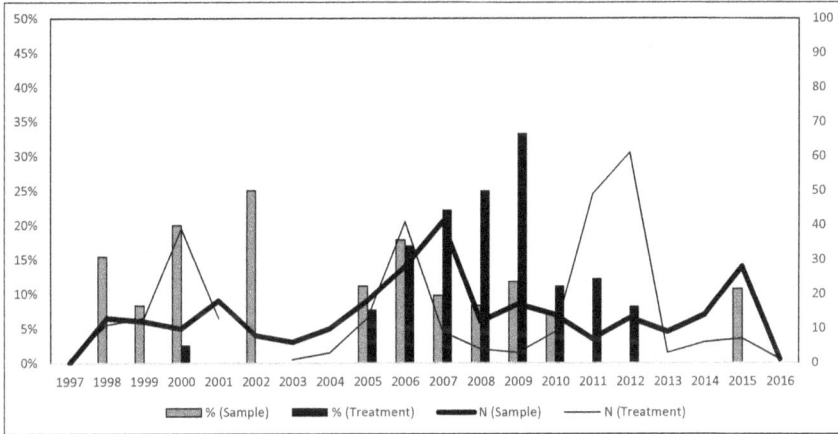

FIGURE 17. Percentage and frequency of references to "rebellious Armenians" in news media over time.

Media's striving for procedural fairness is commonly reflected in a tendency to cite players from opposing sides and a reliance on actors in positions of high authority in reporting about conflicts. Our data show that journalists apply both these strategies when reporting debates about the Armenian genocide. While media strongly support genocide claims, articles also present arguments used by those who challenge acknowledgment and criminalization of denial. They reference political motives of actors (20.2%) and concerns about free speech issues (22.2%), the latter especially in the context of criminalization debates, concerns about Turkey's position in international relations (49.2%), and the health of French-Turkish relations (39.2%). Some articles speak to Armenian militancy (8.8%), potentially weakening the legitimacy of Armenian claims, and many argue that both sides of the divide present at least some legitimate arguments (49%).

Our analysis also confirms media reliance on holders of high political office from both sides of the divide. The most frequently mentioned actor in the sample of articles, in fact, is the Turkish president (previously prime minister) Recep Tayyip Erdoğan (12.4%); two other leading Turkish politicians are also cited relatively frequently (Ahmet Davutoğlu and Abdullah Gül, each just above 4%). On the French side, presidents dominate, all of them proponents of acknowledgment of the Armenian genocide and criminalization of its denial. They include Nicolas Sarkozy (8.6%), Jacques Chirac (5.1%), and François Hollande (5.1%). Other individual actors are cited far less frequently.

Arguments intended to weaken the legitimacy of the Armenian side emerge primarily in the context of political conflicts over acknowledgment and denial, as shown in Figure 17. We see that the percentage of references that highlight the militancy of Armenian insurgency is higher during periods of political or legal disputes (bars, left y-axis). The same applies to the frequency of those references (curve, right y-axis). The figure shows further that this effect is primarily due to reports about political or legal disputes (dark bar graph and line) compared to articles on the genocide as such (gray bar graph and dotted line).

Other rules of the journalistic game reflect the nature of the medium itself. Because of time and space constraints, journalistic reports about mass violence often simplify, focusing on the most dramatic (and quantifiable) events and portraying conflicting parties in overly streamlined ways. Previous studies have found—in reporting on African conflicts—that opposing parties are frequently presented as primordial ethnic or racial groups (e.g., Allen and Seaton 1999; Crilly 2010; McNulty 1999; Thompson 2007). Might this pattern apply to journalistic depictions of Turks and Armenians as well?

Our analysis reveals remarkable patterns. Consider specific forms of victimization. Most articles (45.7%) explicitly speak to killings and many (16.2%) to displacements. Journalists only rarely mention rapes (1.1%), kidnappings (1.2%), the appropriation of Armenian property (1.2%), lack of food and water (4.1%), or disease (1.8%). The rarity of reporting of other forms of victimization starkly contrasts with most historical studies, which engage with the entire range of victimization to which the Ottoman Armenians were exposed. Space constraints are one likely contributor to such omissions.

In line with previous research on other violent conflicts, journalistic references to differentiations within each of the conflicting groups during the unfolding of the genocide are rare. Yet some journalists report dissent within contemporary Turkish society. A March 17, 2015, article in Le Monde ("Editorial" section, p. 15), by staff writer Marie Jégo, addresses Turkish civil society as a motor toward reconciliation with Armenia, listing the many "brave" Turkish intellectuals who engage in difficult "memory work." Furthermore, on April 25, 2007, Sophie Shihab published an article in Le Monde ("International" section, p. 4) about Kurds in the southwest of Turkey who commemorate the genocide and accept (co-)responsibility. Such depictions of conflicting parties within Turkey seek to open up avenues for understanding and reconciliation. In doing so, they simultaneously encourage future acknowledgment of the genocide.

One important constraint on media is the markets in which they operate. Survival depends on sales and ratings. Sales and ratings, in turn, depend on consumers' level of interest and the degree to which reports make sense to them. Especially in the commercialized segments of the media field, journalists thus seek to stir excitement and to dramatize representations. South African dramaturgist Jane Taylor put it well when she wrote about opportunities for dramatization in the realm of grave human rights violations, specifically regarding the role of perpetrators (quoted in Payne 2008:16): "What makes the stories of perpetrators so compelling is, in part, that they are agents: they act upon others. All of the psychological structures of desire, power, greed, fear, identification are invoked in these accounts. Milton's classic dilemma in Paradise Lost was that Satan became the hero of the narrative, because of the inherent interest in his character."

Unsurprisingly, journalists tend to play to preconceptions among consumers of news. In an era of human rights hegemony, we expect them to write about the genocide against the Armenians within the human rights frame; to interpret the violence as criminal, in line with the Genocide Convention; to identify perpetrators; and to link this genocide to others about which the public has reached a broad consensus. In our sample, the relative majority of articles (29.5%) indeed interpreted the aggression against the Armenians as a form of criminal violence and those who executed it as violent criminals. This percentage is especially important, given that half of all articles that do not deal with the violence per se, but rather with disputes over acknowledgment or denial, do not frame the acts of aggression themselves. To support the crime frame, many articles address the *mens rea*, the violators' mental state, as a necessary ingredient of crime, especially the crime of genocide. In fact, 25.8 percent of articles explicitly confirm intent. Within those, journalists most often identify the (Ottoman) state (46.4%) and the Young Turks (5.3%) as perpetrators. An article by *Le Monde* correspondent Jerôme Gautheret of April 23, 2015, provides an excellent example, elaborately reconstructing events and statements by the successors of the Young Turk government. Gautheret here quotes a December 13, 1918, pronouncement from the Turkish Ministry of the Interior: "During the war, our leaders applied . . . the law of deportations in a way that exceeds the infamy of the most bloodthirsty bandits. They decided to exterminate the Armenians, and exterminate them they did. The decision was made by the Central Committee of the CUP [Committee of Union and Progress] and was implemented by the government" (*Le Monde*, April 23, 2015, supplement, p. 5; translated).

Referencing other, generally recognized, mass atrocities is another means of attributing meaning to a debated event. This includes analogical bridging—the referencing of past atrocities that have taken cultural shape to shed light on new or debated episodes of violence. In our sample of articles about the Armenian genocide, a quarter (25.8%) indeed refer to other mass atrocities as points of comparison. Of these, about two-thirds (16.7% of total) cite the Shoah. To be sure, at times journalists reference the Holocaust to draw a distinction with the Armenian genocide, most commonly in reports about the criminalization debate. Yet, because most readers of journalistic reporting understand the Holocaust as the ultimate evil of the twentieth century and because the genocide convention grew out of this dark chapter of human history, frequent bridging indicates that the media seek to appeal to the known in order to dramatize the Armenian genocide.

Media reports resort to analogical bridging especially in the context of disputes over denialism, which supports my central argument about the counterproductive effects of denial in an age of a human rights hegemony. A 2011 article in *Le Monde*, for example, reports on a state visit by President Sarkozy to Armenia. The article quotes the president, who was "profoundly moved" by the genocide memorial. It "evoked memories of Yad Vashem—in Israel—and of the genocide museum of Kigali—in Rwanda." Sarkozy continued that Armenia is "in the heart of all French people [because] from the tragedy of the genocide was born our alliance" (*Le Monde*, October 2011, "Europe" section, p. 4; translated).

In sum, news media, when reporting on the Armenian genocide and struggles over its recognition, reinforce a human rights hegemony. It is true that they strive for balance in their reports, quoting prominent representatives from both sides of the divide. Yet they nonetheless tend to frame the violence as an instance of crimes committed in violation of human rights principles. They point to specific perpetrators and their exterminationist intent. At times, they even use, or report, analogical bridging to the Shoah, thereby comparing the Armenian genocide to that which the public perceives as the ultimate evil in modern history.

Documentary Films, Acknowledgment of Genocide, and Effects of Denialism

Documentary films reinforce the dominant message in U.S. and French news media. An analysis of ten films reveals factual and interpretive denial by Turkish authorities and suggests that filmmaking became one strategy to challenge denialist claims.

Consider the film *Aghet—Ein Völkermord* (Aghet—a genocide), produced in 2010 by ARD, Germany's public media giant. This documentary offers a chronological depiction of the Armenian genocide, supported by archival sources from multiple countries. Footage of Turkish denialism leads into a chronological reconstruction of events before, during, and after the genocide. The film intersperses actors reading excerpts from archival reports, as though they are the author relaying the information, with narration expanding on the reports, accompanied by footage of the atrocities. Focusing on conditions leading to the genocide, its execution, and responsible actors, the film seeks to prove that the Young Turks—under the leadership of Talaat Pasha, Enver Pasha, and Jamal Pasha—carried out a planned, systematic annihilation of the Armenian people. Deportations and death marches are thoroughly covered.

This and other films dramatize their depiction of the Armenian genocide by building analogical bridges to the Shoah. *Aghet* reports, for example, how "in 1934 the body of Talaat Pasha was sent by the Nazis with a pompous state ceremony from Berlin to Turkey" (1:18:50). It establishes a further link by quoting the infamous words attributed to Hitler, "Who still talks today about the annihilation of the Armenians?" (1:19:12). Footage from Nazi Germany explicitly draws parallels to the Armenian genocide (1:18–1:20). The message is further underlined when the film quotes Raphael Lemkin's conclusion that the Young Turks' actions "seemed . . . like a blueprint for the Hitlerian Holocaust and further genocide" (1:20:29) or words by Patrick Devedjian, a French minister and close advisor to President Sarkozy, who challenged Turkish denial with these words: "It is as if the Nazi government members were generally honored in today's Germany" (1:22:26).

We find similar themes and links to the Shoah in other films. *Destination Nowhere: The Witness* (2003) tells the story of Armin Wegner, a German medic during World War I who took many of the iconic photographs of the genocide. Inspired by his traumatic observations on the way to the Syrian Desert, Wegner later raised his voice against Hitler's rise to power. This film thus adds at least an indirect historical link between the Armenian genocide and the Holocaust. *My Son Shall Be Armenian*, a 2004 documentary, follows six people traveling through Armenia to gather stories and connect to their Armenian heritage. Directed by Hagop Goudsouzian, the film frames the violence as genocide. A quotation from a *New York Times* article about "Another Armenian Holocaust" (20:23) is followed by video footage from the Syrian Desert (21:04) and photographs of deportation routes to Deir ez-Zor (21:10). *Screamers*, a 2006 film about an Armenian American metal band with a mission to inform its listeners about genocide, focuses on the Armenian genocide but presents footage from the Holocaust, Rwanda, Yugoslavia (Srebrenica/Sarajevo), and Darfur as well. It also mentions Pol Pot's Cambodia and Stalin's Russia, at times building direct links to the Armenian genocide. Finally, *Secret Histories: The Hidden Holocaust* builds analogical bridging into its title and follows up with explicit references. The narrator reports, over imagery of caves, "Into these caves were tipped literally thousands of women and children," calling them a "Subterranean Auschwitz" (25:45). The film refers to a "Scene of the century's first Holocaust" (29:27) and concludes that Turkish denial is "in some ways identical" to denial by Neo-Nazis when they say that the "Nazi Holocaust against Jews never happened." Other documentaries, such as *Voices from the Lake* (2003), graphically depict the mass violence and use a genocide frame, but without bridging it to the Shoah.

In short, documentary films seem to parallel curricular guidelines, memorials, official recognitions, and a majority of media reports. Filmmakers suggest that denial motivated their drive to acknowledge. Most seek to shed light on the Armenian genocide by building analogical bridges to the Holocaust.

CONCLUSIONS

Case studies from the political and legal fields in France and the United States— begun in chapters 7 and 8, respectively, and continued here—demonstrate the power of human rights hegemony. Power struggles at the level of concrete deci- sion making may yield partial victories to denialist actors. Yet those turn out to be Pyrrhic victories under conditions of human rights hegemony. Just as hegemony prevents grave problems from becoming issues in public conscious- ness and in politics, so it precludes the denial of problems that are broadly rec- ognized. State actors and NGOs are driving forces in securing human rights hegemony and acknowledgment of mass atrocity. Journalists and documentary filmmakers strengthen their case. In the context of human rights hegemony, efforts at denial yield counterproductive consequences, reinforcing the under- standing of the mass violence against the Armenians of the Ottoman Empire as a case of genocide.

Conclusions

Closing the Epistemic Circle
and Future Struggles

The circle of knowledge about the Armenian genocide began to unfold when knowledge repertoires were built up through manifold personal interactions and reflections, through micropolitics of silencing, denial, and acknowledgment. Knowledge entrepreneurs stepped into the picture. Using their privileged access to channels of communication, they shaped rituals and took sides in epistemic struggles in a variety of social fields. In the end, knowledge became objectified and sedimented to establish the "Armenian genocide." It became part of a taken-for-granted historical reality, especially among young generations of Armenians, part of their identity, collective memory, and cultural trauma.

The epistemic process followed a similar logic among Armenians and Turks, but the content of knowledge took radically different shape for these victim and perpetrator peoples. Faced with fierce opposition from the other side, each of these ethno-national groups used public rituals to solidify knowledge repertoires in the in-group. Each also engaged in conflictual strategies to confront the other, in the spheres of law and politics.

The outcomes of these epistemic struggles were mixed. In *Griswold v. Driscoll*, the legal struggle over teaching guidelines in Massachusetts, the court's decision did not confirm the knowledge of either side but it allowed the Massachusetts Department of Education's guidelines to stand. The Armenian genocide thus continues to be a recommended subject of instruction in public schools. In France, legislation acknowledged the history of the Armenian genocide, but the Constitutional Council, on free speech grounds, struck down a later law that sought to criminalize denial of that genocide.

As important as concrete decision-making processes and their outcomes are, we cannot fully grasp their consequences without recognizing that today, judicial and political conflicts unfold in the context of human rights hegemony, a broad recognition of human dignity and condemnation of mass atrocities and violations of basic human rights. Human rights hegemony emerged in the post–World War II era, simultaneously with the Armenian struggle for recognition. It contributed to the generation and sedimentation of knowledge about mass atrocities, including the Armenian genocide. It also produced counterproductive consequences for those who pursued denialist agendas. In the context of a human rights hegemony, denial created and continues to create painful dissonances. It motivates resistance by civil society and governmental actors, and—consequently—further solidifies genocide knowledge. We have observed this pattern in the aftermath of both the *Griswold v. Driscoll* case and the French Constitutional Council decision. My analysis of media reporting and filmmaking provided further support.

Finally, once sedimented over the course of 105 years, knowledge repertoires about the Armenian genocide constitute a matter-of-course understanding of history. Resistance appears vain, even absurd. Survivors can no longer protect new generations from knowledge of a cruel past, and elders of the third generation typically no longer seek to do so. Young Armenians encounter the history of the genocide in stories told at home, in church, and in cultural associations. Some participate in organized group travel to Yerevan on April 24, the official Armenian day of genocide commemoration. Many students, not just Armenians, encounter knowledge about the genocide through school curricula. Others visit memorials, listen to news about commemorative events, and watch documentary films. Learning about the Armenian genocide is now part of the socializing process through which the objectified reality of the Armenian genocide becomes instilled in the minds of new generations. *At this point, the circle of knowledge closes.*

CONTINUING STRUGGLES AND NEW DIVISIONS

Importantly, though, the closing of the epistemic circle is not the end of history. Those who grow up today with knowledge about the Armenian genocide do so in a world different from that of their elders, and the same will be true for their children and their children's children. In this changed world, the reaffirmation of, and struggles over, genocide knowledge take different shape, in everyday interactions, in ritual life, and in political and legal processes. Consequently, knowledge—no matter how sedimented—continues to mutate.

Several historical changes will affect current and future epistemic struggles and mutations of knowledge. Human rights hegemony is well established, but new cohorts (will) also experience challenges to that hegemony. Nationalist forces, new forms of ethnocentrism advanced by populist political leaders, and growing mistrust in democracy are contributing factors. In the homeland, young

Armenians recently experienced new struggles over democracy. In international relations, Turkey continues to play a powerful role, and President Erdoğan is among the growing number of rulers who exhibit nationalist-populist leanings and practices. These include military assertiveness, even support for Turkey's ally Azerbaijan in a new war in Nagorno Karabakh in fall of 2020 that has killed hundreds and threatens to destabilize the region at the time of this writing. Correspondingly, Erdoğan's government has been enforcing denial with a new vengeance, a continuing provocation to young Armenians and to those who solidarize with them. How will they react to a denialist's deadly campaign against their people that, one century earlier, had fallen victim to his genocidal predecessors? What will the consequences be for knowledge formation? What will they be for practice, war and peace? These are among the questions I have to leave unanswered.

We also saw, however, that Turkish knowledge is no longer unified. A multitude of scholars who contributed critical evidence on the Armenian genocide and about Turkish denialism, many cited in this book, are Turks or of Turkish descent. Many have been forced into exile. Their communication now unfolds around the globe, and some of it reaches back into Turkey. Their chances at making inroads within Turkish society will be contingent on multiple factors, including domestic developments within Turkey and geopolitical shifts. At any rate, new chapters will be added to the history of conflicts over genocide knowledge between Armenians and Turks and their respective allies. In this struggle, coalitions of young Turks and Armenians will play an important role. While this book cannot predict the future shape of genocide knowledge, all evidence indicates that struggles will continue but that acknowledgment will solidify.

This book also calls out for future research. For example, we can read the struggle over recognition of the Armenian genocide as one among a growing number of instances in which populist and authoritarian leaders disregard overwhelming evidence. While the story of struggles over recognition of the Armenian genocide provides insights into these leaders' strategies as well as ways in which they can be defeated, future research on this question is desirable. It seems that opportunities will be plentiful. The struggle over recognition of the Armenian genocide sheds light on elite-populace interaction, and several chapters in this book elaborated on sources of denialism, often strategically deployed by leaders. Yet the book has also shown that conditions of receptivity among the populace matter. In the case of the Armenian genocide, these conditions of receptivity include the suffering of Turks and the defeats experienced by the Turkish state in the period preceding and during World War I, and the conditions of the founding of modern Turkey. Additional factors are authoritarianism, centralized control of the educational system, and the recent and massive cleansing rituals that glorify the Ottoman Empire. In addition, Turkey's geopolitical position in a volatile Middle East, a bargaining chip against pressures from the international community, further enables denialism. Yet denial risks counterproductive consequences, as indicated by the final chapter of this book. It does so especially in the context of human rights hegemony and sedimented genocide knowledge.

SEDIMENTATION: APPLYING A METAPHOR
IN THE SOCIAL SCIENCES

"Sedimentation" indeed features centrally in this book. It marks the end of a process that begins with rather fluid elements, thoughts expressed in interpersonal interactions, verbal utterances, and diary or memoir writings. The term, borrowed from the work of Peter Berger and Thomas Luckmann, is one example of the use of metaphors in social science. In geology, *sedimentation* refers to a "process of deposition of a solid material from a state of suspension or solution in a fluid (usually air or water)." The quality of these materials, once deposited, depends on a complex set of factors, "related not only to the density and viscosity of the fluid medium but also to the translational velocity of the depositing fluid, the turbulence resulting from this motion, and the roughness of the beds over which it moves. These processes are also related to various mechanical properties of the solid materials propelled, to the duration of sediment transport, and to other little-understood factors" (www.britannica.com /science/sedimentation-geology).

Translating this definition into the sphere of cultural life, we may think of the density and viscosity of the medium as the shape of network structures in which thoughts and articulations circulate (varying, for example, between diaspora and homelands). Turbulences are the rapidity of social change within which cultural expressions take place (e.g., the breakup of the Soviet Union or the emergence of human rights hegemony). We may liken the features of the material propelled to the variable forms of expression (e.g., spoken word, written text, or ritual performance). The duration of sediment transport is comparable to historical time (105 years), and contributing gravitation is analogous to the power and force expressed in conflictual processes (in the legal and political fields). Importantly, that which is sedimented may be solid, but it is still subject to future mutations: in geology from peat to coal, and—with enough pressure and time—to diamonds. I leave it to the reader to think of the cultural equivalents of these physical materials for the formation of knowledge repertoires regarding the Armenian genocide.

I thus end with two messages. The first is an epistemological lesson that the social and cultural sciences may learn from the natural sciences. Applying the geological concept of sedimentation in sociology reminds us that complex processes require complex and multidimensional theoretical approaches. I attempted to capture those various dimensions in the model of an epistemic circle. Second, and closely related, is a substantive lesson: that knowledge about genocide—including knowledge about the Armenian genocide—is the outcome of processes that lead from thinking and social interaction, through interventions by knowledge entrepreneurs, through ritual affirmation and conflict carried out in various social fields and national and global settings, toward sedimentation. Subsequent generations acquire such knowledge, and this acquisition occurs in new historical contexts. Sedimented knowledge is thus subject to future change. Especially when attacked by authoritarian forces, those who carry the knowledge will continue to experience suffering, and they will be propelled to engage in future epistemic struggles.

NOTES

INTRODUCTION

1. I keep citations to a minimum in this introduction. The authors and works mentioned here will be cited and referenced in the following parts of the book.

2. While the sociology of scientific knowledge shows that historians and their work also reflect their place in history and society, here I do not engage in a sociology of historical knowledge. This book is instead concerned with knowledge in the everyday world of private lives, civil society, politics, and law. Accounts by historians serve as orienting information.

CHAPTER 1. SOCIAL INTERACTION, SELF-REFLECTION, AND STRUGGLES OVER GENOCIDE KNOWLEDGE

1. Gülek is a strategically important mountain pass. Many refugees had to pass through it and thus became easy targets (see Kévorkian 2011:597–599). The reader will encounter a few references to Gülek (or Külek) Station in chapter 2. On events around Yozgat, see Kévorkian (2011:502ff).

2. Little of our knowledge is certified knowledge. We often do not even remember its source, but we think of it as knowledge nonetheless. If knowledge is certified, most of us do not know who certified it. Knowledge about what constitutes valid methods of certification, like all knowledge, varies across social groups, and few have exposed their methodological assumptions to rigorous epistemological inquiry.

3. Quoted from www.ohchr.org/EN/ProfessionalInterest/Pages/CrimeOfGenocide.aspx (last visited June 21, 2020).

4. These video recordings are available online from the Shoah Visual Archives at the University of Southern California (USC) Shoah Foundation, https://sfi.usc.edu/what-we-do /collections (last visited June 21, 2020).

5. Fatma Müge Göçek reports similar observations from interviews with Armenians in Turkey. In those exceptional cases where silence was broken, women were the ones who spoke about the past (personal communication).

6. The credibility of scholarly or other kinds of evidence is itself variable. Attacks by interested actors, doubts in public opinion, and even challenges internal to the world of scholarship have lately experienced new heights, and research on the Armenian genocide is no exception.

7. The notion of interpretive denial poses a challenge to constructionist thought. Constructionists never consider crime an ontological given, because behaviors considered criminal in one place or one era may not be criminal in another. Those responsible for mass violence, historically celebrated as heroes and great state builders, today fear criminal indictments (Giesen 2004b). I contend that we can solve the puzzle if we apply the analytic potential of the sociology of knowledge while we take a philosophically realist position.

8. According to Dariuš Zifonun (2004), self-stigmatization of those who remember, as descendants of the perpetrators, leads to a symbolic transformation of guilt into grace.

9. This section is based on a content analysis of video recordings of Armenian genocide survivors from the Visual History Archives of the USC Shoah Foundation, conducted by Kate Dwyer, an undergraduate student at the University of Minnesota, in the context of a Dean's First Year Student Scholarship. Dwyer also contributed to the writing of this section.

CHAPTER 2. DIARIES AND BEARING WITNESS IN THE HUMANITARIAN FIELD

1. Prashasti Bhatnagar and Erez Garnai contributed to this chapter through their diligent work in the Minnesota History Archives. Dr. Lou Ann Matossian made us aware of the materials analyzed in this chapter and guided us into the archives.

2. Quoted from www2.mnhs.org/library/findaids/P1282.xml?return=brand%3Dfindaids %26q%3Dcharmelite%2520christie (last visited June 21, 2020).

3. We sought to work with volumes 3 through 13, containing Christie's diaries written between January 23, 1915, and December 23, 1919. Because the first of these volumes (no. 3) appears to be missing, the analysis is limited to the period of October 1, 1915, through December 23, 1919 (MHS Box 28).

4. Today, scholars interpret the lack of international response as a signal to the Young Turk government that they could proceed with impunity in their mistreatment of the empire's minority populations.

5. On the significance of Gülek Station, see chapter 1, note 1.

6. Christie's actions and accounts occasionally focus on particular individuals. On August 31, 1917, she observes: "Each day I could write *pages* [underlined in original] of the suffering I see. The very old and the little children suffer the most acutely. I took a boy with me last night to carry a soft bed to old Jizmejian, an exile from Harpoot to whom we have given a little help each week for upwards of two years. Last week he started to come here, fell unconscious in the street, was picked up and taken to his wretched mud room in a filthy yard with crowds of other exiles all about him in adjoining rooms, all as poor as himself. His bedding was wretchedly scant and dirty, and bed sores were forming on his hips. I took my thermos bottle full of tea along, thinking to divide it between him and a blind girl living

near and ill. He told me he had had nothing to eat all day. He drank every drop of four large cups of tea and ate the other food I had brought as if starving. . . . I sent more food today as he has no one about him he can trust to buy for him. In the next yard I found a feeble old woman wretchedly destitute and nearly blind. With her was a 2-year-old baby girl with a face like white wax, and so hungry! The mother is dead and no one knows what has become of the father. The child goes out into the street and eats melon rinds etc. from rubbish heaps. I left money to help in her care: saw other cases about as bad, with ague in nearly every house" (MHS Box 28:159–160).

7. Appropriation of collective property is also an issue, according to an October 6 entry: "Fine congregation today. The people seem to enjoy getting back to their old place of worship. How we had hoped, long ere this to have the new church! The foundations stand, but the outside wall, about half has been carried away with practically all the stones ready for the building and the lime. The trees have been cut down, and the premises left in a state of ruin and desolation. Most of the money that had been put into materials was given from America, but the property was held in the name of the Armenian Protestants of Tarsus. So the chance of receiving damages is extremely small. The stones were carried off and sold by Govt order, confiscated as Armenian property" (MHS Box 28: 255).

8. Remaining diary entries of 1919 center around thankfulness for peace and the reunion with her husband. They contain little more bearing witness or reports about humanitarian aid. In 1920, Carmelite Christie and her husband returned to the United States.

9. On "righteous" Turks who helped Armenians, see Shirinian (2015).

10. I owe this information to Serge Avédikian and his film *Nous avons bu la même eau*.

11. For supplemental materials, see the author's website, www.joachimsavelsberg.com.

12. See the spoken text of many of these testimonies in the film *Aghet—Ein Völkermord*, a documentary produced in 2010 by the Arbeitsgemeinschaft der öffentlich-rechtlichen Rundfunkanstalten der Bundesrepublik Deutschland (ARD), one of the two major German public broadcasting corporations. I discuss the film in chapter 9. It can be viewed at www.youtube.com/watch?v=5UdieWTeUcc&t=514s.

13. See Akçam (2006), Bloxham (2005), Kévorkian (2011), and Suny et al. (2011). For a review of a wealth of scholarship, reflecting overwhelming consent despite controversies on specifics, see Der Matossian (2015).

14. For contemporary literature building on these classics, see chapter 3.

CHAPTER 3. CARRIERS, ENTREPRENEURS, AND EPISTEMIC POWER— A CONCEPTUAL TOOLBOX TOWARD AN UNDERSTANDING OF GENOCIDE KNOWLEDGE

1. On the relationship between the social and the individual in memory, see Olick (1999).

2. Current scholarship builds on Mannheim's suggestion (e.g., Corning and Schuman 2015; Schuman and Scott 1989). Yet a revival of Karl Mannheim's broader contribution is in order. See *The Anthem Companion to Karl Mannheim*, edited by David Kettler and Volker Meja (London: Anthem Press, 2018).

3. David Kertzer (1983) shows that Mannheim really means birth cohorts when he writes about "generations."

4. On their categorization as genocide, see Naimark (2010).

5. Studies on the diffusion of law and policies show similar mixes of path dependency and orientation to current circumstances. In the case of genocide law, countries adopting such laws often build on, but at times expand or contract, the definition presented in the Genocide Convention of 1948 (McElrath 2020).

6. Different from criminal trials, truth commissions allow for, and under specific circumstances explicitly invite, implicatory acknowledgment. The TRC of South Africa is a prime example (Payne 2008).

CHAPTER 4. SEDIMENTATION AND MUTATIONS OF ARMENIAN KNOWLEDGE ABOUT THE GENOCIDE

1. See www.genocide-museum.am/eng/Description_and_history.php (last visited before typesetting of this book on June 21, 2020, recently altered).

2. On religious dimensions of this war, see Tonoyan (2012).

3. Armenian community experiences and learning about the genocide are not limited to Armenia and the two large recipient countries. Events organized by Armenian cultural associations in the United States, for example the Armenian Cultural Organization of Minnesota, show the spread of genocide knowledge in the diaspora of the Middle East and the former Soviet Union. In 2017, one speaker, now in his fifties, who grew up Armenian in the Ukraine and whose grandparents had survived the genocide, reports about his childhood and youth. While "soaked" in Armenian culture, his grandfather, whom he never saw laugh, did not readily speak about the genocide. He does remember, however, the politicization of the Armenian community in Ukraine around the pogroms of the late 1980s in Azerbaijan. Another speaker, now in her fifties, tells about growing up in Iran. She attended an Armenian school in Teheran, where she was a member of the Armenian girl scouts and of the Ararat Society. She recalls many ethnic events as a girl and young woman, including annual April 24 commemorations. She also remembers vividly a picture of her grandparents handed down across generations. A young woman in her late twenties, an immigrant to the United States from her native Syria, reflects on her growing up in the lively Armenian community of Aleppo. There the genocide had been a subject of instruction throughout her education, beginning in kindergarten. In the United States, she is an active member of a traditional Armenian dance group.

4. See, for example, https://cla.umn.edu/chgs/programming/educator-workshops/past -educator-workshops (last visited June 26, 2020).

5. On links between ethnicity and religion, see Wimmer (2013) and Brubaker (2015).

6. A Wikipedia entry on Watertown reports that "Watertown is also the venue for the publication of long-running Armenian newspapers in English and Armenian, including Baikar Association Inc.'s *Armenian Mirror-Spectator* and *Baikar*, and Hairenik Association Inc.'s *Armenian Weekly*, Հայրենիք *(Hairenik Weekly)*, and *Armenian Review*. Hairenik Association also runs a web radio and a web TV station."

7. While the Dashnaks were originally grassroots oriented, the AAA relied on a small professional staff.

8. The majority of these are not Armenian Americans.

9. Other examples include Richard Hovannisian, who grew up in the Armenian world of California to become one of the early American historians studying Armenia and the Armenian genocide (Hovannisian 2010).

10. Dörtyol, a place name meaning "four roads," refers to a location of strategic importance, where the Ottoman military expected a British attack. Deportations were to remove populations that might have welcomed enemy forces. These events preceded the persecution of Armenian intellectuals on April 24 by a good one month. The April 24 arrests and killings prevented potential oppositional action by Armenian leaders against these earlier deportations (for further detail, see Kévorkian 2011:585ff).

11. This situation differs from one in which carriers of opposing memories and meanings converge by necessity or desire. There, we may encounter institutionalized polysemy, as Elizabeth Barna (2020) shows for the Hermitage, Andrew Jackson's plantation outside of Nashville, Tennessee.

12. For a contrasting case, see Gao and Alexander (2017) on the memory of the Nanking Massacre, which disappeared from public consciousness in China. The authors attribute this outcome to the lack of the event's narration as a collective trauma and to missed opportunities to extend psychological identification and moral universalism.

CHAPTER 5. SEDIMENTATION OF TURKISH KNOWLEDGE ABOUT THE GENOCIDE—AND COMPARISONS

1. Also ingrained in Turkish public memory is the 1896 raid on the Ottoman Bank by twenty-eight members of the Armenian Revolutionary Federation (Dashnak), even if the fact is repressed that the raiders primarily sought to attract international attention to the killing of as many as two hundred thousand Armenians under Sultan Abdülhamid II. Western powers intervened diplomatically and the sultan pardoned the surviving attackers, who were allowed to travel into French exile—an outcome that many Turks resented.

2. Here and in the following paragraphs, quotations from Turkish newspapers were translated from Turkish into German by Bayraktar, and from German into English by this author (J.J.S.).

3. Note that the term *Holocaust* is uncommon in the Turkish language. Instead, the Turkish term *Soykırım* applies to both the Holocaust and the Armenian genocide, thus suggesting an equalization of both events, not just their subsummation under the common category of genocide (Bayraktar 2010:209).

4. Here, and in the following quotations, page numbers are missing because I quote from an online publication.

5. These numbers are likely inflated. In addition, the cited death toll includes not just Turks but also Kurds killed. Current Turkish narratives silence the latter aspect of the death toll.

6. Seemingly because of Turkish opposition, this entry appeared only belatedly.

7. Further down, the site specifies: "The CUP government systematically used an emergency military situation to effect a long-term population policy aimed at strengthening Muslim Turkish elements in Anatolia at the expense of the Christian population (primarily Armenians, but also Christian Assyrians). Ottoman, Armenian, US, British, French, German, and Austrian documents from the time reveal that the CUP leadership intentionally targeted the Armenian population of Anatolia. The CUP issued instructions from Constantinople and ensured enforcement through agents in its Special Organization and local administrations. The central government also required close monitoring and data collection on the number of Armenians deported, the amount and type of housing they left behind,

and the number of deportees reaching holding camps. Initiative and coordination came from the highest levels of the CUP ruling circle. At the center of the operation were: Talât Pasa (minister of interior), Ismail Enver Pasa (minister of war), Baheddin Sakir (field director for the Special Organization), and Mehmed Nâzim (leader of demographic planning)."

8. Quoted from https://encyclopedia.ushmm.org/content/en/article/the-armenian -genocide-1915-16-in-depth (last visited June 21, 2020).

9. On new trends within Turkish academia, see Göçek (2015:466–476).

CHAPTER 6. AFFIRMING GENOCIDE KNOWLEDGE THROUGH RITUALS

1. On contested memorials with ambivalent messages, see Wagner-Pacifici and Schwartz (1991) on the Vietnam Veterans Memorial in Washington, D.C.

2. On encounters with genocide memorials as more than engagement with history itself, but as visitors' civic engagement with themselves and others, in the case of the Berlin Holocaust memorial, see Dekel (2013).

3. *Not On Our Watch* is a nongovernmental, international relief and humanitarian aid organization. Based in the United States, it was established in the context of the Darfur conflict to bring global attention to situations of mass atrocity.

4. See www.youtube.com/watch?v=KQuWvY1FlKk (last visited June 21, 2020).

5. They were Hasmik Papian, Armenian opera singer of world renown, and David Ignatius, a *Washington Post* journalist.

6. An Integrity in Journalism Award went to *New York Times* journalist Rukmini Callimachi for her reporting on grave human rights violations. Callimachi's brief address and a video show her work reporting on ISIS and the rape of Yezidi women and girls. The MCs establish the link to the Armenian genocide by reminding the audience of Henry Morgenthau, the late U.S. ambassador to the Ottoman Empire, who bore witness and whose communications informed many articles about the Armenian genocide published in the *New York Times* during World War I. A second prize went to *The Promise*, a film about the Armenian genocide, produced by Survivor Pictures and lead producer Eric Esrailian.

7. Gregorian and Gbowee also introduced the first finalist, Syeda Ghulam Fatima, a Pakistani activist who freed more than eighty thousand bounded workers from a state of quasi-slavery in her native Pakistan. Gareth Evans, former Australian foreign minister, renowned for his human rights work, together with Shirin Ebadi, the first female judge in her native Iran, founder of the Defenders of Human Rights Center in Iran and a Nobel laureate, introduced Tom Catena, a physician operating in the Nuba Mountains of Sudan as the only surgeon for almost two hundred thousand people. Dr. Catena spoke about an "ongoing genocide" in the Nuba Mountains and the government's refusal to allow humanitarian access. Hina Jilani, a former special representative of the UN Secretary General and a human rights defender, and her copresenter introduced Bernard Kinvi, a priest from the Central African Republic, who—during a time of massive violence between Christian and Muslim groups—opened his mission to the threatened populations, irrespective of religion. Finally, George Clooney, known to most as a movie star, but introduced as a cofounder of Not On Our Watch, and Ruben Vardanyan, a Russian social entrepreneur, philanthropist, and cofounder of the Aurora Humanitarian Initiative, introduced Marguerite Barankitse, founder of the Maison Shalom in Burundi.

8. The museum, tucked behind the massive National Museum, hosted a recitation of "unanswered letters" from the years of the genocide on the day preceding the official ceremonies. People spilled out into the hallway, and TV cameras filmed the proceedings. I thank Zara Karakhanyan, who interpreted for me. Following the reading and a candle lighting ceremony, a film showed a group of Armenian artists—participants in a competition on the one hundredth anniversary of the Armenian genocide—on a journey into "Western Armenia." They walked through ruins of the ancient city of Ani and visited iconic buildings in Van, Kars, and other sites. Interviews with deeply moved participants tell viewers that the artists felt as though this was home (one even referred to local Kurds as their guests).

9. Narek Knyazyan received a "Special Prize" for a sculpture entitled *The Last*. It displays a man sitting at the head of long table, alone, shoulders bent forward, head bowed, his right lower arm and his left elbow leaning on the table. Cast in bronze, the work reflects a profound sense of loss, sadness, and mourning. The text on the back of a postcard depicting the sculpture, however, offers a more optimistic interpretation: "The gradually narrowing empty table, as the main axis of the creation, symbolizes the intention to exterminate completely the Armenians by the Ottoman Empire. But if we look at the sculpture on the opposite side, the last from the big family is sitting looking at the widening part of the table in the prospect as one to restore the family and to continue the Armenian gene." Diverse interpretations confirm the polysemic nature of material memorial culture.

10. Events at the University of Minnesota included the Annual Ohanessian Lecture, held in 2015 by Professor Bedross Der Matossian and an international conference, which brought together students from many countries, including Armenia. At a teachers' workshop, Professor Der Matossian and Minnesota historian Dr. Lou Ann Matossian (not related) provided Minnesotan high school teachers with strategies and materials suited to bridge the geographic and temporal divide between the events of 1915 and the students' lives in contemporary Minnesota in an effort to teach effectively about the Armenian genocide.

11. In 2019, a Turkish court sentenced Eren Keskin to three years and nine months in prison on the charge—commonly used nowadays against dissenters—of supporting a terrorist organization. Violent repression is obviously one strategy for keeping opposing knowledge at bay.

CHAPTER 7. EPISTEMIC STRUGGLES IN THE POLITICAL FIELD—
MOBILIZATION AND LEGISLATION IN FRANCE

1. On the complex case of the United States, see Zarifian (2014, 2018). On years of recognition, see Wikipedia, https://en.wikipedia.org/wiki/Armenian_Genocide_recognition (last viewed June 21, 2020). The data in this Wikipedia entry are based on government records. The meaning of *recognition* varies somewhat as different branches of government recognized the genocide with various wordings across countries. I selected the earliest marked year in cases for which several dates were provided.

2. The following analysis has greatly benefited from exchanges with many French colleagues, whom I acknowledge in the preface.

3. See http://melaproject.org/sites/default/files/2017–12/Law%20no.%2090–615%200of% 2013%20July%201990.pdf (last viewed June 21, 2020).

4. See Johan Michel (2011) on the institutionalization of the "crime against humanity" and the advancement of a victim-memorial regime in France.

5. All quotations from Duclert (2015) were translated from French to English by me (J.J.S.).

6. Data were not available for the 1998 National Assembly session.

7. Unofficial English translation. Original French: "Ceux qui oublient le passé sont condamnés à le revivre" (23 January 2012 Senate Proceedings, p. 332).

8. 23 January 2012 Senate Proceedings 1, (unofficial) English translation, pp. 3–8. Official French transcript pp. 332–335.

9. 23 January 2012 Senate Proceedings 3, (unofficial) English translation, pp. 1–3. Official French transcript pp. 341–342.

10. 23 January 2012 Senate Proceedings 3, (unofficial) English translation, pp. 3–4. Official French transcript pp. 342–343.

11. 23 January 2012 Senate Proceedings 1, (unofficial) English translation, pp. 8–11. Official French transcript pp. 335–337.

12. "Condamnant toute forme de négationnisme, qui constitue une atteinte odieuse à la mémoire des disparus et à la dignité des victimes, et réitérant son infini respect pour le peuple arménien et les terribles épreuves qu'il a endurées, il s'est interrogé sur la légitimité de l'intervention du législateur dans le champ de l'Histoire—considérant que l'adoption des résolutions et l'organisation de commémorations constituaient probablement des moyens plus adaptés pour exprimer la solidarité de la Nation avec les souffrances endurées par les victimes" (Commission report submitted to the Senate before the debate of 18 January, 2012, p. 5; official French transcript, http://www.senat.fr/rap/l11-269/l11-2690.html [last viewed October 7, 2020]).

13. See www.acam-france.org/contacts/index_associations_culturelles.php (last viewed April 12, 2019).

14. While similar analyses would be desirable for voting patterns, the distribution of votes is unknown. There is no reason, though, to expect different patterns.

15. 23 January 2012 Senate Proceedings 2, (unofficial) English translation, pp. 1–4. Official French transcript pp. 337–339.

16. See www.lemonde.fr/idees/article/2019/04/05/vincent-duclert-la-commission-sur-le -rwanda-aura-un-pouvoir-d-investigation-dans-toutes-les-archives-francaises _5446212_3232.html (last viewed April 18, 2019).

17. This and the following quotations are translated by the author (J.J.S.).

18. Art. 9.—Il est inséré, après l'article 24 de la loi du 29 juillet 1881 sur la liberté de la presse, un article 24 bis ainsi rédigé: « Art. 24 bis.—Seront punis des peines prévues . . . ceux qui auront contesté . . . l'existence d'un ou plusieurs crimes contre l'humanité tels qu'ils sont définis par l'article 6 du statut du tribunal militaire international annexé à l'accord de Londres du 8 août 1945 et qui ont été commis soit par les membres d'une organisation déclarée criminelle en application de l'article 9 du dit statut, soit par une personne reconnue coupable de tels crimes par une juridiction française ou interna- tionale. »

19. Lewis refused an offer by the Turkish state to cover the court expenses. Soon there- after, the Turkish Republic awarded him a prominent prize; he accepted the award, while declining the substantial monetary award associated with it.

20. The committee's manifesto declares that "le CVUH s'élève contre toute forme d'instrumentalisation de passé et souligne la nécessité d'une action collective de la part de 'tous ceux qui refusent que l'histoire soit livrée en pâture aux entrepreneurs de mémoire' dans un contexte où 'l'information-spectacle et l'obsession de l'audimat poussent constamment à le surenchère, valorisant les provocateurs et les amuseurs public, au détriment des historiens qui ont réalisé des recherches approfondies, prenant en compte la complexité du réel'" (in Adjemian 2012:13).

21. 7 November 2000 Senate Proceedings, (unofficial) English translation, pp. 160–163. Official French transcript pp. 155–158.

22. 7 November 2000 Senate Proceedings, (unofficial) English translation, pp. 163–165. Official French transcript pp. 158–160.

23. 18 May 2006 National Assembly Proceedings, (unofficial) English translation, pp. 30–35. Official French transcript pp. 3647–3650.

24. 12 October 2006 National Assembly Proceedings, (unofficial) English translation, pp. 17–19. Official French transcript pp. 6106–6107.

25. 4 May 2011 Senate Proceedings, (unofficial) English translation, pp. 22–23. Official French transcript pp. 3329–3330.

26. 4 May 2011 Senate Proceedings, (unofficial) English translation, pp. 23–24. Official French transcript pp. 3330–3331.

27. 23 January 2012 Senate Proceedings 2, (unofficial) English translation, pp. 1–4. Official French transcript pp. 337–339.

28. 22 December 2011 National Assembly Proceedings, (unofficial) English translation, p. 13. Official French transcript pp. 27–29.

29. 23 January 2012 Senate Proceedings 4, (unofficial) English translation, pp. 3–5. Official French transcript pp. 346–348.

30. 23 January 2012 Senate Proceedings 1, (unofficial) English translation, pp. 3–8. Official French transcript pp. 332–335.

31. Taken from the council's website in English: www.conseil-constitutionnel.fr/en (last viewed June 21, 2020).

CHAPTER 8. EPISTEMIC STRUGGLES IN THE LEGAL FIELD—SPEECH RIGHTS, MEMORY, AND GENOCIDE CURRICULA BEFORE AN AMERICAN COURT (WITH BROOKE B. CHAMBERS)

1. Social anthropologist Sally Engle Merry and her collaborators (2010) examine the mobilization for women's rights in New York City. Conceding that much of the human rights language in that mobilization stemmed from legal doctrines on both international and domestic levels, codified within the frame of legal logic, they nevertheless demonstrate that the mobilization of values by women's movements—law from below—substantially affected the outcome of the processes at stake.

2. A *next friend* is an "individual who acts on behalf of another individual who does not have the legal capacity to act on his or her own behalf" (https://legal-dictionary.thefreedictionary.com/next+friend).

3. The last point was debated by other respondents. We can neither confirm nor reject this assumption.

CHAPTER 9. DENIALISM IN AN AGE OF HUMAN RIGHTS HEGEMONY

1. This section uses interviews and archival research that Brooke B. Chambers conducted in the Boston area and in Washington, D.C., in 2018.

2. The state, contrary to the plaintiffs' argument, can prioritize the views of one political group over those of another, particularly when the legitimacy of the speech is questionable. Additionally, the plaintiffs' loss of *Griswold v. Driscoll* may have affected the strategizing of the Turkish state and Turkish-American groups in promoting a "contra-genocide" stance within courtrooms. One interviewee argued that this loss "didn't just discourage them, it stopped—they haven't done anything since then, in this regard. Have they tried to influence state departments of education and local school boards? Yes, but to a lesser extent— instead their focus has moved to other areas."

3. In addition to the Armenian Heritage Park, a Holocaust memorial was built on the Greenway in 1995. See www.nehm.org/the-memorial/history/ (last viewed June 21, 2020).

4. All translations here and in the following are by the author (J.J.S.).

5. The CCAF is the representative body of the French Armenian Community, an umbrella for its major political, cultural, educational, religious, and social organizations.

6. Quoted from www.gouvernement.fr/partage/11011-discours-lors-de-la-ceremonie -de-commemoration-du-genocide-armenien-de-1915.

7. On memory-activism in regard to the Israeli-Palestinian conflict, see Gutman (2017).

8. A subset of articles was read by two coders to examine inter-coder reliability, which was in the acceptable range throughout.

REFERENCES

Abel, Richard L., and Philip S. C. Lewis, eds. 1989. *Lawyers in Society, vol. 3: Comparative Theories*. Berkeley: University of California Press.

Adak, Hülya. 2003. "National Myths and Self-N(arr)ations: Mustafa Kemal's Nutuk and Halide Edib's *Memoirs* and *The Turkish Ordeal*." *South Atlantic Quarterly* 102(2):509–527.

———. 2016. "Teaching the Armenian Genocide in Turkey: Curriculum, Methods, and Sources." *PMLA* 131(5):1515–1518.

Adjemian, Boris. 2012. "Le débat inachevé des historiens français sur les 'lois mémorielles' et la pénalisation du négationnisme : retour sur une décennie de controverse." *Revue Arménienne Des Questions Contemporaines* 15:9–49.

Akçam, Taner. 2006. *A Shameful Act: The Armenian Genocide and the Question of Turkish Responsibility*. New York: Henry Holt.

———. 2014. "Textbooks and the Armenian Genocide in Turkey: Heading towards 2015." *Armenian Weekly*, December 4. https://armenianweekly.com/2014/12/04/textbooks/.

Alexander, Ben. 2007. "Contested Memories, Divided Diaspora: Armenian Americans, the Thousand-Day Republic, and the Polarized Response to an Archbishop's Murder." *Journal of American Ethnic History* 27(1):32–59.

Alexander, Jeffrey C. 2002. "On the Social Construction of Moral Universals: The 'Holocaust' from War Crime to Trauma Drama." *European Journal of Social Theory* 5:5–85.

———. 2004. "Toward a Theory of Cultural Trauma." Pp. 1–30 in *Cultural Trauma and Collective Identity*, edited by J. C. Alexander, R. Eyerman, B. Giesen, N. J. Smelser, and P. Sztompka. Berkeley: University of California Press.

Alexander, Jeffrey C., Ron Eyerman, Bernhard Giesen, Neil J. Smelser, and Pjotr Sztompka, eds. 2004. *Cultural Trauma and Collective Identity*. Berkeley: University of California Press.

Allen, Tim, and Jean Seaton, eds. 1999. *The Media of Conflict: War Reporting and Representations of Ethnic Violence*. London: Zed Books.

Arendt, Hannah. 1963. *Eichmann in Jerusalem: A Report on the Banality of Evil*, 2nd ed. New York: Viking Press.

Armenian Weekly. 2012. "Hundreds Join in Celebration at Armenian Heritage Park." https://armenianweekly.com/2012/05/22/hundreds-join-in-celebration-at-armenian -heritage-park/ (retrieved April 3, 2019).

Avédikian, Serge, and Tigrane Yégavian. 2017. *Diasporalogue*. Marseille: Éditions Thaddée.

Bachrach, Peter, and Morton S. Baratz. 1970. *Power and Poverty: Theory and Practice*. Oxford: Oxford University Press.

Baer, Alejandro. 2011. "The Voids of Sephard: The Memory of the Holocaust in Spain." *Journal of Spanish Cultural Studies* 12(1):95–120.

Balakian, Peter. 1997. *Black Dog of Fate: A Memoir*. New York: Basic Books.

———. 2003. *The Burning Tigris: The Armenian Genocide and America's Response*. New York: HarperCollins.

Barna, Elizabeth K. 2020. "Between Plantation, President, and Public: Institutionalized Polysemy and the Representation of Slavery, Genocide, and Democracy at Andrew Jackson's Hermitage." PhD dissertation, Vanderbilt University.

Bastide, Roger. 1948. *Initiation aux recherches sur l'interpénétration des civilisations*. Paris: Centre de documentation universitaire.

Bayraktar, Seyhan. 2010. *Politik und Erinnerung: Der Diskurs über den Armeniermord in der Türkei zwischen Nationalismus und Europäisierung*. Bielefeld: transcript.

Bellah, Robert. 1970. *Beyond Belief*. New York: Harper and Row.

Berger, Peter, and Thomas Luckmann. 1966. *The Social Construction of Reality: A Treatise in the Sociology of Knowledge*. New York: Anchor Books.

Bilder, Richard B. 2006. "The Role of Apology in International Law and Diplomacy." *Virginia Journal of International Law* 46(3):433–473.

Bloxham, Donald. 2005. *The Great Game of Genocide: Imperialism, Nationalism, and the Destruction of the Ottoman Armenians*. Oxford: Oxford University Press.

Blumer, Herbert. 1969. *Symbolic Interactionism: Perspective and Method*. Englewood Cliffs, NJ: Prentice-Hall.

Bourdieu, Pierre. 1984. *Distinction*. Translated by R. Nice. London: Routledge & Kegan Paul.

———. 1987. "The Force of Law: Toward a Sociology of the Judicial Field." Translated by R. Terdiman. *Hastings Law Journal* 38(5):805–853.

———. 1988. *Homo Academicus*. Translated by P. Collier. Stanford, CA: Stanford University Press.

———. 1989. "Social Space and Symbolic Power." Translated by L. J. D. Wacquant. *Sociological Theory* 7(1):14–25.

———. 1994. "Rethinking the State: Genesis and Structure of the Bureaucratic Field." Translated by L. J. D. Wacquant and S. Farage. *Sociological Theory* 12(1):1–18.

———. 1998. *On Television*. Translated by P. P. Ferguson. New York: New Press.

Boyle, Elizabeth Heger. 2002. *The Measure of Mothers' Love: Female Genital Cutting in Global Context*. Baltimore: Johns Hopkins University Press.

Bozarslan, Hamit. 2013. *Histoire de la Turquie : De l'Empire à nos jours*. Paris: Taillandier.

Brubaker, Rogers. 2015. *Grounds for Difference*. Cambridge, MA: Harvard University Press.

Bryce, James, and Arnold Joseph Toynbee. [1916] 2005. *The Treatment of Armenians in the Ottoman Empire 1915–1916: Documents Presented to Viscount Grey of Fallodon by Viscount Bryce*. London: British Parliamentary Blue Book series.

Camic, Charles, and Neil Gross. 2001. "The New Sociology of Ideas." Pp. 236–249 in *Blackwell Companion to Sociology*, edited by J. Blau. Malden, MA: Blackwell.

Caplow, Theodore. 2004. "The Festival Cycle: Halloween to Easter in the Community of Middletown." Pp. 107–119 in *We Are What We Celebrate: Understanding Holidays and Rituals*, edited by A. Etzioni and J. Bloom. New York: New York University Press.

Carzou, Jean-Marie. [1975] 2006. *Un Génocide exemplaire, Arménie 1915.* Mesnil-sur-l'Estrée, France: Firmin-Didot.

Cohen, Stanley. 2001. *States of Denial: Knowing about Atrocities and Suffering.* Cambridge, MA: Polity Press.

Collins, Randall. 2000. *The Sociology of Philosophies: A Global Theory of Intellectual Change.* Cambridge, MA: Harvard University Press.

———. 2005. *Interaction Ritual Chains.* Princeton, NJ: Princeton University Press.

Cooley, Charles H. 1926. "The Roots of Social Knowledge." *American Journal of Sociology* 32:59–79.

Corning, Amy, and Howard Schuman. 2015. *Generations and Collective Memory.* Chicago: University of Chicago Press.

Coser, Lewis A. 1956. *The Functions of Social Conflict.* New York: Simon and Schuster.

———. 1992. "Introduction: Maurice Halbwachs 1877–1945." Pp. 1–36 in *On Collective Memory*, edited by L. A. Coser. Chicago: University of Chicago Press.

Crenson, Matthew A. 1972. *The Un-Politics of Air Pollution: A Study of Non-Decisionmaking in the Cities.* Baltimore: Johns Hopkins University Press.

Crilly, Rob. 2010. *Saving Darfur: Everyone's Favourite African War.* London: Reportage Press.

Dadrian, Vahakn N. 2002. "The Quest for Scholarship in My Pathos for the Armenian Tragedy and Its Victims." Pp. 235–252 in *Pioneers of Genocide Studies*, edited by S. Totten and S. L. Jacobs. New Brunswick, NJ: Transaction.

Dayan, Daniel, and Elihu Katz. 1992. *Media Events: The Live Broadcasting of History.* Cambridge, MA: Harvard University Press.

Dekel, Irit. 2013. *Mediation at the Holocaust Memorial in Berlin.* London: Palgrave Macmillan.

Der Matossian, Bedross. 2014. *Shattered Dreams of Revolution: From Liberty to Violence in the Late Ottoman Empire.* Stanford, CA: Stanford University Press.

———. 2015. "Explaining the Unexplainable: Recent Trends in the Armenian Genocide Historiography." *Journal of Levantine Studies* 5(2):143–166.

Deschamps, Paul. 1923. *La Formation Sociale des Arméniens.* Paris: Bureau de la Science Sociale.

Douglas, Lawrence. 2001. *The Memory of Judgment: Making Law and History in the Trials of the Holocaust.* New Haven, CT: Yale University Press.

Douglas, Mary. 1966. *Purity and Danger.* London: Routledge & Kegan Paul.

Duclert, Vincent. 2015. *La France face au génocide des Arméniens.* Paris: Fayard.

Durkheim, Emile. [1912] 2001. *The Elementary Forms of Religious Life.* Translated by C. Cosman. Oxford: Oxford University Press.

Elias, Norbert. [1939] 2000. *The Civilizing Process: Sociogenetic and Psychogenetic Investigations.* Oxford: Blackwell.

Emirbayer, Mustafa, and Victoria Johnson. 2008. "Bourdieu and Organizational Analysis." *Theory and Society* 37(1):1–44.

Erikson, Kai T. [1966] 2004. *Wayward Puritans: A Study in the Sociology of Deviance*. Boston: Prentice-Hall.

Ferraris, Maurizio. 2014. *Manifesto of New Realism*. Translated by S. De Sanctis. Albany, NY: SUNY Press.

Fine, Gary A. 2001. *Difficult Reputations: Collective Memories of the Evil, Inept, and Controversial*. Chicago: University of Chicago Press.

Frank, David John, Ann Hironaka, and Evan Schofer. 2000. "The Nation-State and the Natural Environment over the Twentieth Century." *American Sociological Review* 65:96–116.

Gao, Rui, and Jeffrey C. Alexander. 2017. "Remembrance of Things Past: Cultural Trauma, the 'Nanking Massacre,' and Chinese Identity." In *The Oxford Handbook of Cultural Sociology*, edited by J. C. Alexander, R. N. Jacobs, and P. Smith. Oxford: Oxford University Press. doi: 10.1093/oxfordhb/9780195377767.013.22.

Garfinkel, Harold. 1956. "Conditions of Successful Degradation Ceremonies." *American Journal of Sociology* 61(5):420–424.

Garland, David. 1990. *Punishment and Modern Society*. Chicago: University of Chicago Press.

———. 2001. *The Culture of Control*. Chicago: University of Chicago Press.

Giesen, Bernhard. 2004a. "The Cultural Trauma of Perpetrators." Pp. 112–154 in *Cultural Trauma and Collective Identity*, edited by J. C. Alexander, R. Eyerman, B. Giesen, N. J. Smelser, and P. Sztompka. Berkeley: University of California Press.

———. 2004b. *Triumph and Trauma*. Boulder, CO: Paradigm.

Glazer, Nathan, and Patrick P. Moynihan. 1970. *Beyond the Melting Pot: The Negroes, Puerto Ricans, Jews, Italians, and Irish of New York City*. Cambridge, MA: MIT Press.

Göçek, Fatma Müge. 2015. *Denial of Violence: Ottoman Past, Turkish Present, and Collective Violence against the Armenians, 1789–2009*. Oxford: Oxford University Press.

Goffman, Erving. 1967. *Interaction Ritual: Essays on Face-to-Face Behavior*. London: Aldine.

———. [1963] 1986. *Stigma: Notes on the Management of Spoiled Identity*. New York: Touchstone.

Goody, Jack. 1977. "Against "Ritual": Loosely Structured Thoughts on a Loosely Defined Topic." Pp. 25–35 in *Secular Ritual*, edited by S. F. Moore and B. Myerhoff. Amsterdam: Van Gorcum.

Gorski, Philip S. 2003. *The Disciplinary Revolution: Calvinism and the Rise of the State in Early Modern Europe*. Chicago: University of Chicago Press.

Gutman, Yifat. 2017. *Memory Activism: Reimagining the Past for the Future in Israel-Palestine*. Nashville, TN: Vanderbilt University Press.

Hagan, John. 2003. *Justice in the Balkans: Prosecuting War Crimes in The Hague Tribunal*. Chicago: University of Chicago Press.

Hahn, Alois. 1982. "Zur Soziologie der Beichte und anderer Formen institutionalisierter Bekenntnisse: Sebstthematisierung und Zivilisationsprozess." *Kölner Zeitschrift für Soziologie und Sozialpsychologie* 34(3):407–434.

Halbwachs, Maurice. 1992. *On Collective Memory*. Chicago: University of Chicago Press.

Higham, John. 1979. *Ethnic Leadership in America*. Baltimore: Johns Hopkins University Press.

Hilberg, Raul. [1961] 2003. *The Destruction of the European Jews*. New Haven, CT: Yale University Press.

Hovannisian, Garin K. 2010. *Family of Shadows: A Century of Murder, Memory, and the American Dream*. New York: HarperCollins.

Hovannisian, Richard G. 1971. *The Republic of Armenia, vol. 1*. Berkeley: University of California Press.

———. 2002. "Confronting the Armenian Genocide." Pp. 27–46 in *Pioneers of Genocide Studies*, edited by S. Totten and S. L. Jacobs. New Brunswick, NJ: Transaction.

———, ed. 1999. *Remembrance and Denial: The Case of the Armenian Genocide*. Detroit, MI: Wayne State University Press.

Kaiser, Hilmar. 2003. "From Empire to Republic: The Continuities of Turkish Denial." *Armenian Review* 48(3–4): 1–24.

Kalberg, Stephen. 1987. "The Origins and Expansion of Kulturpessimismus: The Relationship between Public and Private Spheres in early Twentieth Century Germany." *Sociological Theory* 5:150–164.

———. 1994. *Max Weber's Historical-Comparative Methodology*. Chicago: University of Chicago Press.

———. 2005. *Max Weber: Readings and Commentary on Modernity*. Malden, MA: Blackwell.

———. 2014. *Searching for the Spirit of American Democracy: Max Weber's Analysis of a Unique Political Culture, Past, Present, and Future*. Boulder, CO: Paradigm.

Karakaya, Yağmur. 2018. "The Conquest of Hearts: The Central Role of Ottoman Nostalgia within Contemporary Turkish Populism." *American Journal of Cultural Sociology* 8:125–157. doi: https://10.1057/s41290-018-0065-y.

Karakaya, Yağmur, and Alejandro Baer. 2019. " 'Such Hatred Has Never Flourished on Our Soil': The Politics of Holocaust Memory in Turkey and Spain." *Sociological Forum* 34(3):705–728.

Keck, Margaret E., and Kathryn Sikkink. 1998. *Activists beyond Borders: Advocacy Networks in International Politics*. Ithaca, NY: Cornell University Press.

Kertzer, David I. 1983. "Generation as a Sociological Problem." *Annual Review of Sociology* 9:125–149.

Kettler, David, and Volker Meja, eds. 2018. *The Anthem Companion to Karl Mannheim*. London: Anthem Press.

Kévorkian, Raymond. 2011. *The Armenian Genocide: A Complete History*. London: I.B. Tauris.

Kezer, Zeynep. 2019. "Lifescapes Disrupted: Armenians, Kurds and the State in Eastern Turkey." In *Cultural Violence and Destruction of Communities: New Theoretical Perspectives*, edited by F. M. Göçek and F. Greenland. London: I.B. Tauris.

Kidron, Carol A. 2009. "Toward an Ethnography of Silence: The Lived Presence of the Past in the Everyday Life of Holocaust Trauma Survivors and Their Descendants in Israel." *Current Anthropology* 50(1):5–27.

Knoblauch, Hubert, and René Wilke. 2016. "The Common Denominator: The Reception and Impact of Berger and Luckmann's *The Social Construction of Reality*." *Human Studies* 39:51–69.

Krog, Antjie. 1998. *Country of my Skull: Guilt, Sorrow, and the Limits of Forgiveness in the New South Africa*. New York: Broadway Books.

Landsman, Stephen. 2005. *Crimes of the Holocaust: The Law Confronts Hard Cases*. Philadelphia: University of Pennsylvania Press.

Langer, Lorenz. 2014. "Entscheidungsbesprechungen." *Aktuelle Juristische Praxis* 9:1240–1246.

Lauterpacht, Hersch. 1943. "The Law of Nations, the Law of Nature, and the Rights of Man." *Transactions of the Grotius Society* 29:1–33.

Leo, Per. 2014. *Flut und Boden: Roman einer Familie.* Stuttgart: Klett-Cotta.

Levi, Primo. [1986] 2017. *The Drowned and the Saved.* New York: Simon & Schuster.

Levy, Daniel, and Natan Sznaider. 2010. *Human Rights and Memory.* University Park: Pennsylvania State University Press.

Lipstadt, Deborah. 1993. *Denying the Holocaust: The Growing Assault on Truth and Memory.* New York: Free Press.

Lukes, Stephen. 1975. "Political Ritual and Social Integration." *Sociology* 9(2):289–308.

Mamigonian, Marc A. 2015. "Academic Denial of the Armenian Genocide in American Scholarship: Denialism as a Manufactured Controversy." *Genocide Studies International* 9(1):61–82.

Mannheim, Karl. 1952. "The Problem of Generations." Pp. 276–320 in *Essays on the Sociology of Knowledge,* edited by P. Kecskemeti. London: Routledge & Kegan Paul.

———. [1936] 1985. *Ideology and Utopia: An Introduction to the Sociology of Knowledge.* Translated by L. Wirth and E. Shils. San Diego, CA: Harcourt.

———. 1986. *Conservatism: A Contribution to the Sociology of Knowledge.* Edited and translated by D. Kettler, V. Meja, and N. Stehr. London: Routledge & Kegan Paul.

Marrus, Michael. 2008. "The Nuremberg Doctors' Trial and the Limitations of Context." Pp. 103–122 in *Atrocities on Trial: Historical Perspectives on the Politics of Prosecuting War Crimes,* edited by P. Heberer and J. Matthäus. Lincoln: University of Nebraska Press.

Marutyan, Harutyun. 2007. "Iconography of Historical Memory and Armenian National Identity at the End of the 1980s." Pp. 89–113 in *Representations on the Margins of Europe: Politics and Identities in the Baltic and South Caucasian States,* edited by T. Darieva and W. Kaschuba. Chicago: Chicago University Press.

———. 2010. "Can Collective Memory of Genocide Lead to Reconciliation? A View from Yerevan." Pp. 24–38 in *Prospects for Reconciliation: Theory and Practice,* edited by H. Kharatyan-Araqelyan and L. Neyzi. Bonn, Germany: Institut für Internationale Zusammenarbeit des Deutschen Volkshochschulverbandes.

———. 2014a. "Trauma and Identity: On Structural Particularities of Armenian Genocide and Jewish Holocaust." *International Journal of Armenian Genocide Studies* 1(1):53–69.

———. 2014b. "Museums and Monuments: Comparative Analysis of Armenian and Jewish Experiences in Memory Policies." *Études Arméniennes Contemporaines* 3:57–79.

Mauco, Georges. 1932. *Les Étrangers en France : leur rôle dans la vie économique.* Paris: Armand Colin.

McElrath, Suzy. 2020. "The Global Criminalization of Genocide, 1950–2015." PhD dissertation, Department of Sociology, University of Minnesota, Minneapolis.

McNulty, Mel. 1999. "Media Ethnicization and the International Response to War and Genocide in Rwanda." Pp. 268–286 in *The Media in Conflict: War Reporting and Representations of Ethnic Violence,* edited by T. Allen and J. Eaton. New York: St. Martin's Press.

Mead, George H. 1934. *Mind, Self, and Society: From the Standpoint of a Social Behaviorist.* Chicago: University of Chicago Press.

Merry, Sally E., Peggy Levitt, Mihaela Şerban Rosen, and Diana H. Yoon. 2010. "Law from Below: Women's Human Rights and Social Movements in New York City." *Law & Society Review* 44:101–128.

Meyer, John W., Francisco O. Ramirez, and Yasemin Nohoglu Soysal. 1992. "World Expansion of Mass Education, 1870–1980." *Sociology of Education* 65(2):128–149.

Michel, Johann. 2010. *Gouverner les Mémoires: Les Politiques Mémorielles en France*. Paris: Presses Universitaires de France.

———. 2011. "L'institutionalisation du crime contre l'humanité et l'avènement du régime victimo-mémoriel en France." *Canadian Journal of Political Science* 44(3):663–684.

———. 2016. "A Study of the Collective Memory and Public Memory of Slavery in France." *African Studies* 75(3):395–416.

Milgram, Stanley. 1963. "Behavioral Study of Obedience." *The Journal of Abnormal and Social Psychology* 67(4):371–378.

Minnesota Historical Society. n.d. Thomas and Carmelite Christie and Family Papers. St. Paul, MN.

Minow, Martha. 1998. *Between Vengeance and Forgiveness: Facing History after Genocide and Mass Violence*. Boston: Beacon Press.

Mitgutsch, Anna. 2016. *Die Annäherung*. München: Luchterhand.

Mkrtchyan, Tigran, ed. 2015. *Global Forum against the Crime of Genocide*. Yerevan: Ministry of Foreign Affairs.

Morgenthau, Henry. 2003. *Ambassador Morgenthau's Story*. Detroit: Wayne State University Press.

Mouradian, Claire. 2003. "Les Déportations Ethniques de Masse en URSS." Pp. 332–346 in *Une si longue nuit. L'apogée des régimes totalitaires en Europe, 1935–1953*, Edité sous la direction Stephane Courtois. Paris: Éditions du Rocher.

Mouradian, Claire, Raymond Kévorkian, and Yves Ternon. 2015. *Le Génocide des Arméniens de l'Empire ottomane*. Paris: Éditions du Mémorial de la Shoah.

Mouradian, Claire, and Anouche Kunth. 2010. *Les Arméniens en France*. Du chaos à la reconnaissance. Toulouse: Éditions de l'Attribut, Collection Exils.

Naimark, Norman M. 2010. *Stalin's Genocides*. Princeton, NJ: Princeton University Press.

Neier, Aryeh. 2012. *The International Human Rights Movement: A History*. Princeton, NJ: Princeton University Press.

Neurath, Paul Martin. [1943] 2005. *The Society of Terror: Inside the Dachau and Buchenwald Concentration Camps*. London: Paradigm.

Nonet, Philippe, and Philip Selznick. 1978. *Law and Society in Transition: Toward Responsive Law*. New York: Octagon Books.

Novick, Peter. 1999. *The Holocaust in American Life*. Boston: Houghton Mifflin.

Olick, Jeffrey K. 1999. "Genre Memories and Memory Genres: A Dialogical Analysis of May 8, 1945 Commemorations in the Federal Republic of Germany." *American Sociological Review* 64:381–402.

———. 2016. *The Sins of the Fathers: Germany, Memory, Method*. Chicago: University of Chicago Press.

Özbek, Esen Egemen. 2016. "Commemorating the Armenian Genocide: The Politics of Memory and National Identity." PhD dissertation, Carleton University, Ottawa, Ontario.

Panossian, Razmik. 2006. *The Armenians: From Kings and Priests to Merchants and Commissars*. New York: Columbia University Press.

Payne, Leigh. 2008. *Unsettling Accounts: Neither Truth nor Reconciliation in Confessions of State Violence*. Durham, NC: Duke University Press.

Pendas, Devin. 2006. *The Frankfurt Auschwitz Trial, 1963–1965: Genocide, History, and the Limits of the Law*. Cambridge: Cambridge University Press.

Polian, Pavel. 2004. *Against Their Will: The History and Geography of Forced Migrations in the USSR*. Budapest: Central European University Press.

Polletta, Francesca. 1998. "Legacies and Liabilities of an Insurgent Past: Remembering Martin Luther King, Jr., on the House and Senate Floor." *Social Science History* 22(4):479–512.

———. 2006. *It Was Like a Fever: Storytelling in Protest and Politics*. Chicago: University of Chicago Press.

Power, Samantha. 2002. *A Problem from Hell: America and the Age of Genocide*. New York: Harper.

Presser, Lois. 2018. *Inside Stories: How Narratives Drive Mass Harm*. Oakland: University of California Press.

Rebérioux, Madeline. 1990. "Le génocide, le juge, et l'historien." *L'Histoire* 138:93–95.

Riesman, David, Nathan Glazer, and Reuel Denney. [1950] 2001. *The Lonely Crowd, Revised Edition: A Study of the Changing American Character*, 2nd ed. New Haven, CT: Yale University Press.

Riley, Alexander. 2008. "The Role of Images in the Construction of Narratives about the Crash of United Airline Flight 83." *Visual Studies* 23(1):4–19.

Rydgren, Jens. 2007. "The Power of the Past: A Contribution to a Cognitive Sociology of Ethnic Conflict." *Sociological Theory* 25(3):225–244.

Sands, Philippe. 2016. *East West Street: On the Origins of "Genocide" and "Crimes Against Humanity."* New York: Alfred A. Knopf.

Sarafian, Ara. 1994. *United States Official Documents on the Armenian Genocide*. Watertown, MA: The Armenian Review.

———. 2004. *United States Diplomacy on the Bosphorus: The Diaries of Ambassador Morgenthau 1913–1916*. Princeton, NJ, and London: Gomidas Institute.

Savelsberg, Joachim J. 1992. "Law that Does Not Fit Society: Sentencing Guidelines as a Neo-Classical Reaction to the Dilemmas of Substantivized Law." *American Journal of Sociology* 97(5):1346–1381.

———. 2015. *Representing Mass Violence: Conflicting Responses to Human Rights Violations in Darfur*. Oakland: University of California Press.

———. 2020a. "The Representational Power of International Criminal Courts." Pp. 281–323 in *Power in International Criminal Justice: Towards a Sociology of International Justice*, edited by M. Bergsmo, M. Klamberg, K. Lohne, and C. Mahony. Brussels: Torkel Opsahl Academic EPublisher.

———. 2020b. "Writing Biography in the Face of Cultural Trauma: Nazi Descent and the Management of Spoiled Identities." *American Journal of Cultural Sociology* (OnlineFirst).

Savelsberg, Joachim J., and Ryan D. King. 2007. "Law and Collective Memory." *Annual Review of Law and Social Science* 3:189–211.

———. 2011. *American Memories: Atrocities and the Law*. New York: Russell Sage Foundation.

————. 2015. "Institutionalizing Collective Memories of Hate: Law and Law Enforcement in Germany and the United States." *American Journal of Sociology* 111(2):579–616.

Savelsberg, Joachim J., and Hollie Nyseth Brehm. 2015. "Representing Human Rights Violations in Darfur: Global Justice, National Distinctions." *American Journal of Sociology* 121(2):564–603.

Scheffer, David. 2012. *All the Missing Souls: A Personal History of the War Crimes Tribunals.* Princeton, NJ: Princeton University Press.

Scheler, Max. 1992. *On Feeling, Knowing, and Valuing: Selected Writings.* Edited by Harold Bershady. Chicago: University of Chicago Press.

Schenck, Naomi. 2016. *Mein Großvater stand vorm Fenster und trank Tee Nr. 12.* München: Berlin Hanser.

Schnapper, Dominique. 2010. *Une sociologue aux Conseil constitutionnel.* Paris: Gallimard.

Schneider, Joseph. 1985. "Social Problems Theory: The Constructionist View." *Annual Review of Sociology* 11:209–229.

Schuman, Howard, and Amy D. Corning. 2000. "Collective Knowledge of Public Events: The Soviet Era from the Great Purge to Glasnost." *American Journal of Sociology* 105(4):913–956.

Schuman, Howard, Barry Schwartz, and Hannah D'Arcy. 2005. "Elite Revisionists and Popular Beliefs: Christopher Columbus, Hero or Villain?" *Public Opinion Quarterly* 69:2–29.

Schuman, Howard, and Jacqueline Scott. 1989. "Generations and Collective Memories." *American Sociological Review* 54:359–381.

Schütz, Alfred. [1932] 1967. *The Phenomenology of the Social World.* Translated by G. Walsh and F. Lehnert. Evanston, IL: Northwestern University Press.

Schwartz, Barry. 1991. "Social Change and Collective Memory: The Democratization of George Washington." *American Sociological Review* 56(2):221–236.

————. 2003. *Abraham Lincoln and the Forge of National Memory.* Chicago: University of Chicago Press.

————. 2009. "Collective Forgetting and the Symbolic Power of Oneness: The Strange Apotheosis of Rosa Parks." *Social Psychology Quarterly* 72(2):123–142.

Schwartz, Barry, and Howard Schuman. 2005. "History, Commemoration, and Belief: Abraham Lincoln in American Memory, 1945–2001." *American Sociological Review* 70(2):183–203.

Seckinelgin, Hakan. 2019. "Memories That Forget: The Conceptual Grammar of Forgetting the Armenian Genocide in Turkey and Its Implications for Social Relations." Lecture presented on April 9, 2019, at the Institut d'études avancées de Paris, Paris.

Semprún, Jorge. 1981. *Aquel Domingo.* Barcelona: Planeta.

Senate Select Committee on Intelligence. 2014. *The Senate Intelligence Committee Report on Torture.* Brooklyn, NY: Melville House.

Shils, Edward. 1981. *Tradition.* Chicago: University of Chicago Press.

Shils, Edward, and Michael Young. 1953. "The Meaning of the Coronation." *The Sociological Review* 1(2):63–81.

Shirinian, George N. 2015. "Turks Who Saved Armenians: Righteous Muslims during the Armenian Genocide." *Genocide Studies International* 9(2):208–227.

Sikkink, Kathryn. 2011. *The Justice Cascade: How Human Rights Prosecutions Change World Politics.* New York: Norton.

Simmel, Georg. [1955] 1964. *Conflict and the Web of Group Affiliations*. Edited and translated by K. H. Wolff and R. Bendix. New York: The Free Press.

Smelser, Neil J. 2004. "Psychological Trauma and Cultural Trauma." Pp. 31–59 in *Cultural Trauma and Collective Identity*, edited by J. C. Alexander, R. Eyerman, B. Giesen, N. J. Smelser, and P. Sztompka. Berkeley: University of California Press.

Smith, Philip. 2005. *Why War? The Cultural Logic of Iraq, the Gulf War, and Suez*. Chicago: University of Chicago Press.

———. 2008. *Punishment and Culture*. Chicago: University of Chicago Press.

Smith, Philip, and Alexander Riley. 2009. *Cultural Theory: An Introduction*. Malden, MA: Blackwell.

Smith, Roger W., Eric Markussen, and Robert Jay Lifton. 1999. "Professional Ethics and the Denial of the Armenian Genocide." Pp. 271–295 in *Remembrance and Denial: The Case of the Armenian Genocide*, edited by R. G. Hovannisian. Detroit: Wayne State University Press.

Smith-Lovin, Lynn, and Charles Brody. 1989. "Interruptions in Group Discussions: The Effects of Gender and Group Composition." *American Sociological Review* 54(3):424–435.

Stein, Arlene. 2014. *Reluctant Witnesses: Survivors, Their Children, and the Rise of Holocaust Consciousness*. Oxford: Oxford University Press.

Steinberg, Stephen. 2001. *The Ethnic Myth: Race, Ethnicity, and Class in America*, 3rd ed. Boston: Beacon Press.

Stryker, Robin. 1989. "Limits on Technocratization of Law." *American Sociological Review* 54(3):341–358.

Suny, Ronald G., Fatma Müge Göçek, and Norman M. Naimark, eds. 2011. *A Question of Genocide: Armenians and Turks at the End of the Ottoman Empire*. Oxford: Oxford University Press.

Swidler, Ann, and Jorge Arditi. 1994. "The New Sociology of Knowledge." *Annual Review of Sociology* 20:305–329.

Sykes, Grasham M., and David Matza. 1957. "Techniques of Neutralization: A Theory of Delinquency." *American Sociological Review* 22(6):664–670.

Ternon, Yves. 1999. "The 'Lewis Affair.'" Pp. 237–248 in *Remembrance and Denial: The Case of the Armenian Genocide*, edited by R. G. Hovannisian. Detroit: Wayne State University Press.

Thompson, Allan, ed. 2007. *The Media and the Rwanda Genocide*. Ottawa, CA: Pluto Press.

———. 2019. *Media and Mass Atrocity: The Rwanda Genocide and Beyond*. Waterloo, ON: Centre for International Governance Innovation.

Thompson, E. P. 1975. *Whigs and Hunters*. New York: Pantheon.

Tonoyan, Artyom H. 2012. "Religion and the Conflict over Nagorno Karabakh." PhD dissertation, Institute of Church-State Studies, Baylor University, Waco, TX.

Tsutsui, Kiyoteru. 2017. "Human Rights and Minority Activism in Japan: Transformation of Movement Actorhood and Local-Global Feedback Loop." *American Journal of Sociology* 122(4):1050–1103.

Türkmen, Buket. 2019. "The Actors of Democracy Watch in Turkey: Towards a Non-negotiated Public Sphere?" Lecture presented on March 12, 2019, at the Institut d'études avancées de Paris, Paris.

Turner, Victor W. 1969. *The Ritual Process: Structure and Anti-Structure*. Chicago: Aldine.

Unger, Roberto M. 1976. *Law in Modern Society*. New York: Free Press.

Üngör, Uğur Ümit. 2015. "On Memory, Identity, and Genocide." *Testimony Between History and Memory* 120(1):51–61.

Vinitzky-Seroussi, Vered, and Chana Teeger. 2010. "Unpacking the Unspoken: Silence in Collective Memory and Forgetting." *Social Forces* 88(3):1103–1122.

Wagner-Pacifici, Robin, and Barry Schwartz. 1991. "The Vietnam Veterans' Memorial: Commemorating a Difficult Past." *American Journal of Sociology* 97(2):376–342.

Weber, Max. 1978. *Economy and Society*. Berkeley: University of California Press.

Weil, Frederick. 1987. "Cohorts, Regimes, and the Legitimation of Democracy: West Germany since 1945." *American Sociological Review* 52(3):308–324.

Weissman, Fabrice. 2011. "Silence Heals . . . From the Cold War to the War on Terror, MSF Speaks Out: A Brief History." Pp. 177–198 in *Humanitarian Negotiations Revealed: The MSF Experience*, edited by C. Magone, M. Neuman and F. Weissman. New York: Columbia University Press.

Welzer, Harald, Sabine Moller, and Karoline Tschuggnall. 2002. *Opa war kein Nazi: National-sozialismus und Holocaust im Familiengedächtnis*. Frankfurt am Main: Fischer.

Werfel, Franz. [1936] 1983. *The Forty Days of Musa Dagh*. New York: Carroll & Graf (German Orginal: *Die vierzig Tage des Musa Dagh*, Frankfurt: Fischer, 2012).

Werth, Nicolas. 1998. "Un État contre son peuple. Violences, répressions, terreurs en Unions soviétique." Pp. 39–312 in Stephane Courtois et al., *Le Livre noir du communisme. Crimes, terreur, répression*. Paris: Robert Laffont, coll. Bouquins.

Wimmer, Andreas. 2013. *Ethnic Boundary Making: Institutions, Power, Networks*. Oxford: Oxford University Press.

Wolfgram, Mark A. 2019. *Antigone's Ghosts: The Long Legacy of War and Genocide in Five Countries*. Lewisburg, PA: Bucknell University Press.

Zarifian, Julien. 2014. "The Armenian-American Lobby and Its Impact on U.S. Foreign Policy." *Society* 51:503–512.

———. 2018. "The Armenian and Turkish Lobbying, and the (Non-)Recognition of the Armenian Genocide by the United States." Pp. 117–138 in *Congress and Diaspora Politics: The Influence of Ethnic and Foreign Lobbying*, edited by C. Campbell, D. Dulio, and J. Thurber. New York: CUNY University Press.

Zerubavel, Eviatar. 2006. *The Elephant in the Room: Silence and Denial in Everyday Life*. Oxford: Oxford University Press.

———. 2016. "The Five Pillars of Essentialism: Reification and the Social Construction of an Objective Reality." *Cultural Sociology* 10(1):69–76.

Zifonun, Dariuš. 2004. *Gedenken und Identität: Der deutsche Erinnerungsdiskurs* (Wissen-schaftliche Reihe des Fritz Bauer Instituts, vol. 12). Frankfurt/New York: Campus.

INDEX

Enver Pasha, 92, 202
epistemic power, 53, 59, 61–62, 65, 132–61
Erdoğan, Recep Tayyip, 10, 29, 128–29, 156, 199, 207
Erikson, Kai T., 115, 131
ethnic revival, 82
European Court of Human Rights (ECHR), 168, 185
European Parliament, 133
European Union (EU): Turkey's membership issue, 10, 89, 101, 156, 158, 168. *See also* French mobilization and legislation
Evans, Gareth, 216n7
evidence, credibility of, 212n6(ch1)

factual denial, 24, 26, 27
Family of Shadows (Hovannisian, G.), 29
Faurisson, Robert, 151
field (term), defined, 33–34
Fine, Gary A., 3, 5 fig.1, 53, 60, 76
flexibility of knowledge, 55–56
fluidity of knowledge, 66
The Forty Days of Musa Dagh (Werfel), 141
France: Armenians in, 66, 76–77, 79, 142; boycott by Turkish organizations, 101; Constitutional Council (CC), 134, 136; context of memory laws, 136–38; Enlightenment in, 55; epistemic efficacy, 143–49; French Armenian civil society, 140–43; French political field in context, 139–40, 140 fig.10; French repatriates from Algeria, 138; French-Turkish relations, 199; genocide exhibitions, 82–87; laws pertaining to Armenian genocide, 135–36; Marando, 43; Paris Turkish embassy attack, 100; political field in, 132–35; Shoah Memorial exhibit, 82–86, 104, 105; stories of silencing in, 20. *See also* epistemic politics; French mobilization and legislation
France, Anatole, 84, 141
Frank, Anne, 34
Frankfurt Auschwitz trial, 59, 94, 164. *See also* Auschwitz
French Armenian Community, 220n4
French Guiana, 138
French intellectuals, 141–42, 152, 168
French mobilization and legislation, 132–61; agency of historians and, 150–54; Armenian genocide laws, 158–61; Boyer Law, 135–36, 144 table2, 150, 153–54, 158–60; Constitutional Council, 158–61; epistemic effects and, 140–43; foreign policy and, 154–58; political

debate and, 143–49; political mobilization of scholarship, 149–50
French repatriates, 138
French Revolution, 55
French triangle, 140, 140 fig.10, 149, 160
Front National, 136

Gao, Rui, 215n12
Garland, David, 61, 184
Garnai, Erez, 212n1
Gautier, Charles, 157
Gayssot, Jean-Claude, 136
Gayssot Act of 1990, 136, 138, 145, 150, 151, 152, 168
Gbowee, Leymah, 127, 142, 216n7
generations, 213n3; contenting with, 65; experiential motivation of, 16; generation units, 54–55; knowledge and, 17; knowledge transmission between, 57, 66, 102–3; silencing and, 64. *See also* birth cohorts
genocide (term): claiming term, 70; defined, 18; emergence of, 57; history of, 18; Turkey's preventing use of, 89; use of, 68
Genocide Convention of 1948, 18, 57, 68, 188, 214n5(ch3)
genocide knowledge: affirming through rituals, 113; core features of, 107; diaspora and, 214n3; epistemic circle, 5 fig.1; struggles over, 15, 32; toward understanding of, 53. *See also* carriers; denialism; entrepreneurs; epistemic power; humanitarian field; silencing; Turkish knowledge
genocide knowledge in Armenia: epistemic shifts of 1960s, 70–71; overview, 66, 66–69, 87; polysemy and reinterpretations of 1980s, 71–76; postwar memories, 69–70
genocide laws: Armenian genocide laws, 158–61; current circumstances and, 214n5(ch3); Genocide Convention of 1948, 18, 57, 68, 214n5(ch3)
Germany: Armenisches Hilfswerk (German Armenian aid organization), 48; Baader-Meinhof group, 98–99; criminal trials, 107–8; Nuremberg Trials, 94, 164; recognition of Armenian genocide, 134; Talaat Pasha assassination in, 100; Turkey and, 102; Verfassungsgericht, 160. *See also* Nazi Germany
Gidden, Anthony, 61
Giesen, Bernhard, 18, 164, 212n7
Giles, Bruno, 157
Ginsberg, Allen, 175
Glasnost (openness), 71–72

Founded in 1893,
UNIVERSITY OF CALIFORNIA PRESS
publishes bold, progressive books and journals
on topics in the arts, humanities, social sciences,
and natural sciences—with a focus on social
justice issues—that inspire thought and action
among readers worldwide.

The UC PRESS FOUNDATION
raises funds to uphold the press's vital role
as an independent, nonprofit publisher, and
receives philanthropic support from a wide
range of individuals and institutions—and from
committed readers like you. To learn more, visit
ucpress.edu/supportus.

www.ingramcontent.com/pod-product-compliance
Lightning Source LLC
Chambersburg PA
CBHW050346270326
41926CB00016B/3625